BETWEEN THE ROPES

Wrestling's Greatest Triumphs and Failures

Brian Fritz & Christoper Murray

D0029102

ECW Press

Published by ECW PRESS
2120 Queen Street East, Suite 200, Toronto, Ontario, Canada M4E 1E2

Library and Archives Canada Cataloguing in Publication

Fritz, Brian
Between the ropes : wrestling's greatest triumphs and failures /
Brian Fritz and Christopher Murray.

ISBN 1-55022-726-2

1. Wrestling—United States. 2. Total Nonstop Action Wrestling.
3. World Wrestling Entertainment, Inc. 4. World Championship Wrestling, Inc.
5. Extreme Championship Wrestling. I. Murray, Christopher, 1981– II. Title.

GV1195.F75 2006   796.812'0973   C2006-900492-7

Developing editor: Michael Holmes
Typesetting: Gail Nina
Cover and text design: Tania Craan
Cover photos: Lee South, Courtesy of TNA Wrestling
Photos page 220, 229, 243 and 276: Lee South, Courtesy of TNA Wrestling
All other photos: from the collection of Brian Fritz

PRINTING: Transcontinental

DISTRIBUTION

CANADA: Jaguar Book Group, 100 Armstrong Avenue, Georgetown, ON, L7G 5S4
UNITED STATES: Independent Publishers Group, 814 North Franklin Street,
Chicago, Illinois 60610

PRINTED AND BOUND IN CANADA

ECW PRESS
ecwpress.com

CONTENTS

Acknowledgements

I would like to thank so many people for helping not only with this book, but also by being a part of *Between the Ropes*. Chris Murray actually came up with the idea of writing this book, and really jump-started the process. He has been a tireless worker on this project and has always been a big part of the success of the show.

Brian Dickerman has been there from day one, which I cannot thank him enough for. He has made a lot of sacrifices to be a regular part of the show, and I know there were times when he preferred to be somewhere else. I've always said that without him, there would be no *Between the Ropes*, because he is the lifeblood of what we do.

Larry Brannon (Vito DeNucci) has been a great addition to the show, and I'm glad that he is a part of it. I know it is tough for him, considering the wonderful family he has and giving up some valuable time from them. For that, I thank him and his wife Amy.

Thanks to B. Randall Myers for teaching me so much about working in radio and for helping to get *Between the Ropes* off the ground and keeping it on the air. You were never afraid to tell me the truth when no one else would speak up, even if you thought it was something I didn't want to hear.

Over the years, we've had a bunch of different producers, and all of them have helped out a lot. The long list includes B. Randall, Craig Bullock, Andy Garcia, Jim Ferran, August Schalkham, and Mike Tuck. Now for long-time listeners of the show — you won't recognize most of those names, since we decided to use dumb nicknames instead. But in the end, they've all come through.

A special thank you goes out to Marc Daniels, who first gave me the opportunity to do *Between the Ropes* and has given the show a home on the radio.

To my good buddy Jerry Lynn for his great friendship and for being a great part of our wonderful driving singing duo, which no one else will truly appreciate. Steve Corino, Shane Douglas, and Simon Diamond have all been good friends as well and I hope we all have good times ahead. Also, I need to thank Mick Foley for his unintentional words of wisdom in helping me write the book.

Thanks also go out to the hundreds of guests who have shared their time and been on the show. I hope that all of you enjoyed the conversations we have had over the years.

Michael Holmes of ECW Press gave Chris and I the opportunity to do this book, which I appreciate. He has always believed in this project from day one.

To my parents, Robert and Janet, who have always been there for me. It was my dad who introduced me to wrestling as a teenager even though he was not a big fan of it. Still, he watched it with me to spend some quality time together as I was growing up. Regardless of the motive, I was hooked and haven't stopped watching since. My mom was always there to listen to me shout about what I had just seen in wrestling, nodding her head and laughing at my excitement.

More than anyone else, I would like to thank all of the people who have ever tuned in to *Between the Ropes*, who enjoy the program and have supported it. In the end, it is the fans that make or break you, who tell you what is good and what isn't. We've been very fortunate to have a loyal group of people who have appreciated what we have done, and hopefully, what we will continue to do.

— Brian Fritz

Fritz did most of the thanking for both of us, but I do want to make some quick mentions. Right off the bat, many thanks to my mother, Liz, father, Dennis, and brother, Matt, for their support and belief in me and this project.

Also, thanks to my good friends — Craig Mitchell, Joe Antico, Mike Malone, Nick Labetti, and Trevor Labetti — for trekking with me to Madison Square Garden, the Meadowlands, the Nassau Coliseum, and other venues all over the Tri-State Area for wrestling events throughout the years. There've been some good matches and plenty of laughs along the way.

Thanks to the good people at ECW Press for taking a chance on us, particularly Michael Holmes, for his guidance and assistance in offering the opportunity and making this book a reality.

Thanks to writers like Dave Meltzer and Wade Keller, who covered professional wrestling in print long before it was fashionable, and Mick Foley, who opened the door for literature on wrestling with his first autobiography, and proved that wrestling fans can read.

Thanks to Brian Dickerman and Larry "Vito DeNucci" Brannon, as well as Randy "B. Randall" Myers before him, for providing two hours of the best wrestling radio anywhere in the world each and every week. Great radio guys, and even better people.

Most of all, thanks to Brian Fritz for allowing me to be a part of the ride for the past seven years, and for being a true friend I'm lucky to have gotten to know. Looking forward to being there for the next step in the journey, whatever that may be.

Last but not least, thanks to every single person who has listened to *Between the Ropes* over the years, and every single person that has picked up this book. You guys and girls have made this all possible, and I hope we are able to continue entertaining you, both in print and on the airwaves, for years to come.

— Christopher Murray

Foreword

I've had the privilege of being able to wrestle around the world, holding world championships for ECW, the NWA, and the AWA. Sitting now in a hotel room in Tokyo getting ready to go out and perform, I fondly remember the time I met Brian Fritz and first heard about the *Between the Ropes* radio program.

Ever since my first appearance on the show back in my ECW days, followed by my many, many, many appearances since, I have held the *Between the Ropes* show dear to my heart. Brian Fritz and his program have always greeted me with open arms, and I consider *Between the Ropes* to be my radio home.

To me, Fritz, Dickerman (never call him Dickerson, trust me), and now Vito, have hosted the number one pro wrestling radio show for the past seven years. These are three guys who love the sport. Wrestling is fun for all of them. They enjoy the lighter side of the sport, especially when I am there, and don't have the attitude that they're ashamed to follow wrestling, as most of the media does. They speak with the top stars in wrestling, including Ric Flair, me, Steve Austin, me, John Cena, me, and anyone else who has ever been anyone in this industry.

BTR with its 4th host, Steve Corino

I met Fritz back in 1999, when I was just a

young rookie in ECW. He was the first "media" guy to actually act like he cared about me as a person, and not just some wrestler. And he did. That is the way he is. For the ten years that I have been involved in pro wrestling, I have seen friendships come and go, but I can say that Brian Fritz will be my friend far past my time in wrestling.

I joke that when I come on *Between the Ropes*, I am a cohost, but in all reality, I feel like the fourth member of the family. That is the way these guys make me feel. There are no rules, no script, and nothing off-limits. Most of the time when I have been in studio, it has been a nonstop two hours of fun that can not be surpassed.

Seven years ago, I was the new kid on the block, hoping to get exposure from the show. Now, I consider Fritz one of my true friends. And for that I am grateful. They say in pro wrestling you can count your true friends on one hand. Well, I am glad Brian Fritz is one of them.

Congratulations to *Between the Ropes* for being given the chance to write this book. And for those who read it, I hope you enjoy it as much as I enjoy being a part of the *Between the Ropes* family.

Steve Corino
4th Host of *Between The Ropes*
And, oh yeah, Pro Wrestler

Introduction

Sports entertainment. Professional wrestling. Regardless of what you call it, for millions of fans, it's a fun distraction from the daily grind a couple of times each week. But these fans continually find themselves defending their passion to everyday people, who view wrestling as little more than a fake sport that appeals only to the dregs of society.

Fake. The four-letter F-word that can send a wrestling fan over the edge. Sure the punches and kicks are pulled and the in-ring action is mainly choreographed, but the fakery ends there. Outside the ring, pro wrestling is much different. Real men. Real women. Real families. Real injuries. Real problems.

A case can be made that the behind-the-scenes aspects of wrestling are just as intriguing as the storylines on television. The often blurred line between fact and fiction associated with a wrestling "angle" clears up on the other side of the curtain. What's left is a captivating reality that few people have ever had the opportunity to see.

The reality is that pro wrestling is a bizarre business. It's not just the storylines of man-on-woman violence, racial gang warfare, necrophilia, or mock terrorist beheadings that make you scratch your head. The industry itself is often exempt from the rules and regulations adhered to by everyday society. This is world in which performers are labeled as independent contractors, yet they can only work when and where their promoter dictates. This is world where a wrestler can be rescued from a fatal plane crash, and immediately check himself out of the hospital for fear the public would find out that a babyface (a.k.a. "good guy") and a heel (a.k.a. "bad guy") were flying together. This is a world where men shy of their fortieth birthday drop dead with alarming regularity, and hardly anyone — inside or outside the business — bats an eye. Yet for all of these potential misgivings, the allure still remains for many, many people.

Over the last decade, pro wrestling has had more than its share of ups and downs. Some have been played out out in the open for the world to witness, others were not as public. In this book, we take a look at some of the major events that have shaped professional wrestling during this period. In addition to enjoying a number of fascinating stories, you will get to read what the participants of these industry-changing events said at the time. We have had the privilege of speaking with nearly every wrestling superstar — past and present — on our *Between the Ropes* radio program (don't worry, you'll hear enough about the show by the time this book is complete), and to have heard their candid opinions and insights that are usually kept quiet. Through these men and women's own words, you will better understand the popularity of this sports and entertainment hybrid among millions of people. You'll also get a glimpse of what wrestling is like once the cameras stop rolling.

For those of you who have never watched pro wrestling and have picked up this book because you were interested to learn, or because we begged you to buy it, hopefully you will be both entertained and enlightened by what you discover. Those who follow the sport regularly, and may already know some of the stories, can now read the wrestlers' own thoughts for the first time. Fasten your seatbelts for an exciting journey through the wild and wacky world of professional wrestling. Get ready to step *Between the Ropes*.

BETWEEN THE ROPES

PART I

Brian Fritz and Brian Dickerman

Brian, I just don't think there is a place for a show on pro wrestling on this station. I'd rather stick to real sports.

Those were the immortal words of Dick Sheets, the program director at WQTM back in July 1997 when I approached him about doing a radio show strictly on professional wrestling. I can't blame the guy for shooting down the idea either, but that doesn't mean I liked it.

Seriously, I was just a rookie in the radio business, only twenty-four years old and having worked at Central Florida's Sports Radio 540 The Team for less than a year. I had never been on the air before, much less hosted a show, and I truly had no idea what I was trying to get into. Dick knew I was greener than grass, and wasn't about to put me on the air, especially hosting a show on pro wrestling.

Dick was always hard on me during my early days at the radio station, and rightfully so. I had to pay my dues like everyone else when it came to the different duties there. I wanted to be on the air in some capacity, whether it was part of a show or simply doing the sports updates. But I was far from ready.

He would grill me on a regular basis, making me cut demo tapes and picking them apart with his keen ear. I wasn't too happy with his assessment most times, but he was the boss, and he knew best. Who was I to say he was wrong? He was a respected radio man, who had been running major radio stations longer than I had been walking on God's green earth. The man at least took the time to speak with me and go over the little things, making sure that I was truly prepared when I finally got to pop my radio cherry.

But just because Dick shot down my idea then, it didn't mean that I forgot about it. Wrestling was hot. I mean scorching, fireball hot. You had two big promotions fighting one another, putting on kickass programming each and every week, trying to one-up each other. The war between the WWF and WCW continued to heat up week after week, as the two sides showed nothing but contempt for one other. This was one of the great times in wrestling history, and I was soaking it up.

World Championship Wrestling was hitting an unbelievable peak, with the nWo crashing the show, taking their no-holds-barred attitude to new levels. The World Wrestling Federation had its own uncontrollable group in Degeneration X, who would stun people with their brash behavior on television. Plus, a new star had burst onto the scene like no one had done before. Stone Cold Steve Austin. On top of all this, Extreme Championship Wrestling, a renegade promotion out of Philadelphia, was pushing the limits inside and outside the ring with its outlaw performers and unbelievable wrestling, throwing out the rules of the past to create its own wrestling genre which caught on with its fanatical fan base.

Wrestling was big — bigger than ever before — and I wanted to talk about it on the radio. I was sure there was an audience for it, since millions of people were tuning in every week and spending an enormous amount of cash on wrestling tickets, pay-per-views, and merchandise. You couldn't walk down the street with someone wearing an nWo or a Stone Cold shirt. Wrestling was in, and I wanted to discuss it on the air.

But that would have to wait, because the station I worked at wasn't interested in a program unless it was about a real, bona fide sport. Luckily, I had several things going for me. First, the popularity of wrestling was not going away. In fact, it continued to grow with Steve Austin's battles against his boss, Vince McMahon, and an emerging supernova star in The Rock. Plus, there was no letdown in the bitter WWF vs. WCW war.

Brian Dickerman

Next, I was introduced to Brian Dickerman, a guy who worked down the hall for our rock station, 101.1 WJRR. Hell, the guy will probably kill me for printing his first name here, but he will just have to live with it. At least I didn't call him Dickerson — just ask him about that sometime.

Dickerman was another longtime wrestling fan who had watched for years and shared the same passion I did. We quickly became friends. Dickerman could share memories of watching the USWA, his favorites — the Von Erichs — wrestling in Memphis, or some of the other territories that were hot back in the '80s. He was an encyclopedia of the wrestling business.

> **DICKERMAN:** Growing up, I lived on that four o'clock ESPN wrestling show. It was originally WCCW, but over the years it switched to AWA, and eventually Global before they cancelled it for "real" sports. After watching all that wrestling and reading the various magazines available at the grocery store, I knew way too much about professional wrestling.

For the next year, I worked hard to improve, and finally got some opportunities to do some small things on the air. Dickerman and I continued to become better friends; we talked about wrestling all the time. Plus, I kept talking about my idea to do a show on wrestling. I just wouldn't let it go. I never spoke with Dick again about starting the show, but I spoke with almost everyone else about my idea. I believed it was a big thing just waiting to happen.

Most people rolled their eyes about it, even as big as wrestling was becoming. One of them was the man I consider to this day as my mentor in radio: Randy Myers, better known as B. Randall.

Randy showed me the ropes around the station, helped me learn how to produce shows, and taught me the ins and outs of radio. He was a machine, doing all of the small things many people miss and explaining how important they were. But he's also a hard-headed guy, never afraid of sharing his thoughts, and never pulling his punches.

"Are you kidding me? It's wrestling, it's not real. Who would want to listen to a show about that? It won't work."

> **B. RANDALL:** At first, I thought exactly that. Pro wrestling was a product of television, a soap opera, so to speak, and unlike true sports such as baseball or football, it would never be accepted on the radio. On one hand, we at Sports Radio 540 The Team were in the business of broadcasting sports

games and sports talk radio, not rehashing the latest TV shows. Besides, was pro wrestling even a sport? I didn't think so, and for that reason, didn't think it belonged on our radio station. However, on the other hand, it was a product that did appeal to the same audience we were targeting as a radio station, so just maybe it would work. After all, young men all from all over the country were tuning in every Monday night, giving the WWF and WCW some of the highest ratings on cable television. The question was, could we get those same ears to tune in to a talk show about what they we're watching?

He just didn't like wrestling at the time, but my persistence paid off.

The more Dickerman and I talked about it, and the more popular wrestling became, the more intrigued B. Randall became. Before long, he, like millions of others, got sucked in. He was never big on the matches, but he enjoyed the craziness that happened outside of the ring. He bit — hook, line, and sinker — into the shock TV mentality, and started to buy into my idea for a show.

Fritz, B. Randall Myers and Dickerman

B. RANDALL: The storylines and characters at the time were some of the best in years. The Rock, Stone Cold Steve Austin, Mankind, and of course, the whole McMahon family, were making the shows very entertaining to watch. But it was when pro wrestling became the focal point of conversation every Tuesday that I realized that this radio show just might work. I told Fritz I was in, and would do whatever was needed to get the show not only on the AM station, but to stream it online as well. I figured if we bombed over the air, the show would still have life on the fan-crazed World Wide Web.

It had been almost a year since I had unsuccessfully pitched my idea. During that time, I was busting my ass at the station. Whatever work they had for me, I was up for it. I helped B. Randall produce the morning show. On nights or weekends, I ran Atlanta Braves baseball or different football games. During basketball season, I started covering the Orlando Magic for the station. I was working more than fifty hours a week while still attending college, but I knew I still had to prove myself.

In June 1998, I finally received the break I needed. Dick Sheets was removed as program director at the station. At the time, Dick was the program director for two stations — Sports Radio 540 The Team, and 101.1 WJRR. The powers that be decided it was too much for one person and removed him from his duties with 540 so he could focus on the rock station. His replacement was the afternoon show host, Marc Daniels.

While I didn't know Marc too well at the time, he knew how hard I was working. We had a big staff meeting where we discussed the direction of the station. Then he uttered the magical words: "If anyone has an idea for a new show, please let me know. We are open to some new ideas."

This was the break I had been looking for. All I needed was the opportunity to speak with him about the show and why it would work. I thought about how I should sell him on wrestling and what I needed to focus on.

Wrestling is huge right now: check. I know wrestling, having followed it closely for years: check. I would work hard on the show to make sure it sounded up to par: check. But I was still worried that I would once again hear those dreaded words, "I'd rather stick to real sports."

After the big meeting, I had my chance to sit down with the new boss and pitch my show. The amazing part was that I didn't even have to sell him on it. Maybe he'd already heard about my idea and knew what I was going to say. And while he never admitted it, Marc was a closet wrestling fan. He bit onto what was out there at that time. I told him I wanted to do a show on wrestling and explained that it wouldn't be just about what everyone saw on television. We would talk about the happenings behind the scenes and talk with the people behind the characters, providing an in-depth look at sports entertainment. His response was, "I like it. Get me a demo tape."

I was in. Who would have thought it? I still had to make that demo tape, but I knew Marc would go with it. It was an easy choice to have Dickerman cohost the show. He was in on the idea from the beginning, and was excited about the opportunity.

> **DICKERMAN:** I don't think either of us really knew what we were going to do, but we loved wrestling and couldn't wait to talk about it on the radio.

B. Randall heard the news that the boss wanted a demo tape. The guy who had previously said it would never work quickly wanted in on the project. Unbelievable. But he was a good friend, and I knew he could produce the show. I also knew he would keep me on the right track each week and would let me know whether or not something worked.

> **B. RANDALL:** Did I ever think at the time we'd be writing a book about this some day? Not at all! But pro wrestling was gaining popularity and I wasn't about to be left out. If anything, I would probably meet some stars along the way and maybe snag some free tickets the next time WWF *Raw* came to town.

The team of Fritz, Dickerman, and B. Randall was born, and we went to work on a demo tape. It was simple: thirty minutes of talking about wrestling in the format that we wanted. No frills, no production, just straight talk about what was happening in the wrestling world.

We banged it out and gave the tape to Marc. Our future was in his hands. Looking back on it now, I know we probably weren't ready to be on the air. I was nowhere near prepared when it came to how to put a show together, how to keep it flowing, and how to present it in the best way possible. I was a rookie when it came to hosting, but I had to start somewhere. Luckily, Marc knew that too, but he also understood how big of a phenomenon wrestling had become. He gave the thumbs up and the show was good to go.

I couldn't believe it. It took me a year of clinging onto an idea no one else really believed in. Now it was a reality. Dickerman hadn't really thought it would happen, so he never got attached to it. B. Randall had thought it was a bad joke. Now, it was happening. I didn't care what anyone had said in the past, this was going to work, and we had the right guys to make it happen.

> **DICKERMAN:** If you go back and listen to the first show, it's probably some of the worst radio you'll ever hear, but you could have fooled us. We were so excited to be doing a show about pro wrestling. We thought it was the greatest thing on earth.

We were quickly getting everything in place. I would host the show with Dickerman, while B. Randall would be on the air and produce. Things were coming together. I didn't care much for the timeslot we were given — Tuesday nights from 11pm to 2am — all that mattered was that we were going to be on the air. It was early August, 1998 and we knew that we had about three weeks before launch. The next order of business was a name. I had multiple ideas floating around in my head all having to do with a ring or a mat. For some reason, I thought we should use the term "squared circle." Thus, the name of the show became *Inside the Squared Circle*. Now all we had to do was get the word out.

At this point, I need to mention Chris Murray and how he became part of the crew. Chris and I had already known each for

Dickerman and Chris Murray

about a year. But the roles were reversed, where I'd been helping out with his project. During the early boom period of the Internet, Chris was working on an e-mail wrestling newsletter, *SDNV Newsletter*. When the show began, I brought Chris aboard to help out. Chris had a lot of good contacts and is simply awesome at writing up great releases and getting them to the right places in cyberspace. I definitely needed his help spreading the word on the new show, and he was a key part of its initial success. It was shortly after the launch of the show that the *SDNV Newsletter* bit the dust. God rest its soul. I don't know how the online wrestling community has survived without it, but somehow, someway, we have all made it through its untimely passing.

We were a week from our debut show and began sending out releases to various wrestling websites. We wanted to make sure everyone knew about the show and that everyone in Central Florida tuned in. Word was spreading fast.

Word may have spread too fast. Out of nowhere, I was pulled into Marc Daniels's office about an e-mail he received. It was from a guy in Washington D.C. claiming he owned the *Inside the Square Circle* name, and was preventing us from using it. He went so far as to threaten us with a cease-and-desist letter. Less than a week from our first show, we had to change names.

We all brainstormed to come up with different names: *On the Mat*, *Inside the Ring* . . . nothing sounded right. None rolled off the tongue. Then, it hit me — *Between the Ropes*. Eureka! We had a name and started the process of spreading the word. Yeah, it did seem weird that we had to change the name before we even hit the air, but at least it happened before and not after we started.

On August 25, 1998, *Between the Ropes* hit the airwaves for the first time on WQTM Sports Radio 540 The Team. I was beyond giddy just to be on the air. Doing the show that I wanted. The show that I believed in. The show that most said no one would listen to. It didn't matter.

WCW

Chapter 1

In any industry with roots that can be traced back more than 100 years, it is virtually impossible to consider any one event as more important than any other. Pro wrestling has seen it all. From Frank Gotch and George Hackenschmidt, to Gorgeous George, to Hulkamania, to Austin 3:16, wrestling has constantly reinvented itself to adapt to the ever changing world around it.

Yet, the biggest industry transformation in recent times produced negative results for the business as a whole. It was early 2001, and the monstrosity known as professional wrestling was finally slowing down, after experiencing its greatest popularity surge in the United States. The world of "sports entertainment," Vince McMahon's favorite euphemism for avoiding the negative stigma associated with wrestling, had dominated cable television, network television, pay-per-view, the Internet, and even music and publishing. Pro wrestling had become firmly entrenched in the mainstream fabric of American society.

Three companies — the World Wrestling Federation, World Championship Wrestling, and Extreme Championship Wrestling — battled for their piece of the extra-large pie. But as the boom period waned, one company's slice grew larger at the expense of the others, until it ultimately controlled the entire pie. That company was the WWF, and just as it became comfortable leading this three-car race, the checkered flag came out. The competition was over.

Along the way, WCW and ECW offered some memorable moments. For a brief time, WCW dominated the business by reinvigorating older stars and introducing fresh talent from around the world to a new audience. ECW, while never reaching the level of its resource-laden counterparts, made a profound impact with its more aggressive, more athletic brand of wrestling that was eventually copied on a larger scale by the "Big Two." Unfortunately, WCW and ECW, for all the good they gave their fans, also had their share of problems, both on and off camera. In just a matter of weeks in early 2001, two companies guilty of a laundry list of sins were finally sentenced to death, leaving one man, arguably the most sinful of them all, in charge of the only game in town.

Chapter 2

Complicated. If there was one word to describe the legacy of World Championship Wrestling, that would be it. From the original purchase, to the final sale, to the thirteen years of ups and downs in between, WCW rarely traveled the simple road. To this day, former wrestlers, referees, and office workers alike recite identical tales of chaos and turmoil that permeated the WCW infrastructure. And with the only man who could save the company he'd already rescued once no longer in the picture, WCW's shoulders were finally pinned to the mat.

The common belief among wrestling fans is that Ted Turner created World Championship Wrestling out of the ashes of the National Wrestling Alliance. While there is a modicum of truth to that notion, the actual origin of WCW is, in a word, complicated.

Jim Crockett Promotions, the preeminent NWA territory thanks to hours of national programming on Turner's Superstation WTBS, attempted to challenge Vince McMahon's World Wrestling Federation empire in the late 1980s. Major attempts to promote on pay-per-view and run live events in traditional WWF markets failed miserably, in part because of underhanded McMahon sabotage.

By 1987, the WWF had transitioned to pay-per-view television for its major events and made a killing. *WWF WrestleMania III* garnered 400,000 pay-per-view buys, which represented an incredible eight percent of a market still in its formative years. Crockett was ready to put his annual year-end extravaganza, *Starrcade*, on pay-per-view on Thanksgiving night and reap the same rewards. Vince McMahon had other ideas. To ensure a calamity for *Starrcade '87*,

McMahon scheduled his own pay-per-view, the *Survivor Series*. Using his leverage with the cable and pay-per-view communities after several profitable broadcasts, he issued an ultimatum. Any cable company carrying *Starrcade* could not air the *Survivor Series* and would not have access to the next *WrestleMania*. It was a dirty trick, but McMahon held all the cards. Nearly 200 cable companies sided with the WWF, leaving only five companies willing to air *Starrcade*. Instead of the millions he expected to rake in, Crockett drew only 15,000 buys on his biggest night.

Still fuming over McMahon's devious tactics, Crockett sought revenge. His next idea was to invade McMahon's home base, New York City. He couldn't book Madison Square Garden because of the McMahon family's exclusivity with the arena, so he chose Long Island's Nassau Coliseum instead. The *Bunkhouse Stampede* was scheduled for pay-per-view on January 24, 1988. McMahon had another trick up his sleeve. To counter the Crockett show, the WWF aired a free special the same night on the USA Network called *The Royal Rumble*, from Hamilton, Ontario, Canada. The show drew an 8.2 Nielsen rating, a record for a WWF show on USA that stands to this day, while the Bunkhouse Stampede fell flat with the pro-WWF New York audience and consumers at home.

With his balance sheets deep in the red, Crockett saw the hand-writing on the wall and sought an exit from the wrestling business. With bankruptcy looming, Crockett made the decision to sell. He found a buyer in Ted Turner, who wanted to keep wrestling on his network. Months of negotiations ended on November 21, 1988 when Crockett sold the assets of his company to Turner's corporation for approximately $9 million and guaranteed employment in wrestling for members of his family. Turner renamed the company World Championship Wrestling Inc. and soon followed with a phone call to nemesis Vince McMahon to let him know, "I'm in the rasslin' business."

Turner's purchase of Jim Crockett Promotions was met with guarded optimism within the industry. Early on, the organization experienced little turnaround under the new regime. Over the next several years, Jim Herd, Kip Frye, and Bill Watts oversaw the WCW operation while George Scott, Ole Anderson, and Dusty Rhodes tried their hand at creative booking. None of the combinations bore fruit. Bill Shaw from TBS huddled with fellow members of the Turner hierarchy to choose a new leader for the wrestling division. Senior employees like Tony Schiavone, who had worked as a commentator dating back to the Crockett NWA days, and Keith Mitchell, head of WCW production, appeared to have the inside track. But Shaw and the Turner vice presidents shocked everyone by promoting C-level announcer Eric Bischoff to the top of WCW ladder. Bischoff, whose previous wrestling experience came as an advertising salesman, announcer, and then booker in the dying days of Verne Gagne's AWA, impressed Turner officials with his flashy presentations and forward thinking about invigorating a company that was averaging $6 to $7 million in losses per year. With his Ken-doll good looks, ambitious demeanor, and a corporate attitude, Bischoff assumed the newly created role of Executive Vice President of World Championship Wrestling in mid-1993.

One of Bischoff's early goals was to improve the look of the WCW television product. He despised the dark, dingy feel of the weekly shows, and set to drastically upgrade the entire production. To do so, he struck a deal with Disney to tape television at the MGM Studios. With the resources of a professional soundstage, and an enthusiastic crowd drawn from the theme park, the idea made plenty of sense. The decision also saved the company a bundle of cash because they could tape several months of programming over a one-week stretch in Orlando. But the fiscal savings came at a price. In taping television so far in advance, the promotion was locked into future storylines. Plus, fans in attendance and insider fans who learned the results of the tapings knew how storylines would develop and when titles would change hands.

One such instance came in October during a WCW tour of Western Europe. An argument between Sid Vicious and Arn Anderson, both of them drinking heavily, escalated into a violent situation when Vicious stabbed Anderson repeatedly with a pair of scissors. Both men survived the melee, but Bischoff, entrenched in his first crisis, fired Sid amidst international media attention, which

Fritz and Arn Anderson

ruined plans to switch the WCW World Title from Vader to Sid at that year's *Starrcade*. In fact, Sid had already been filmed wearing the belt at the Orlando tapings. Bischoff made the call to put Ric Flair back on top, and booked Flair, who promised to retire if he had lost as a storyline stipulation, over Vader in an emotional match in his hometown of Charlotte, North Carolina to capture the WCW Championship once again.

MGM Studios remained the home for the majority of WCW's television tapings, but also became the site for Eric Bischoff's biggest coup. As WCW taped on Soundstage B, a syndicated television series called *Thunder in Paradise* was shooting next door on Soundstage A. Along with Chris Lemmon and Carol Alt, the star of the show was none other than wrestling legend Hulk Hogan. The Hulkster had left the WWF in June 1993. He'd worked some big money wrestling dates in Japan, but now spent the majority of his time on the TV series, portraying R.J. "Hurricane" Spencer, an ex–Navy SEAL dishing out his own brand of vigilante justice to wrongdoers with the help of his partner (played by Lemmon) and a specially equipped speedboat called Thunder.

WCW's business was still floundering at the time with rumors that Turner was seriously considering shutting down the wrestling operation. But Bischoff had a plan, and saw Hogan as the man to put WCW on the mainstream map. With the help of Ric Flair, Bischoff met regularly with Hogan on the *Thunder in Paradise* set. Hogan hesitated over the idea of returning to wrestling, especially with the Vince McMahon steroid trial looming and his expected testimony for the prosecution. Bischoff arranged a face-to-face sitdown between Hogan and Ted Turner, where an unprecedented contract offer was put on the table: $2.1 million guaranteed through the end of the year, plus 25% of any increase in pay-per-view revenue from shows which Hogan worked. The enormous complexity of the deal marked a change in attitude in the Turner hierarchy toward WCW. The purse strings loosened, giving Bischoff a chance to compete with the WWF for new talent. In Bischoff's mind, the Hulkster was just the start.

> **STING:** I knew what I was dealing with. It was Hulk Hogan. He had gone beyond where I had ever been. It was one of those things where you have to accept it, because it's the truth. And sometimes the truth hurts. I was okay with it.

Chapter 3

WCW announced the Hogan signing in a crawl on the June 4, 1994, edition of WCW *Saturday Night*. A mock press conference at Disney soon followed to commemorate the contract signing. The plan was for Hogan to work with Ric Flair for most of the year, the dream program not fully exploited by the WWF two years earlier. In Hogan's first WCW match, he pinned Flair at the inaugural *Bash at the Beach* pay-per-view in Orlando on July 17. NBA star Shaquille O'Neal stood by in Hogan's corner. The event drew a 1.02 buyrate, WCW's record high to that point. The rematch was scheduled for an August 28 *Clash of the Champions* TBS special, with Flair regaining the title to set up a third match. However, Hogan balked at losing the belt and hindering his momentum. The two instead wrestled to a countout, with Flair going over, but not winning the title. The third match took place at *Halloween Havoc* on pay-per-view from Detroit on October 23. A steel cage was added to the equation, along with Mr. T as guest referee and a stipulation that Flair would retire if he did not win the title. Hogan came away victorious, and Flair went home temporarily to give the champion the entire spotlight. The pay-per-view drew another strong 1.0 buyrate, a 100% improvement from 1993.

Business crept upward for the Hogan-led WCW. New faces, many of them Hogan's cronies from the WWF, popped up. The biggest acquisition came in November, when "Macho Man" Randy Savage surprised the wrestling world by leaving his commentary position with the WWF to return to the ring with WCW. The $400,000 per year WCW contract didn't hurt.

RANDY SAVAGE: It was a total change. I kind of knew what I was getting into, but I really didn't realize how much different until I got there. First of all, coming from the sticks, the minor leagues of wrestling, and then to the WWF, getting a break and being guaranteed an opportunity with Vince McMahon, who I'll be grateful to forever. It was a first-class organization. Then I got to WCW and you don't know who is in charge. A lot of different cliques. If you're a good soldier there, you die. If you're a good soldier with Vince, you'll do good. Nobody cares, and that's just the way it was down there. I'll guarantee when it comes to the history of WCW, that's not the way to have longevity in a territory and make it rock.

As Hogan worked with Vader in early 1995, Bischoff continued to conceive of ways to make things profitable for the first time and surpass the WWF as the dominant player in the industry. But even Bischoff himself could not forecast the events that would soon provide him with the elusive chances to challenge the leader.

Bischoff walked into a rare face-to-face meeting with Ted Turner at the CNN Center in July 1995, planning to discuss a satellite deal to broadcast WCW programming into China. During the meeting, Turner posed a surprising question to his wrestling vice president: "Eric, what do we have to do to compete with the WWF?" A stunned Bischoff blurted out, "Give me prime time." Up until that point, WCW's flagship show had aired late Saturday afternoons on TBS. Bischoff never believed he'd get his wish, but Turner turned to Scott Sassa, President of the Turner Entertainment Group, and pulled the trigger — "Scott, give Eric two hours every Monday night on TNT." WCW *Monday Nitro* was born.

Running head-to-head with the established WWF *Monday Night Raw* program on the USA Network sounded like a suicide mission. Most pundits espoused the theory that the two shows would split the wrestling audience. Bischoff didn't care. He wanted to show up Vince McMahon, and there was no better way than by invading the WWF's established wrestling night. The Monday night wrestling war kicked off on September 4, 1995. But on this night, only one side made it to the battlefield. With *Raw* preempted by U.S. Open tennis on USA, Bischoff wisely debuted WCW

Monday Nitro unopposed, to potentially the entire wrestling viewing audience. Viewers who sampled *Nitro* from the Mall of America in Minneapolis, Minnesota, witnessed Brian Pillman pin Japan's Jushin "Thunder" Liger, Ric Flair defeat Sting via disqualification, and Hulk Hogan pin Big Bubba Rogers in the main event. The biggest surprise came in the form of the shocking WCW return of Lex Luger, who had appeared on a WWF house show the previous night. Luger's WWF contract had expired and he had verbally agreed to stay, but Bischoff seized the opportunity and stole Luger from under McMahon's nose with a big money offer that proved to be the opening salvo in what would become a bitter war.

> **ERIC BISCHOFF:** I was definitely trying to become number one, and I was doing it in a very, very aggressive way that probably, in some people's minds, bordered on being unethical because of the aggressiveness and unique nature of some of the things I was doing. But it wasn't because I was trying to put anyone out of business. I was just trying to firmly establish myself as number one, and that came at the expense of WWE. There's no question about that and it certainly didn't have anything to do with how I felt about Vince McMahon personally because I didn't know Vince McMahon. I had no reason to like him or hate him. It was really just me doing what I felt I had to do in a very unique business to become number one. So it wasn't emotional. There was no hatred involved.

Nitro drew a respectable 2.9 Nielsen rating for its maiden voyage. But how would the show fare against competition? On September 11, *Nitro* defeated *Raw* in the ratings by a 2.5 to 2.2 margin. The WWF returned the favor the following week with a 2.5 to 2.4 victory. The shows traded results for the remainder of the 1995, using tactics which included Bischoff's underhanded ploy of giving away results of taped editions of *Raw* during his live *Nitro* broadcast before the matches aired. It was admittedly a dirty maneuver, but this was war.

> **RANDY SAVAGE:** It was a huge rivalry. In fact, a few times I was asked to go out there and knock Vince, but I said that wasn't the deal when I came

in. You should have told me that, because that's the guys in the front office or the promoters or the guys who think they're in charge. That's their job if they want to go in that direction. I've seen that happen a lot of times before where that backfires. A couple of times over a few adult beverages after a good *Nitro*, it was predicted that Vince would be out of business in six months. And I'm thinking to myself, "I don't think these guys know Vince McMahon." He's a street fighter. You measure a guy when they're down, not when they're up.

The first several months of 1996 remained even. Airing against one another from 9pm to 10pm eastern, neither *Nitro* nor *Raw* could take the upper hand for any length of time. Bischoff refocused on the creative direction of company, and found his next great inspiration on the opposite side of the globe. As part of a business relationship and talent exchange with New Japan Pro Wrestling, Bischoff attended one of the promotion's big Tokyo Dome events. New Japan's business had been on fire thanks to an interpromotional angle between New Japan and the UWFI, a pro wrestling promotion utilizing a "shoot," or stiff, style of action. The success of the storyline motivated Bischoff to try to duplicate the issue in the United States. Of course, the WWF would have no part of doing business with WCW. But Bischoff didn't need the WWF initials, just the talent.

In early 1996, WCW's aggressive talent acquisition strategy paid off again with the signings of top WWF stars Razor Ramon and Diesel. The pair received mega-contracts of $750,000 each per year to make the jump. Bischoff was willing to spend the cash to facilitate his version of an invasion angle. The storyline kicked off on the May 27, 1996, *Nitro*, the first two-hour edition of the show. During a routine match between Mike Enos and Steve Doll, Scott Hall, the former Razor Ramon, made his way through the crowd and into the ring to disrupt the program. In his trademark Razor Ramon Puerto Rican accent, Hall cut a promo calling out Ted Turner and the WCW talent, intimating an allegiance with the WWF. The following week, Kevin Nash, formerly Diesel, arrived on the scene with Hall, again overtly teasing that they were working for Vince

McMahon. Hall and Nash popped up week after week in unexpected situations to interrupt *Nitro* and torment the performers. Viewers were intrigued by the apparent arrival of WWF talent to challenge WCW talent in their own backyard. The ratings quickly shifted toward WCW, as *Nitro* defeated *Raw* by a full ratings point, 3.4 to 2.3, on June 17.

The invasion angle took off for good at the *Bash at the Beach* pay-per-view on July 7 in Daytona Beach, Florida. WCW assembled a team to battle Hall and Nash, now The Outsiders, and a mystery partner in a six-man tag. Sting, Randy Savage, and Lex Luger represented Team WCW. The big question surrounded the third member of the opposition. Would it be another WWF defector? Not exactly, but it did turn out to be a man forever linked to the Stamford, Connecticut–based promotion. As The Outsiders dominated Sting and Savage, Hulk Hogan calmly walked down the aisle to presumably save his WCW brethren. Instead, the Hulkster shocked the world by dropping the big leg on Savage and joining forces with Hall and Nash. Hogan then revealed in a post-match interview, "Mean Gene, the first thing you need to do is tell these people to shut up if you want to hear what I got to say. The first thing you got to realize, brother, is this right here is the future of wrestling. You can call this the New World Order of wrestling, brother. . . . That's why these two guys, the so-called Outsiders, these are the men I want as my friends. They're the new blood of professional wrestling, brother. And not only are we going to take over the whole wrestling business, with Hulk Hogan and the new blood, we will destroy everything in our path. As far as I'm concerned, all of this crap in the ring represents these fans out here. For two years, brother, I held my head high. I did everything for the charities. I did everything for the kids. And the reception I got when I came out here — you fans can stick it, brother."

The New World Order — nWo — had arrived.

Chapter 4

The weeks and months ahead showcased the nWo as a dominating force over WCW. Hogan won the WCW World Title from The Giant at the August *Hog Wild* pay-per-view and proceeded to spray-paint "nWo" on the prestigious gold belt. The group added new members along the way, with The Giant turning on WCW to wear black, Ted Dibiase jumping from the WWF to join as a manager, and the 1-2-3 Kid from the WWF becoming the sixth nWo member, Syxx. Most *Nitro* shows ended with the nWo destroying any and all WCW talent in sight and spray-painting their group's initials on the victims.

As 1997 arrived, WCW's business rocketed to unprecedented levels. In 1996, the company turned a profit for the first time thanks to revenue from the additional hour of *Nitro*. Ratings increased week after week, pay-per-view buyrates were up 26% since the arrival of Hall and Nash, and live event attendance was up a strong 56%. Life couldn't be sweeter for Bischoff and company, or could it?

The white-hot success of the nWo led Bischoff to add a January pay-per-view to the schedule, the first nWo pay-per-view. By this point, Bischoff had been revealed in the storyline as a member of the nWo working to destroy WCW from within. Several minor names were added to the group as well. The event, nWo *Souled Out*, came off as a bad show, with the nWo winning most of the matches against WCW wrestlers. *Souled Out* also did a poor buyrate, less than half of December's *Starrcade*, in one of the rare examples of the nWo failing to exhibit the Midas touch.

As the nWo continued gaining momentum, while running

roughshod over WCW, the seeds were planted for an inevitable showdown between the nWo's Hogan and WCW's Sting. To Bischoff and WCW's credit, the company built the storyline slowly before considering the match. It started at *Fall Brawl '96* when the nWo trotted out Sting, in black and white garb, as part of their War Games team. The situation turned out to be a ruse as the real Sting ran in at the end of the match to aid Team WCW. But this would be the last we'd see of Sting in the ring for nearly sixteen months. He ditched the colorful face paint and spiked blonde hair in favor of a black trenchcoat, white face paint, and a baseball bat, a near carbon copy of the character from the movie, *The Crow*. He retreated to the rafters of the arenas, watching the action with a stoic disposition. As the nWo continued to dominate, WCW fans yearned for Sting to be their savior.

> **STING:** What prompted the change was the fact that wrestling was changing and wrestling fans were changing. It had to be faster-paced. It had to be bigger moves. It had to be more cutting edge. It had to be darker. Even Hollywood and the movies were doing that, too. When Kevin Nash and Scott Hall made that first vignette of the nWo, that was cutting edge, and I knew it was going to work before it ever aired. I watched it in the studio with them and I was freaking out. I was like, "This is going to change our company." And it did. They would tag me up from time to time with Hulk, and he was still red and yellow, and he was starting to get booed out of the building and I knew it was probably right around the corner for me, too. Hulk had to change his character and became Hollywood Hulk Hogan. Scott Hall gave me an idea of coming out with a dark jacket and to paint my whole face, and the character slowly developed into what it developed.

WCW's ratings held steady in the 3.2 to 3.5 range throughout the summer of '97. The WWF had expanded *Raw* to two hours earlier in the year to compete with WCW. As business improved for WCW, so did the company's mainstream perception, thanks to a clever, albeit expensive, celebrity signing. Bischoff brought in controversial pro basketball superstar Dennis Rodman, fresh off an NBA championship with Michael Jordan and the Chicago Bulls, to be a member of the nWo. Basketball's bad boy teaming with wrestling's premiere group of bad guys worked like magic. Rodman agreed to step in to the ring at the 1997 *Bash at the Beach* for a $750,000 payday and a percentage of revenues over a certain threshold. Rodman teamed with WCW World Champion Hulk Hogan to battle Lex Luger and The Giant, back as a WCW baby-face, which ended with Hogan submitting to Luger's torture rack maneuver, setting the stage for a title match. The pay-per-view only managed a pedestrian 0.78 buyrate, but it provided the company with valuable publicity on news and sports shows around the country. A bigger Rodman payoff would come one year later.

Luger's title shot was the featured bout on August 4 as part of a special three-hour *Nitro* commemorating the 100th episode. The expanded show broke the 4.0 ratings barrier for the first time during the Monday night wars, a 4.4 composite, capped by Luger winning the title. His reign didn't last long as Hogan regained the strap five days later at the *Road Wild* (formerly *Hog Wild*) pay-per-view. Those strong ratings were about to become the norm. An unopposed two-hour *Nitro* on August 25 drew a whopping 5.0 rating with an amazing 5.7 for the second hour. When *Raw* returned on September 8, the margin of difference favored *Nitro*, 4.3 to 2.2. WCW could do no wrong.

> **MIKE TENAY:** If you can think back to the days of WCW, the most successful time when *Monday Nitro* was really exploding on the scene and the pay-per-views were doing great, we really had something for every wrestling fan. Maybe we had an opening match cruiserweight situation with a Rey Mysterio, a Juventud Guerrera, a Dean Malenko, that type of match. Then we might follow that up with a lucha libre six-man tag. You might see a tag-team match next maybe involving the Harlem Heat or the Steiner Brothers. And then from there we'd go on with such recognizable names at the top of the card — the Hogans, the Savages, the Flairs, and the like.

Sellout crowds and record buyrates became a regular occurrence as WCW geared up for its biggest show in history. The long awaited Sting vs. Hogan match was on tap for the December 28

Dickerman, Rey Mysterio Jr. and Fritz

Starrcade '97 extravaganza. But just before the final push, WCW received a gift of epic proportions. Already with all of the momentum in the wrestling war, WCW was about to be handed the competition's biggest superstar. The WWF asked out of Bret "The Hitman" Hart's long-term, big money contract, and permitted him to negotiate a record three-year, $7.5 million contract with WCW. The infamous McMahon doublecross in Hart's final WWF match at *Survivor Series '97* in Montreal quickly made Hart the hottest name in wrestling. But in the company's first major sign of creative weakness, Hart's debut with WCW came off flat. Instead of having him wrestle as a babyface on *Starrcade*, Hart refereed a match between Eric Bischoff and Larry Zbyszko for control of the *Nitro* show. But *Starrcade* didn't need Hart to be a success. Over 17,000 fans sold-out the MCI Center in Washington D.C. to the tune of over a half million dollars in gate receipts and an eye-popping 1.9 buyrate — or 650,000 pay-per-view buys — to witness Sting's return to the ring and subsequent victory over Hulk Hogan, the first significant win for WCW over the nWo.

Eric Bischoff sat on top of the world when 1998 rolled in. With business on fire and ratings reaching new heights each week, the Turner brass asked Bischoff to add another two-hour prime-time wrestling show for TBS. On January 4, 1998, WCW *Thunder* debuted on Thursday nights. From a business perspective, Bischoff originally wanted to split the nWo and WCW brands to theoretically double revenues by managing each as a separate entity. The nWo would control *Nitro*, while WCW would run *Thunder*. But a trial nWo *Nitro* before *Starrcade* bombed aesthetically and in the ratings, which changed his mind. The storyline continued with the nWo and WCW battling for supremacy.

Bret Hart's arrival in WCW was expected to continue the positive momentum. Coming off the WWF screwjob, Hart personified the term, "sympathetic babyface." He proved immediately he could draw money for the company when his first pay-per-view match at January's *Souled Out '99* helped the show draw a 1.0 buyrate, more than double the previous year's nWo pay-per-view experiment. But Hart's push quickly slowed down. He never entered the main event picture, as Hogan — who some blamed for selfishly sabotaging Hart's run — Sting, and Randy Savage feuded over the WCW World Title. The squandering of this golden opportunity symbolized the early cracks in WCW's armor.

> **BRET HART:** I think that there were certain guys that just maybe had it in for me. I don't even know which guys those are. I've had it suggested to me over the years that Hogan took a big part in making sure that I never got off the ground. I've also had people say it was Flair. I've had people say it was Kevin Sullivan or it was Kevin Nash. I really don't know who it was. I always had a pretty good rapport with Eric Bischoff, but he always seemed to be answering to somebody else and he always seemed to be answering to a committee of people that were all nameless faces that seemed hell-bent on making sure I sat on the bench for most of the time I was there.

Chapter 5

Luckily for WCW, despite missing out with Bret Hart, there was another rising star on the horizon and, for once, he was a home-grown talent. Bill Goldberg, a football standout at the University of Georgia who had a cup of coffee with the NFL's Atlanta Falcons, debuted to little fanfare in September 1997. He rarely spoke on the microphone, opting to do his talking in the ring. Week after week, he annihilated opponents at the snap of a finger with his trademark spear and jackhammer moves. In early 1998, his record was still unblemished, and fans started to take notice with loud "Goldberg!" chants before and after his appearances.

With ratings for *Nitro* remaining strong, Eric Bischoff received the green light to expand to three hours from 8pm to 11pm eastern each Monday night. On paper, the idea looked feasible, as the company had been so hot, it could easily fill an extra hour of programming and enjoy the additional advertising revenue. But after already adding *Thunder* to the mix for two hours on Thursday nights, five hours of weekly prime-time television would prove quite challenging over the long haul.

Early on, the ratings held up. The first permanent three-hour *Nitro* on January 26, 1998, drew a 4.7 rating. *Thunder* also did well on TBS, with ratings in the low 4.0's for its first few weeks. *Nitro* stayed consistently in the mid-to-high 4.0's through the first quarter of 1998. In fact, an unopposed *Nitro* on February 16 drew a 5.1 rating, a new record. The honor lasted exactly one month, as another unopposed show on March 16 garnered a 5.6. However, slowly but surely, the WWF's *Raw* gained momentum on the shoulders of edgy programming and the emergence of Stone Cold Steve Austin, Degeneration X, and The Rock. Appearances by Mike Tyson leading up to *WrestleMania XIV* and the Austin vs. McMahon feud storyline helped the WWF turn the corner. Fans tiring of the older WCW stars and constant pattern of nWo dominance began sampling what the WWF presented. *Nitro*'s ratings didn't immediately deteriorate as much as *Raw* attracted new viewers. The turning point came on April 13, 1998, when *Raw*, for the first time in eighty-three head-to-head matchups, defeated *Nitro* by a 4.6 to 4.3 margin. WCW felt the heat, but there was little it could do facing preemptions for *Nitro* by the NBA playoffs.

The cracks in the WCW armor grew larger as the WWF crept back in the previously one-sided Monday night wars. Bischoff, in particular, exhibited signs of frustration. He fired Syxx, who had been sidelined with a broken neck, to spite Kevin Nash and Scott Hall, who were complaining to him about their storylines. Syxx immediately jumped back to the WWF and became a key player as X-Pac in the revamped Degeneration X stable. Bischoff then went off on Ric Flair for missing a WCW *Thunder* event despite company approval to attend his son's amateur wrestling tournament. Bischoff even went so far to file a $2 million lawsuit against his legendary star.

> **RIC FLAIR:** I was mad at myself for allowing myself to be put in the position that he put me in. I won't forgive him for what he did to me. There will be no reason he can ever give me to why he did it. I'm over it, and I've learned that you get bigger and you get better every day or you live in the past, and I'm going down that road now to hopefully getting bigger and better every day in terms of the past and the life that I lead.

The foundation was slowly crumbling. Last but not least, Bischoff tried to rally the troops by challenging Vince McMahon to a fight on WCW television at the May pay-per-view. To no one's surprise, McMahon declined.

When *Nitro* got back on track following the basketball playoffs, the company turned to Goldberg to help reverse its fortunes.

Despite not being in the main-event picture, Goldberg was, by far, WCW's most popular attraction. His winning streak remained intact, although WCW, for some odd reason, decided to artificially inflate the numbers. Along the way, Goldberg won the WCW United States Title from Raven on the April 20, 1998, *Nitro* in Colorado Springs, Colorado. He chalked up his 100th win at the *Great American Bash* against Konnan. But the biggest match of Goldberg's rookie career came on *Nitro* on July 6, 1998. In his hometown of Atlanta, in front of more than 40,000 screaming fans — a WCW record — in the Georgia Dome, Goldberg challenged Hulk Hogan for the WCW World Title. Hogan agreed to drop the strap, especially in front of the enormous crowd, in exchange for the promise he'd be the man to finally beat Goldberg down the road. The amazing night saw a packed house cheer in unison as Goldberg overcame all obstacles to spear and jackhammer his way to the WCW Championship.

> **TERRY TAYLOR:** A lot of people don't know that most of that Goldberg stuff was mine, from the undefeated streak to calling him by the one name to short matches. Mike Tyson was beating people up in ninety seconds, and you'd see Mike Tyson fight and he was ferocious and beat people so quickly, but when you think about it, you paid fifty bucks and really didn't see anything. And that's what we did with Goldberg. We wanted people to want to see more, so we didn't have him go long.

In a vacuum, the Georgia Dome show could be considered nothing but an overwhelming success, between the live gate and the television ratings. *Nitro* scored its first ratings victory over *Raw* in five weeks, 4.8 to 4.0, with the Goldberg vs. Hogan bout itself drawing an unbelievable 6.9 rating. But in the grand picture, WCW had wasted a big payday on pay-per-view by giving away Goldberg's title victory on free television just to claim one Monday night victory. The decision-making continued to befuddle observers.

Believe it or not, Goldberg's title victory got lost in the shuffle. Six days later, WCW held the annual *Bash at the Beach* pay-per-view and again brought in Dennis Rodman to compete. But

Rodman didn't come from the NBA alone. Superstar Karl Malone of the Utah Jazz also signed on to face Rodman as part of the tag-team main event. WCW lucked into great fortune as Rodman's Bulls had just defeated Malone's Jazz in the NBA Finals. A memorable scene of Rodman and Malone fighting for a loose ball on the floor during one of the games provided plenty of free publicity for the match. In the ring, Rodman and Hogan defeated Malone and Diamond Dallas Page, but WCW was the real winner after a 1.5 buyrate (about 600,000 buys) for the event, the second largest in company history.

It should be noted that while WCW's pay-per-view main events were generally poor, and this tag-team match was no exception, the undercard usually featured strong matches. Wrestlers like Chris Benoit, Eddie Guerrero, Chris Jericho, Dean Malenko, Raven, cruiserweights from Mexico, and other international stars busted their butts to make WCW events worth watching.

Chris Jericho and Dickerman

CHRIS JERICHO: I don't think it's intentional, but I do think some guys get held back. Well, not necessarily held back, because I think guys are used to the highest potential to the people that are in charge see them as. I don't see that the people in charge see that. The fans see it and the wrestlers see it, but I think the powers that be don't see things that way for whatever reason. I don't know why. I can't figure them out for myself, but I think that's the problem with WCW. There are so many guys that are ready to break through to the upper echelon and become main event draws. I just don't think, for whatever reasons, I don't know why, that the people in charge see that.

The success of celebrities in the ring led WCW to try it again with the August *Road Wild* show. The time, it wasn't a basketball player, a football player, or even a figure skater. WCW signed Jay Leno. Yes, the late-night talk show host was going to wrestle. The angle started when Hulk Hogan and Eric Bischoff hijacked *The Tonight Show* on NBC. Leno brought out Diamond Dallas Page to chase them off, leading up to a tag-team match on pay-per-view. The match went surprisingly well, with Leno pinning Bischoff to win for his team. But the show didn't replicate the business success of the previous month, doing a 0.93 buyrate. Evidently, the crossover between wrestling fans and Leno's audience was slim to none. Who knew?

Once the celebrity bug wore off, WCW tried another blast from the past to spark the top of the cards. In came The Ultimate Warrior to feud with Hulk Hogan, eight years after their *WrestleMania VI* showdown. Known now solely as The Warrior, his gimmick consisted of appearing and disappearing in a cloud of smoke to mess with Hogan's psyche. The execution of the storyline and match came off as badly as it sounded on paper. The public didn't care either, as the show drew only a 0.78 buyrate. For the record, *Nitro* did win the ratings battle the following night thanks to a free replay of the Goldberg vs. Diamond Dallas Page WCW Title match that got cut off the pay-per-view after a technical snafu. But the numbers began to slip into the low 4.0's thereafter, while *Raw* took off into the 5.0's consistently.

While ratings slowly began to drop, live attendance held firm. In fact, WCW drew two monster crowds in domes for *Nitro* events — over 30,000 at the Astrodome in Houston on November 30 and close to the same total in St. Louis at the TWA Dome on December 21. Both shows were part of the build to *Starrcade*. This year's show would be headlined by Goldberg defending his WCW World Title against Kevin Nash, who earned the shot by winning the sixty-man, three-ring battle royal at the November *World War 3* pay-per-view. Coincidentally, Nash also became the head creative booker for WCW at around the same time. He decided he would be the man to finally pin the still-undefeated Goldberg. Hogan had gone on hiatus, claiming to be running for the presidency of the United States after former wrestler Jesse Ventura shockingly won the gubernatorial election in Minnesota. Nash orchestrated the *Starrcade* match so that Scott Hall interfered and stunned Goldberg with an electric taser behind the referee's back. Nash followed with a jackknife powerbomb and, for the first time in history, pinned Goldberg's shoulders to the mat for a count of three. On December 27, 1998, Kevin Nash became the new WCW World Champion, and the invincible aura of Goldberg was destroyed. Soon, the fortunes of the entire company would follow.

Even with the Goldberg streak ended and his momentum neutered, there was still reason for optimism to begin 1999. After all, the final *Nitro* of 1998 drew a 4.6 rating, the highest number since the post–*Halloween Havoc* show. At the arenas, WCW averaged an unheard of 8,000 paying fans per live event in 1998, which included a mind-boggling string of twenty-three consecutive sold-out events. No wrestling promotion in the world had ever hit that mark up to that point. The average pay-per-view buyrate was just under 1.0. In total, WCW grossed approximately $200 million in revenue and a whopping $55 million in profit. The company that had never made a dime before 1996 had raked in $55 million in twelve months. With all of the good fortune, how could things fall apart so quickly? The first *Nitro* of 1999 foreshadowed that answer.

TERRY TAYLOR: WCW had a lot of problems. This is not a knock on Eric. Eric was the one who turned it around. We were in the boiler room saying we're taking on water. So, we called up to the captain of the Titanic, and we're saying we are down here in the boiler room and it's pretty wet. Something is going on and we're taking on water. We're starting to sink. He would say that this is the biggest, the most expensive, the most elaborate ship of all time and it's unsinkable. Things kept going wrong and got worse and worse. It's not his fault. He was busy and misled. I think there are a few things he would do differently, I know he would do differently, because when he came back, he wasn't just throwing the money around any more. You can't just give wrestlers money. Most of them will hate me for this, but a lot of the guys need the motivation of money or they don't work as hard. It's human nature. There isn't a guy alive who will work harder than me if I get paid more.

Chapter 6

Just as the quality decision-making and well-planned booking of
1996 and 1997 resulted in the exorbitant profits of 1998, the questionable choices of that same year would lead to problems down
the road. The misspent push of Bret Hart, Goldberg's title win on
free television, and Nash's victory over Goldberg at *Starrcade*
proved the fallibility of WCW's braintrust. To atone for these mis-
takes and return to the road to riches, the company needed to set a
positive tenor with the January 4, 1999, *Nitro* from another full
Georgia Dome. In retrospect, this show became a turning point in
WCW history — for all the wrong reasons.

The aftermath of Goldberg's first loss left fans demanding a
rematch, and WCW promised to deliver on this all-important
Nitro. But something funny happened over the course of the three-
hour buildup. Led by booker Kevin Nash, WCW didn't want to
restore Goldberg just yet. The title would leave Nash's waist, but
Goldberg wouldn't be the recipient. To weasel out of the advertised
main event, WCW concocted a far-fetched storyline in which Miss
Elizabeth, a heel, claimed Goldberg had been stalking her. Police
arrested Goldberg and took him downtown for questioning,
meaning his title opportunity was gone. But lo and behold, Hulk
Hogan made a surprise return from his bogus presidential campaign. Hogan stepped up and offered to take Goldberg's place in
the main event against Nash. It wasn't the promised rematch, but
the fans were at least in line for a title match. The two original nWo
members faced off in the middle of the ring. After one minute of
trash-talking, Hogan stuck his right index finger into Nash's chest.

The champion took an exaggerated fall to the mat, and acted as if he was unconscious. Hogan covered him and got the three count to win the title. Then Nash popped right up and embraced Hogan to reveal the storyline farce. The real scam was behind the scenes as Hogan and Nash selfishly schemed to protect each other's careers, with Hogan allowing Nash to beat Goldberg in exchange for regaining the title. Fans in the Georgia Dome were upset by the slap in the face. Viewers at home were upset. And wrestlers in the locker room realized the new political climate and were rightfully upset.

> **BOBBY HEENAN:** I didn't hate the business as much as I hated the lack of intelligence when it came to producing the show. Like when Mark McGwire hit seventy home runs that year, he came to Atlanta and he wanted to meet Goldberg. So Goldberg went over to Turner Field, and McGwire ripped his shirt off and rubbed his bat on his shirt and went out and hit seventy home runs that year. Vince McMahon would have had McGwire and Goldberg in Louisville picking out wood. He'd have them taking batting practice. He'd have been doing everything to show it. We never aired it or showed it because that was McGwire and Goldberg's idea and it wasn't theirs, and I don't think they knew how to do it. They never sent a camera crew over or anything, and this was the hottest story going when McGwire hit seventy. And then what do they do? They have 40,000 people in the Georgia Dome and they beat Goldberg. Please!

The ratings elucidated the damage done by the one finger title change. The January 4 show drew a 5.0, a strong number, but still short of *Raw*'s 5.7. Four weeks later, the margin grew to a 5.8 to 4.7 in favor of the WWF. Two weeks later, *Raw* smoked *Nitro* by two full ratings points, 5.9 to 3.9. The story got even worse for WCW on March 1, when *Raw* drew a 6.4, its first 6.0 with competition, to *Nitro*'s 4.3. The ship had certainly begun to take on water. To prove that it wasn't merely *Raw* siphoning away WCW's viewers, *Thunder*'s ratings experienced the same downturn. The first *Thunder* of 1999 popped a 4.3 rating. By April 1, the rating had fallen to a 3.1 and continued to descend.

The booking throughout the early half of the year did little to reverse the slide. Fan favorite Ric Flair was portrayed as an insane lunatic, with poorly contrived skits set in a mental institution. The lure of the nWo had long since worn off from overexposure and oversaturation. With an abundance of new members over the past year, the New World Order cracked into two factions — the black and white nWo Hollywood, and the black and red nWo Wolfpack. By this point, fans were bored with the entire concept. In addition, the WCW World Title bounced from Hogan to Flair in a steel cage match at March's *Uncensored* pay-per-view, to Diamond Dallas Page in a four-way match at April's *Spring Stampede*. WCW then booked two title switches in one night on the April 24 *Nitro*. Sting captured the belt in the first half of the show, only to lose it back to Page at the end of the night. The excessive changes did little but devalue the credibility of the title, rendering it worthless as a drawing tool.

If anyone felt WCW was still a threat in the Monday night wars, the June 14 battle proved otherwise. *Raw* more than doubled *Nitro* that night — 6.6 to 3.2. A month earlier, an unopposed *Raw* had drawn an 8.1 rating, one-tenth of a point shy of the all-time wrestling cable record.

WCW tried to get back in the game by spending money on non-wrestling talent. Dennis Rodman returned, which turned into a disaster after multiple no shows. The company tried to appeal to the hip-hop community by bringing in Master P and his No Limit Soldiers. The idea fell flat as the southern WCW fans booed the babyface rappers in favor of the heel West Texas Rednecks, led by Curt Hennig, who preferred country music. Heavy metal group Megadeth also made an appearance on *Nitro* to poor ratings and fan indifference. Instead of spending money on fresh wrestling talent, WCW handed out a three-year contract at close to a half-million dollars per year to UFC fighter Tank Abbott, an out-of-shape brawler known solely for his punching power. Perhaps the biggest failure was the idea of bringing in legendary rock band KISS to perform on the August 23 *Nitro*. One would think Bischoff and company should have realized by now that fans didn't care about concerts on their wrestling shows. The $500,000 experiment resulted in the lowest *Nitro* ratings since July 1996 — over three years! The show managed only a 2.9 composite rating, with the actual concert pulling a 2.2 rating.

> **ERIC BISCHOFF:** A lot of times when I hear people talking about WCW, it's that the company was financially mismanaged. They had an unlimited amount of money to spend. They didn't know how to control their expenditures. That is completely untrue. We had a budget that was approved a year in advance just like anybody else. The only reason that we had money to spend is we were making so much money. The company went from being a $24 million a year company that was losing $10 million a year in the process when I took it over in 1993, to a $300, $350 million company that was making $30 to $40 million a year after I took it over two or three years later. So certainly I had a lot more money to spend, and I had a lot of freedom within the Turner organization that was based on the success that I created, not on the fact that Ted Turner was willing to throw unlimited amounts of money at WCW just because he wanted to or had some vendetta against Vince McMahon.

As business rolled downhill, the frustration among the wrestlers, particularly mid-card performers, reached the boiling point. Despite all of the fiscal problems, the old guard — Hogan, Nash, Savage, Flair, Piper, etc. — continued to dominate the main event positions. The company desperately needed an influx of fresh names in their main events, but the veterans refused to pass the torch. As a result, talent looked north for employment. Chris Jericho's contract expired and he jumped ship to the WWF for a three-year deal in July 1999. Raven quit the company, walking out on a $275,000 per year guaranteed contract, after speaking out publicly about the company's problems. He returned to ECW for around half the money.

> **CHRIS JERICHO:** I felt that I didn't have a chance to really spread my wings to my fullest potential in WCW. I think in a year to two years that will be a great place to be. Right now, I think there is a certain kind of person that gets the chance to expand to the utmost of their character's creativity, and I don't think I was one of those chosen few in WCW.

The sky was falling in on WCW's world, and the Turner hierarchy finally took notice. On September 9, 1999, Eric Bischoff was relieved of his WCW duties and sent home pending reassignment within the Turner organization. In layman's terms, he was fired, but would still collect the money on his expensive multiyear contract.

DIAMOND DALLAS PAGE: What Eric pulled off there was unbelievable. I was around Eric Bischoff when he told me he was going to kick Vince McMahon's ass. I told him he was out of his mind. I don't doubt anything he says anymore. He told me he was going to run this company back when we were job guy announcers. He pulled it off.

A lot of people don't understand this, but when Eric Bischoff was here, there were a lot of people stabbing him in the back. There were a lot of people undermining what he was doing. There were a lot of people that he was trusting, that were not delivering the goods.

Bischoff was replaced by Bill Busch, an accountant who went from Vice President of Strategic Planning to Executive Vice President of WCW. His first responsibility was to cut costs wherever possible. Since he didn't know much about wrestling, the search was on for someone to handle the creative direction full-time. If WCW couldn't compete with the WWF, why not raid the men who scripted their popular product? Busch and WCW did just that by signing the WWF's head writers, Vince Russo and Ed Ferrara.

J.J. DILLON: There was a mutual friend that we had both known out of Connecticut who had called me and said that Vince [Russo] wasn't happy for one reason or another and wanted to know if there was any interest. I was in a position to ask the questions. Russo was petrified that Vince [McMahon] would find out, so it was a cloak-and-dagger type of thing. But it ended up where he was flown down to Atlanta and we met out at the airport for a weekend with Bill Busch, who was in charge at that time. Brad Siegal came in and talked to him, and Harvey Schiller came in and talked to him, and a decision was made by them to offer him a job.

Russo's influence in revitalizing the WWF product was undeniable. His "crash TV" style of producing a wrestling television show changed the business for the better. He convinced McMahon to shift away from the cartoonish aspects of the WWF product in favor of more reality-based storylines. Sprinkled in was a greater emphasis on violence, sex, and obscene language, to appeal to the young male demographic. The formula worked to perfection. But Russo was not the savior he sold himself as. For all of his good ideas, he contributed just as many, if not more, bad ones. Luckily, he had a safety net in the form of Vince McMahon, who filtered out most of the junk. That aspect of Russo's résumé did not become evident until he arrived in WCW, well after Bill Busch signed him on October 3 for just under $600,000 per year.

> **ED FERRARA:** One of the things we said when we first came in was that we were not going to change things overnight. We need to take our time. We need to change what we can as we can and not overdo it. If we try and do too much too soon, there is going to be a backlash.

The Russo-Ferrara duo started on the October 18 *Nitro*. The feel of the entire product changed immediately, with a heavy focus on angles and skits as opposed to in-ring action. The show drew a 3.3 rating, up from the previous week's 2.6. Russo booked a WCW World Title tournament after a weird, worked shoot angle at *Halloween Havoc* in which Hogan deliberately laid down for Sting in the main event, again cheating fans out of an advertised title match. The tournament concluded at WCW *Mayhem* in Toronto on November 21, with Bret Hart pinning Chris Benoit in the finals. This set the stage for Hart vs. Goldberg for the title at *Starrcade* and Russo's grand idea to turn the company around.

From the MCI Center in Washington D.C. on December 19, Russo took a page out of the WWF playbook, albeit an unscripted play, by reprising the *Survivor Series '97* Montreal screwjob. This time, Hart played the role of perpetrator instead of the victim. As Hart applied the Sharpshooter on Goldberg, guest referee Rowdy Roddy Piper, in his best impersonation of Vince McMahon, called for the bell without Goldberg submitting. Hart feigned anger over the cheap victory, but his true feelings would come out the next night. On *Nitro* from Baltimore, Hall and Nash, the WCW Tag-Team Champions, interfered on behalf of Hart in his rematch with Goldberg. WCW United States Champion Jeff Jarrett, who jumped to WCW with Russo and Ferrara from the WWF, joined in with spray paint. The foursome inscribed "n-W-o" on Goldberg to end the show. Russo's grand idea was now apparent — the reformation of the New World Order.

Chapter 7

Could Hart, Hall, Nash, and Jarrett replicate the 1996 success of Hogan, Hall, and Nash? Russo hoped so. Although not his fault, WCW lost $15 million in 1999. That's right, $15 million! The most money any wrestling company had ever lost in one year. (All of this coming just twelve months after the company netted $55 million in profit.) The freefall was unfathomable. Russo felt he could turn things around. All he needed was time. His first two months on the job did not go well. *Starrcade* capped the year off with a miserable 0.32 buyrate, a 72% decrease from the Goldberg vs. Nash debacle the previous year. For Russo to succeed, he needed plenty of luck. He got it, but as it turned out, it was all bad.

Hoping to improve ratings, WCW cut *Nitro* back to two hours — from 8 to 10pm eastern. The idea was to cut out the filler and focus on the main storylines. Without a third hour to drag down the ratings, the composite would be artificially propped up. Too bad it didn't work. The last three-hour *Nitro* drew a 2.9 rating. The January 3 two-hour show did a 3.3. But to compensate for the loss of advertising revenue from axing the third hour, ratings needed to hit the mid-4.0's. WCW never got close.

But the real bad luck came in the form of the injury bug. It started with Goldberg suffering a severe gash in his arm from a glass-breaking stunt gone awry on *Thunder*. The injury required forty stitches to close, and kept the company's top babyface on the shelf for several months. WCW Champion Bret Hart joined him on the injured list with a severe concussion, originally suffered at *Starrcade*. He'd continued to work with it unknowingly until doctors refused to medically clear him. He would never wrestle again. Then Jeff Jarrett went down with a concussion of his own. With three of WCW's top stars out, the *Souled Out* pay-per-view looked dead in the water.

> **BRET HART:** I think I was a catalyst. I set a lot of things in motion. It's funny what one kick to the head can do, but I think it affected everybody. . . . They just started trying to get their engines going and got torpedoed with about five or six big torpedoes.

With the event in shambles, Russo made a gutsy decision — strip Hart of the title, announce a battle royal for the gold at *Souled Out*, and book Tank Abbott, who could still not wrestle his way out of a paper bag, to win the WCW World Title. Upon hearing this, Bill Busch decided Russo possessed more guts than brains. Already frustrated by the lack of progress under Russo, Busch made the call to remove him from power. He devised a committee led by Kevin Sullivan to handle the creative direction. The decision was made for Sid Vicious to wrestle Chris Benoit for the vacant World Title on the show.

> **ED FERRARA:** When we worked together in the WWF, we established a really good routine, a very good working relationship. There was a lot of give and take, but we had a lot in common. . . . When we went to WCW, things changed. Obviously, Vince was brought in at a higher level than I was. Vince is very much a cowboy. He wanted to do things his way 24/7. I had been in the television business for over ten years and I know about the politics of TV in that maybe you might have the most brilliant, creative idea in the world but you've also got some corporate suits above you that you need to have their blessing to get these ideas through. You've got to play the game a little bit. You're not going to change the world with a revolution in that sense. In the corporate world, you've got to change it from within. I feel that Vince, rather than trying to make little concessions making the people above him feel like he was making an attempt to play their game, he went back at them from day one, and refused to bend and really engendered a very antagonistic relationship both ways.

The new *Souled Out* main event was set, but Chris Benoit didn't want the shot. In fact, he wanted out of WCW entirely. He and several other wrestlers disapproved of the choice of Sullivan. The Canadian, in particular, had a personal issue with Sullivan — dating back to the time Sullivan's wife left him to be with (and eventually marry) Benoit. A group of seven wrestlers — Benoit, Eddie Guerrero, Dean Malenko, Perry Saturn, Shane Douglas, Billy Kidman, and Konnan — confronted Busch on the afternoon of the pay-per-view and asked either for their unconditional releases or that Sullivan be removed as head of creative. Busch asked them for time to make a decision. In the meantime, the company booked Benoit to win the title, even though chances were good he would be leaving. Benoit reluctantly agreed. The next day at *Nitro*, Busch told all of the wrestlers they were being sent home pending a resolution. Benoit gave the belt back and went home with his comrades. The title was vacant again. Two days later, on January 19, Busch decided to support Sullivan and sent full contract releases to Benoit, Guerrero, Malenko, Saturn, Douglas, and Konnan. Kidman had agreed to stay. Konnan began to waver on his decision since he had no guarantee of employment elsewhere. Douglas felt the same way. The other four immediately flew to WWF headquarters for secret meetings to negotiate contracts. Douglas was unaware they went without him and felt betrayed.

SHANE DOUGLAS: I'm one of those people who value friendship from people who want legitimate friendship, but when it turns out not to be, I wash my hands of it. I don't have time in my life to deal with people who are false friends. I choose to keep myself away from that. When that whole thing went down, my exact words to every single one of them was that every single person in this meeting has the right and the obligation to decide for themselves what is best for them and their families. They had brought up that we stick together as a group. I think they felt a lot more emboldened by walking in there and having a lot more guys like me stand behind them, I guess thinking that would help strengthen their position. I can tell you right now, on the record, that at no time would I have ever walked away from a $1.9 million contract. I'm a kid that grew up in the

Fritz, Dickerman, Shane Douglas, Rey Mysterio Jr. and B. Randall Myers

projects eating pancakes five or six days in a row, so $1.9 million to me was like hitting the lottery. We sat in the stands at the Cincinnati Gardens that day going in to have this meeting. We had talked about how we should contact the WWF and talk about if they are interested in bringing us in. Not one person in those stands that afternoon ever said that they were going to go into that meeting and offer up their resignation or request a release. Had they done so, I would have never walked into that meeting. I was intelligent enough to know that we weren't going to make that kind of money in the WWF, that the pay scale simply wasn't there to make what I was making. I would never have walked into that meeting requesting for a release when I was making that kind of money. So when we walk into that meeting, the six people that had spoken before me, I got about a half-sentence out of my mouth explaining why I was there and my explanation was simple. For $1.9 million, your company has a right and an obligation to get a return out of the character for that kind of investment, and if Kevin Sullivan was going to be coming into a position of power and was telling people that I was faking this biceps tear, it was clear that he had no intention of ever using my character and would undermine everything that I try and do. So I wanted to make Bill Busch aware that this investment was in jeopardy because of Kevin Sullivan. That was my intention of what that meeting was for.

The foursome, sans Douglas and Konnan, signed with the WWF and debuted in short order. Busch's tactic of standing behind Sullivan and ridding WCW of disgruntled performers did nothing other than cripple the talent roster through the loss of four premiere ring workers.

EDDIE GUERRERO: Take this into consideration on how bad the politics were over there. You take a guy like myself, who grew up in this business, and also Dean Malenko. Look at Chris Benoit who sacrificed and busted his ass to get where he's at. You take guys like that who give their heart, their bodies, their all to wrestling. Hey, when *we* don't want to go to work, you know there's something wrong. It got to the point where we would go to work with knots in our stomach because of the politics and the B.S. that we would be dealing with. To us, it became torture. I was looking for excuses

Chris Murray and the late Eddie Guerrero

not to go to work and this is because I love wrestling. For them to kill my
thrill to go to work, that's pretty bad.

Sid Vicious eventually won the WCW World Title following a
series of matches with Kevin Nash. By this point, most people no
longer cared. The January 31, 2000, ratings, which coincidentally
featured the WWF debuts of Benoit, Guerrero, Malenko, and
Saturn, saw *Raw* pummel *Nitro*, 6.6 to 2.8. Even worse, an unopposed *Nitro* in its normal 8 to 10pm timeslot lost to a preempted
Raw in a late night 11pm to 1am timeslot, 4.3 to 3.6. More wrestling
fans stayed up well past midnight on a weeknight to watch *Raw*
than would watch *Nitro* in prime time. *Nitro's* numbers remained
in the mid-to-high 2.0's, topping the 3.0 mark again only a handful
of times. The biggest revenue stream, pay-per-view, completely fell
apart, with record-low buyrates month after month for *Souled Out*
(0.25), *SuperBrawl* (0.15), and *Uncensored* (0.13). Ric Flair and Hulk
Hogan were brought back to stop the bleeding, but the wound was
too deep.

Brad Siegel, President of Turner Entertainment Networks, had
had enough. He felt the Sullivan regime had done little to improve
matters.

SHANE DOUGLAS: Kevin Sullivan should never have made a dime of his
money. He's a piece of garbage with the brain about the size of a pea. He
was telling me on the phone one time when I was with ECW that the nWo
was his idea, and I later find out from talking with Eric Bischoff and several
other people on the inside that it was Bischoff's inception and that Kevin
Sullivan, at most, had a steering influence. The results speak for themselves. Go back and look at what the ratings did under Kevin Sullivan. Go
back and look at what characters he created when he was in charge. It's
laughable. It is absolutely laughable that a company the size of WCW and
a conglomerate the size of AOL–Time Warner would actually take a guy like
this seriously, and that he stayed in power for two to three months. I used
to sit at home weekly thinking the phone was going to ring because the ratings were falling faster that a rock in a swimming pool, and week after
week he would roll out characters like The Dog. Here was a guy who was

giving it his all and trying to play the character. But let's face it, The Dog is an incredibly backhanded thing in the wrestling business. It's the kind of thing that people make fun of the wrestling business for, and with good reason. So I knew time was limited for Kevin Sullivan and I would just ride it out.

BILLY KIDMAN: Nobody liked working for Sullivan. Let's face it, because his ideas were all from the '70s. He pushes his friends. He hates a lot of guys and he uses his political power to bury them. He hates most of the young guys. He hates the small guys. He's just a miserable little man.

Siegel made the call to bring back Vince Russo, this time with Eric Bischoff. The unlikely tag team, in a sense, would handle creative and appear as television characters. Siegel wisely barred Bischoff from financial decisions, and asked Bill Busch to run the business end of the company. Refusing to work with Bischoff again, Busch quit, forcing Siegel to spend the bulk of his time on wrestling matters. It was now the Russo and Bischoff show, in perhaps the final attempt to save the company.

BOOKER T: I always had a very good relationship with Eric Bischoff. I'm really glad to see him back. Vince Russo, I didn't really know a lot about him, but I'm a team player. Right now, I'm pretty much letting these guys do what they need to do as far as getting us back in this war with WWF. Hopefully, we'll get back in that war and back on top of the ratings. I prefer to sit back rather than being too quick to jump the gun and say, "I don't like this." I like the direction it is going with younger guys like myself getting a chance. Guys like Billy Kidman and The Filthy Animals getting a chance. Like guys like Hulk Hogan and those guys did once upon a time, it's time for a change as far as the young guys to pull the show. There is a younger audience and it is about time.

Chapter 8

The new era began on April 10, 2000. The Russo and Bischoff duo blew up existing storylines and vacated all of the championships. The new direction saw the older, established stars, dubbed the Millionaire's Club, battle the up-and-coming talent, the New Blood. On paper, it sounded like a good idea, a rarity for WCW at this point. By mingling with the older names, the younger stars would receive a rub and make the leap into the top tier. The first show drew a 3.1 rating, about a half-point better than the recent average.

> **HULK HOGAN:** Sometimes people make excuses for failure. It's all about digging in. If Hulk Hogan was in their way, they should have moved me. I think the young guys have always had a chance. They just need to step up and take what is theirs. In this business, you make your own breaks. No crybabies, be a man and step up to the plate. If you want something, take it.

But while the idea of having young talent working with, and going over, established stars seemed sound, the results got lost in translation. Wins by Billy Kidman over Hulk Hogan, Mike Awesome over Kevin Nash, and Shane Douglas over Ric Flair suffered from outside interference, cheating, or other illegal means that portrayed the up-and-comers as weaker than their opponents. The execution left plenty to be desired and hindered the elevation process.

Despite the initial bump in business, after fans had sampled the Russo-Bischoff era, the numbers plateaued at previous levels. The latest attempt to spark life into the company came from Russo. And in typical Russo fashion, the idea blew up in his face and likely closed the coffin on WCW's future. On the April 26 *Thunder*, taped the night before in Rochester, New York, David Arquette, who appeared on the show to promote his new wrestling movie featuring WCW cameos, won the WCW World Title, pinning Eric Bischoff in a tag-team match in which the title could change hands. Yes, B-level actor David Arquette became the king of the mountain in WCW. The lineage of the title now included Flair, Sting, Hogan, Goldberg, and David Arquette!?! Russo believed making Arquette champion would result in a deluge of important mainstream publicity. It worked, if you count a tiny blurb in *USA Today* as major publicity. It also worked in revolting wrestling fans, as evidenced by the ensuing *Nitro*, which drew a dismal 2.5. Arquette's reign lasted until the May 7 *Slamboree* pay-per-view, where Jeff Jarrett won a three-way triple-decker steel cage match to regain the strap. The big draw of Arquette on pay-per-view resulted in a 0.14 buyrate. A 2.5 rating and a 0.14 buyrate in exchange for the credibility of the WCW World Title. Quite the bargain.

Russo flung more and more wild ideas at the wall, hoping one would stick. Goldberg turned heel at the *Great American Bash*. Fans pelted the ring with garbage in protest. The insanity continued the next month at *Bash at the Beach*, when, for the second time in nine months, someone laid down in a World Title match. This time, WCW Champion Jeff Jarrett purposely laid down for Hulk Hogan, who pretended not to know what was transpiring. WCW followed with a convoluted, worked-shoot angle, featuring promos by Hogan and Russo designed to stir controversy, but which only generated confusion, apathy, and an angry Hogan storming out of the building. The night climaxed with Booker T winning the WCW World Title, despite Hogan walking out with his own belt. The entire scenario started as a storyline, but Hogan felt it went too far, and filed a real defamation lawsuit against WCW.

Amidst all of the craziness, Brad Siegel made another change at the top. The Russo-Bischoff era was over. Siegel handed Russo complete autonomy; Bischoff was sent home for the second time. The company also went into full cost-cutting mode, after losses for the month of July alone hit $7 million. Estimates for annual losses were in the $80 million range — more than five times the red ink of 1999. By this point, Turner himself had taken notice. For first time since the days of Bill Watts in 1993, the Turner hierarchy legitimately explored severing ties with the wrestling industry.

> **JEFF JARRETT:** You could point so many fingers down there, but, in reality, the problem was this: it was a corporate structure. There was never one boss and nobody's ass was ever on the line. It's just that in a nutshell. . . . In WCW, you had different department heads, it was a corporate environment. And another thing, as good as the guaranteed contracts were, there really was no incentive for a guy to bust his ass, because you knew the check was coming every two weeks. Everybody has to be held accountable. In WCW, no one was held accountable. I think the corporate environment was the biggest failure. If you look back, it was a catastrophe from day one.

As the parent company, Time Warner, pondered the future of WCW, Vince Russo delivered another whopper on the September 25 *Nitro*. Russo, who had taken a more hands-on approach on television, booked himself into the main event of *Nitro* in a steel cage match against WCW Champion Booker T. For reasons only Russo could comprehend, he scripted himself to win the title after Goldberg interfered and speared him through the cage, meaning Russo reached the floor first and won the match. The title lineage now read Flair, Sting, Hogan, Goldberg, Arquette, and Russo. To underline the impact of Russo's title victory, the ratings for the next four weeks went 2.6, 2.5, 2.3, and 2.2.

Chapter 9

As the leaves changed in late 2000, rumors gathered steam that Time Warner was looking to sell World Championship Wrestling. Earlier in the year, SFX Entertainment, a live events promotions company, negotiated to purchase WCW, but passed on the $600 million asking price. In October, published reports cited Mandalay Sports and Entertainment, in affiliation with Eric Bischoff, as potential candidates. But Mandalay eventually bowed out. The World Wrestling Federation made inquiries, but were forced to withdraw when Viacom, the WWF's new television partner, demanded exclusivity for all WWF-produced programming. Time Warner wanted to keep the wrestling shows on its family of networks. WCW stayed put for the time being and the search continued for potential buyers.

> **MIKE SANDERS:** To be honest, I don't know what they were thinking. I was told, and I don't know how true this is, but I was told several years ago that if you were doing a 2.5 or a 2.7 rating, you were hot. Then we burst onto the scene doing 5.0's and 6.0's and I think their expectations were that was what we've got to have. They put a lot of pressure on people, but at the same time, they put a lot of constraints on people who were trying to improve the show. We want you to take it all the way, but we'll only give you this much to do it with. Did they give up? Maybe. I don't know.

Amidst all the uncertainty, Vince Russo, perhaps realizing his days were numbered after the expected sale of the company, notified management that he could not work due to post-concussion syndrome suffered during his in-ring ventures.

Fritz, Sid Vicious and Dickerman

> **STACY KEIBLER:** WCW was complete insanity. I didn't know who my boss
> was week to week and who I was going to. When I became more a part of
> the storylines, nobody knew who to ask. Things were just all over the
> place. Someone will tell you one thing and then someone else will tell you
> something else. It was crazy.

Ed Ferrara and Bill Banks took over the writing. With the year-
end spectacular, *Starrcade*, approaching, Sid Vicious returned to
challenge new WCW Champion Scott Steiner, who'd defeated
Booker T for the gold at *Mayhem*. Steiner retained his belt and, in
traditional WCW fashion, got into a backstage fight the next night
with Diamond Dallas Page after cutting an unscripted promo belit-
tling Page on television. The most excitement in WCW at that point
occurred behind the curtain.

For comparison purposes, at the end of 1998, *Nitro*'s ratings had
consistently surpassed the 4.0 mark, pay-per-views averaged close
to a 1.0 buyrate for the year, more than 8,000 fans on average paid

for each live event, and the company netted $55 million in profit. Inside forty-four months, the scorecard read as follows — ratings in the low 2.0's, an average buyrate of 0.17, 2,600 paid fans per show, and more than $60 million in losses. These kinds of numbers, along with the upcoming finalization of the merger with America Online forced Time Warner to speed up plans for a sale.

In January 2001, Eric Bischoff reemerged as the leading suitor. After pairing with Mandalay proved fruitless, Bischoff amassed a team of investors led by Fusient Media Ventures, a company specializing in raising capital to purchase and reinvigorate floundering brands. On January 11, 2001, the sale of WCW became a reality. Bischoff would assume the role of President of WCW while Fusient's Brian Bedol, who'd previously founded the Classic Sports Network (later ESPN Classics), would serve as CEO. The sale, for an estimated $70 million, required basic due diligence and, upon completion, the company planned to shut down for several weeks to reorganize before a grand relaunch. In the interim, the company produced lame-duck shows, which resulted in a record low 2.1 rating for *Nitro* on February 11, in preparation for the "new WCW."

But just like the formation of the company, the end proved to be . . . complicated. The due diligence revealed some financial question marks that resulted in the offer being lowered to around $48.7 million — $5.7 million down and annual payments of $2.15 million over twenty years. Before negotiations could continue, the entire landscape changed in March, when Jamie Kellner took over as CEO of Turner Networks after the AOL merger. His first order of business — cancel all wrestling programming. The twenty-nine-year tradition was officially over.

LARRY ZBYSZKO: The end was very sad. I was very frustrated because I saw it coming. Me and a couple of other guys tried to get to the upper echelon and say this thing was hot but you guys are killing it. You don't understand what you're doing here. We didn't know it at the time, but they already knew that AOL was going to cancel it and they didn't want to screw up their AOL–Time Warner deal. They wouldn't listen, and the truth was, they didn't care. They really just killed the thing. It was sad. A lot of people that worked really hard for ten, eleven years to build that thing up to what they had at number one. It was big and it got out of control. It was mismanaged. I don't think anyone from Time Warner wanted it except for Ted Turner. It was on TBS for thirty years and the idiots cancelled it.

Without the television timeslots, perhaps the most valuable WCW asset, the Fusient deal died. Bischoff and company attempted to secure another cable home, but met resistance from most networks about airing wrestling. Fusient officially bowed out for good and back into the picture came the WWF.

With the television issue now nonexistent, the WWF sauntered in and quickly closed a deal to purchase the brand name and trademarks of WCW, the rich video library, and the contracts of twenty-four wrestlers, mostly mid-card, lower-paid talent. AOL–Time Warner assumed responsibility for the remaining contracts, virtually all high-priced talent, and any outstanding lawsuits. The total purchase price ended up being mere peanuts — $2.5 million. The WWF planned to deliver the ultimate WCW vs. WWF dream program to strengthen their already hot core business.

While the WCW name would reappear on WWF programming, for all intents and purposes, World Championship Wrestling was no more. Incompetent management, the inability to create new stars, and resistance to change all contributed to the end. The final *Nitro*, on March 26, 2001, featured appearances by Vince and Shane McMahon on TNT, the latter onsite in Panama City, Florida, announcing that he had technically purchased WCW as part of the future invasion storyline. On the show, Booker T won the WCW World Heavyweight Title from Scott Steiner, and in the main event, Sting wrestled Ric Flair.

SCOTT HUDSON: As a fan, it was awe-inspiring. It's one thing to think of the big picture of it being the last *Nitro*. It's the last time of WCW as a separate entity would ever appear on television. It was the last time I would be with most of those wrestlers, and all of the crew. It was a very emotional night. But to top it all off with Sting and Flair, two total pros both in and out of the ring, it was a tremendous honor to announce that match. . . . It was

"The Nature Boy" Ric Flair and Fritz

appropriate for those two guys to take us out because they were there when WCW as a whole was formed, and they were there at the finish.

Fittingly, the two men on whose backs WCW was built competed for the final time on the final show, a symbolic end to the sad and tragic story that was World Championship Wrestling.

RIC FLAIR: It was terrible. I was extremely happy for wrestling the day they closed the doors to WCW. I was unhappy for people who lost work. We had become almost a humiliating product. What was being put on the air each week was not wrestling. It wasn't anything that the NWA or WCW could possibly have dreamt they could go to in terms of an all-time low. I was just glad that Vince McMahon was able to come along and salvage what was left of it and, of course, take the careers of some guys that were fortunate enough to move along with the company and keep them wrestling. I feel terrible for the people who lost their jobs. People that had been there for twelve years got a two-month severance package. I do personally begrudge several people, whose names I won't mention, for literally putting their self-interest ahead of business and, excluding myself, ahead of 120 other people.

PART II

Jerry Lynn chokes Brian Fritz

Over the years, we have been lucky enough to speak with some of the biggest stars in professional wrestling. But even more rewarding has been the opportunity to get to know some of them on a personal level.

The one thing I value the most in my life are the friendships I have made and I've been fortunate to have made friends with many from the wrestling world. The first person that comes to mind was also the first wrestler that I ever met: Jerry Lynn. It was back in early August 1998, at an NWA show in Sanford, Florida. One of the featured matches on the card that night pitted Jerry against Rob Van Dam.

Before the show began, Dickerman and I found Jerry walking around, taking pictures with fans and signing autographs, which is the norm for a guy who has always been very giving to fans. We introduced ourselves, and Jerry was very receptive to coming on the show. He even invited us to hang out with him following the show at a nearby sports bar. We were in!

That evening, we met up with him to grab a bite to eat and talk a little wrestling. It was a Thursday night, and the replay of WCW *Thunder* just happened to be playing on a big-screen TV near our table.

"Man, would l love to get my hands on that asshole!" exclaimed Jerry as Eric Bischoff was shown walking to the ring. We quickly found out that Jerry was not a big fan of Easy E, or WCW for that matter, especially after the way he'd been unceremoniously given his release from the company a year earlier. After all, in WCW he had been given that incredibly imaginative name, *The Amazing JL!*

Jerry Lynn and Fritz meet for the first time

I know it has been said before by others, but it needs to be said again — not only is Jerry one hell of a talent in the wrestling ring, he's an ever better person. Without a doubt, he is one of the smartest people when it comes to wrestling, because he understands the small details. I think a lot of people can come up with the overall idea, but what propels something from average to good or good to great are the little details that tie everything together. Jerry understands these things and enjoys laying out all the fine points. He really gets it, and any promotion that has him helping out is very lucky.

Outside the ring, Jerry can be quite the character. The guy loves death metal and is always mentioning these insane band names like Dying Fetus, Rancid Rectum, or whatever other disgusting name you can conjure up having to do with the human body. He is always telling me about some hardcore band with a gross name that he is listening to. Hell, I can't understand what those bands are screaming, but Jerry loves that stuff.

What most people may not know is that Jerry also has a great sense of humor. Mind you, it can be a little strange sometimes, but he is always cracking people up. It wasn't too long ago that I first witnessed one of the most bizarre displays that, as we found out, has been one of Jerry's longest running pranks. Basically, he will sneak up to a friend in public, squat down, grab their leg and begin dry-humping it! It's one of the craziest things I've ever seen, but funny as hell. I am proud to say that so far, I have only been a witness to this phenomenon, but I'm sure I will fall prey to it sooner or later.

Luckily, it looks like Jerry has finally outgrown staying up all night and partying. There have been several times when he kept me out on the town until dawn as we hopped from club to club, only to end up eating breakfast at sunrise before he flew back home. Early in the night, Jerry would always say something like, "I promise, we won't be out too late tonight. I need to get some sleep before I fly out in the morning." The next thing I knew, it would be four in the morning and he would be asking if we could get a bite to eat before I dropped him off at the airport! I don't know how he did it. No matter how long he had wrestled, or how banged up from his match, he was ready to go out on the town.

While Jerry and I like talking about wrestling, I most enjoy the times we sit around and chat about our lives and crack jokes with one another. It's always a good time being hanging with Jerry. He is truly one of the best guys you will ever meet. He always goes out of his way for his fans and even more for his friends. I cannot say enough about the quality of person he is. He has to be, since he is such a puss in the ring!

JERRY LYNN: With all the travel and moving from city to city in the wrestling business, a lot of friends come and go or flake off. Well Fritz is no flake. He's listened to me bitch about the business, helped me out when I've missed flights, and even put up with a little death metal. (Just a little, I don't want him to poop himself.) He has literally given me the shirt off his back. I can't say enough to put him over, but I can say he is one who will always be a close friend.

On that same evening in Sanford, Dickerman and I also met Rob Van Dam for the first time. RVD was looking a little rough, sporting two black eyes following a stiff match at the ECW *Heatwave* ,where he and Sabu teamed up against Hayabusa and Jinsei Shinzaki from Japan. But Rob was Rob; maintaining his easygoing, carefree attitude regardless of what his face looked like.

"Now, of course, I'm going to be your first guest on your show, right?" asked Rob. "After all, I am the whole f'n show!" That is true Rob.

We, of course, assured him that he would be on the first show as we exchanged e-mail addresses. And he very well could have been, if he had replied to the e-mails I sent him! It only took me three months and a favor from a mutual friend to get Rob on the show.

Anyway, that night over dinner, Dickerman and I sat there a bit in awe, considering the surroundings. Among the people at the table with us were Rob and his future wife Sonya, Jerry, Sabu, and the late Bobby Duncum Jr. It was a bit surreal for a couple of marks like us. At one point, I leaned over to Dickerman and said, "Can you imagine us sitting here with these guys? RVD, Jerry Lynn, Sabu . . . this is pretty cool."

"What do you mean Sabu? Where is he?" Dickerman asked. I pointed out that he was right behind him, but no one would have known it was him, as he was wearing shorts and a T-shirt along with cowboy boots and a neon-orange hat on backwards. Let's just say that Sabu wasn't too worried about the fashion statement he was making.

Though Rob Van Dam is a high-flying wrestler, he is one of the most grounded guys you will meet outside of the ring. He is a true family man, who loves his wife and would like nothing more than to spend the rest of his life with her. I admire the guy for it.

I will admit that after his first appearance in the studio on the show, I was not too fond of RVD. He thought it would be funny to drop a curse word and watch me rush to hit the dump button so it wouldn't make it onto the air. And it wasn't like he did this once or twice, but over and over again. He would try and fake me out too, by finishing a sentence, pausing, then dropping an F-bomb. At the time, it really pissed me off, but that's just Rob being Rob. He likes to find ways to amuse himself. It wasn't too long after that incident that I began helping him out with his Web site and we became friends.

> **ROB VAN DAM:** Early in my career, before the hundreds and hundreds of interviews I've done building my professionalism, I didn't have the control to choose which words would come out of my mouth at real-time talking speed. When you're not writing the sh%t down and actually speaking straight from the f*cking heart — oh f*ck — a word or two might slip from the lips. Now, I have that sh#t under control, and if Fritz would ever like to have "The Whole F*cking Show" on his program again, you bet your Go$ da*n a$$ I'd do it.

Several years later, Rob was interested in doing a "shoot interview," which he planned on selling through his Web site. He asked me to conduct the interview, which I was more than happy to do, and I got a nice weekend in Los Angeles for my help. It was an interesting couple of days hanging out with RVD on the West Coast, especially when it came to knocking out the interview. Let's just say that I had a little trouble seeing him at times through the haze in the air.

You will not find a more confident or passionate person in or out of wrestling than Rob either. He loves entertaining fans and showcasing the amazing skills that he possesses. It just kills me to see the life sucked out of him working in WWE, considering that the company has no clue of what a great talent they have in him. He identifies with the crowd in such a spiritual way through his breathtaking moves, but the promotion will not utilize him correctly. Rob exudes something different, something unique, in the way he can connect with the crowd. The wrestling world got to see that when he worked in ECW and his fans have been hoping to see that same swagger, that same athletic artist showcasing his skills once again. Regardless, Rob will always wear a smile on his face and make the best of any situation. That is his best quality, and what makes him a true success.

> **ROB VAN DAM:** Last year, I convinced Vince to do an ECW reunion pay-per-view. For one night, we all got to express ourselves with true freedom,

like we did in the old days. Let's just say we rocked the industry hard. We made history, and we were loved for it. Best night in wrestling I can remember in years. I get high off positive energy, whether it's appreciation from the fans, life throwing good shit my way, or when I'm amusing myself watching Fritz hit the dump button at the studio. Most people don't get my sense of humor. That's okay, it's mostly for me anyway. Most people don't get my views. Whatever, I don't get theirs and I'm not looking for a change. The important thing to remember is that happiness is underrated. Wow! I feel that perhaps I can spread positive energy through this book. Fritz is a tool, and I will use this book as an outlet for my means! Be joyous, readers! Hey, if this makes it to the book, I bet this is the part where it takes a strange turn.

Anyway, what I'm really trying to say is that I'm glad Fritz is my friend, and we still sell the video we made together — no, not that one — the one where he interviewed me on my career, at my store, dude. ECW! ECW! ECW!

* * *

Being in radio, we're always looking for new avenues to promote our program and reach new listeners. Remote broadcasts can be a popular way to achieve some exposure. Airing live from a different location around town allows fans to get an up close and personal view of the show, and helps attract new listeners who just stroll by to check out the commotion. Plus, remotes are a fun way to break up the monotony of the regular in-studio grind.

By May 1999, the show had been on the air for three-quarters of a year. It was doing quite well, but we were still open to any ideas that would help spread the word about *Between the Ropes*. With that in mind, over a few drinks at a local establishment while watching WWF *Raw* with some guys from the radio station and pro wrestler Jerry Lynn, the seeds were planted for one of the craziest stunts in WQTM history.

The name Jerry Lynn may not be familiar to the casual wrestling fan. But most people who have followed the business will readily admit that Lynn was one of the most underutilized and underrated talents to come down the pike in recent memory. A former ECW Heavyweight Champion, Jerry Lynn's career began in Minneapolis in the late 1980s as a student of renowned wrestling trainer Brad Rheingans, a 1976 fourth-place Olympic Greco-Roman wrestler who turned pro after losing out on a chance for a medal at the boycotted 1980 games. Lynn earned his stripes bouncing around smaller promotions in Minnesota and Memphis, as well as the Global Wrestling Federation in Dallas, which briefly aired a daily afternoon show on ESPN. Lynn's notoriety in the States garnered him an opportunity to work in Japan for Michinoku Pro Wrestling, an organization based around smaller, more athletic performers, and therefore tailored perfectly to his style.

Lynn's first big break domestically came in 1995, when he signed with WCW. He donned a purple and yellow mask with matching tights as the high-flying Mr. JL. Not surprisingly, WCW did little with him in two years. The WWF brought Lynn in for their new light-heavyweight division in 1997, but before they could sign him to a contract, he started with ECW, quickly becoming one of the company's most solid and consistent workers. Lengthy programs with Justin Credible and ECW Television Champion Rob Van Dam turned Lynn into a bona fide star as ECW started on national television in the fall of 1999. In a mild surprise, he captured the ECW Title on an October 2000 pay-per-view in his hometown. He was a major player in ECW until the promotion folded in 2001. He subsequently signed on with the WWF, and quickly won the Light Heavyweight Title, but wasn't used much thereafter. After departing the Fed, Jerry joined the upstart TNA promotion and was easily the company's most valuable performer in its opening year. His strong matches on pay-per-view week in and week out solidified the X Division as the company's signature.

As I mentioned earlier, Jerry had been a good friend of *Between the Ropes* since appearing on one of the early episodes. In the spring of '99, he was living in Central Florida, which made it easy to get him involved in our outrageous plan. The idea was conceived for the *Coach & Company* program. Coach Marc Daniels, a popular local sports radio personality for over a decade, hosted the afternoon show and was scheduled for a remote from Church Street Station in downtown Orlando. As part of the broadcast, Marc planned to give away a pair of seats to a live WWF event coming to town. These were, by far, the hottest tickets in town at the time. To help out with the contest, Jerry came down to the remote. Ironically, he was an ECW wrestler and we were giving away WWF tickets. Regardless, Jerry wasn't coming down just to hang out, chat with the fans, and sign some autographs. As a tribute to the burgeoning popularity of hardcore wrestling, Jerry agreed to piledrive someone through a wooden table to the concrete below. The victim wouldn't be just anyone, it would be me, Brian Fritz.

Sometimes you agree to do something before thinking. That was the case for me in this unique situation. The only difference this particular time was that I agreed to do something that was actually dangerous . . . very dangerous.

It all started during a conversation Dickerman, Jerry Lynn, and fellow wrestling fan and radio bigwig Pat Lynch were having one night at a remote broadcast from a local restaurant. Pat threw out a simple question to Jerry: "Would you ever put someone through a table for the hell of it?" Well, Jerry is usually up for about any-

"Would you be up for me putting you through a table?"

thing. "Sure. Would you be up for me putting you through a table?" Pat rejected the idea quicker than my prom date rejected me. Dickerman passed as well. They enjoyed watching others put their bodies on the line but had no ambition to do it themselves.

Of course, this conversation got back to me, and I was game. What the hell? I figured it would be cool to try and I never thought twice about it. Plus, I wanted to stand out from the others and do something they wouldn't do. I wanted to prove I had the grapefruits to take a piledriver through a table!

I figured that if I was willing to take the maneuver, I might as well try and get some attention for it. So, I had a conversation with my boss, Marc Daniels, and together we concocted the idea to do it during his remote afternoon show three weeks later. That didn't leave us much time to put it together. Now, I had not known Jerry too long, so I had to somewhat talk him into doing it. But after some nudging, he was happy to drive me headfirst through a table with his patented cradle piledriver, the same move that had finished off many opponents over the course of his wrestling career.

> **JERRY LYNN:** It's very strange, weird, and really retarded when people find out you wrestle and approach you to ask you (in a very enthusiastic way involving screaming, wailing, and gnashing of teeth) to chop them, or give them the cradle piledriver. Unless it's a close friend or relative, I have to refuse, mainly because I'm off the clock. I need to get paid to do that! Plus, I don't want my ass sued! Right from the moment I said yes to Fritz, I was a little nervous. A few days before the show, I called Fritz and voiced my concern. Fritz reassured me there was nothing to worry about. In reality, it finally dawned on me: I'm a wrestler. I have nothing to sue for!

The weeks went by and the event drew closer. Jerry appeared on the afternoon show with Marc and said he couldn't wait to drive me through the table. Dickerman and I talked about a few different things we could do at the event for a short buildup. But there was one thing missing — a table!

The station never helped us obtain a table and the event was quickly approaching. The day before it was to take place, ECW came to town for a house show. Dickerman and I drove the radio station van to the show, which ironically turned out to be a great decision. As we pulled up to the building, we noticed a huge tent containing lots of wooden tables. Well, how hard would it be to just grab one of them? We did just that. Immediately following the show, we grabbed one of the tables and tossed it into the van. We were really lucky to get one, too. A bunch of the rabid ECW fans were so jacked up following the house show, they began slamming one another through the tables! It was the craziest thing I've ever seen. These wrestling fans were so wild for that hardcore wrestling that they were bodyslamming and powerbombing one another through tables!

The next afternoon, Dickerman, B Randall, Jerry and I met downtown at the broadcast site. Marc was already on the air hosting his show while Jerry came up with a quick storyline for us. Anything would be better than just the two of us walking over to the table.

We weren't performing this feat in an isolated area or even on grass. The table was set up on the brick sidewalk at Church Street Station, near all of the popular nightclubs in downtown Orlando. There was really no room for error. I had never taken a bodyslam much less a piledriver. Regardless, I was about to take my first bump. Minutes before we began, Jerry pulled me to the side and instructed me on how to take a piledriver. We practiced it once, but I pulled my head out. "If you do that during the move, you'll get killed," explained Jerry. Well, that quickly hit home, and the picture was starting to get really clear to me. I finally realized that I could, in fact, get hurt. Luckily, it was Jerry who I was performing the move with and I had nothing to worry about. We practiced one more time, I kept my head tucked, and we were good to go.

B. RANDALL: Having worked in radio for about five years before *Between the Ropes*, I had seen some crazy promotions and stupid stunts performed for attention. This, however, was pretty damn dangerous. So here was the plan: piledrive Fritz on a sidewalk in downtown Orlando, with nothing but an old wooden folding table between his head and the cement. One wrong move could change his world. Surprisingly, we got little resistance from station management (maybe because half of them still didn't know we were on the air) and proceeded to promote the stupid stunt. At the time, I guess I wasn't really thinking about how dangerous it really was. After all, I wasn't doing it, and besides, didn't they do this every Monday night without incident? I was all for it. I wanted to get paid and figured if we could get the attention of local media and potential advertisers, the show would be a success. Fritz was pumped to do it, Jerry Lynn was up for it, and the listeners seem intrigued. It was a go!

Following a commercial break, it was show time. Marc asked if I was ready and I turned to the small crowd and said no. Yes, I did say "small crowd." It was in the middle of a Monday afternoon, and not too many people decided to skip out on work to watch me get spiked through a table. I started pleading my case to the people there, saying I had changed my mind. Marc was a bit perplexed and didn't understand what was going on. Then, Jerry walked up behind me and called out my name. I turned around and he planted me with a kick to the gut. As I was bent over, he whacked me across my back with a chair! It was a plastic fold-up chair and stung only for a second or two. There was no way I would have allowed him to hit me with a metal chair, especially since I am allergic to pain. Anyway, he whacked me with the chair and I crumpled to the ground.

Now, this is where it turns really cheesy, as in a bad-movie-on-cable-in-the-middle-of-the-night cheesy. Two masked men, one wearing a Sting mask (Dickerman), and another wearing a Japanese mask (B. Randall), ran out and lifted me onto the table. Jerry then climbed on top, propped my limp body up, and tucked my head between his legs. I could already start to feel this rickety table start to give under our weight, but it had just enough strength left.

"He's got him up there!" Marc screamed on the radio. "He's got him up! Oooooohhhh!"

For those listening to the broadcast, it sounded like an explosion going off as I was driven headfirst through the table. Truth be told, my head did hit wood, but just barely. Jerry showed how truly good

Splat! Jerry Lynn's cradle piledriver puts Fritz through a table

he was at his craft, protecting me as we crashed through that old table. *Splat!* Right onto the concrete sidewalk.

I laid there lifeless as Jerry jumped up and posed for the small congregation. Most were cheering in amazement. Several of them, including my dad, who is not a wrestling fan at all, stood there in utter disbelief. I guess it's not easy for a father to watch his son put his life on the line as part of a ridiculous stunt.

> **DICKERMAN:** I leaned over to Fritz to ask if he was okay, but got no response. I thought he was really messed-up. I mean, a piledriver through a table isn't exactly a safe maneuver. He ended up being fine, he just couldn't hear me through my stylish Sting mask. Once we determined he wasn't dead, it was time for the fun to continue.

It wasn't over for me yet. Several weeks earlier, I lost a bet with one of the other radio jocks and had to shave my head bald per the stipulation. Well, I lost, and I really wasn't looking forward to sporting the "Stone Cold" look. But a bet is a bet, and it was time to pay up.

Jerry Lynn as "The Barber," giving Fritz a mowhak

The electric clippers appeared and Jerry did the honors. He happily shaved off all of my hair. Well, not exactly all of it. He decided to have a little fun at my expense and left a mohawk. When he was done showing off his barber skills, he splashed me with some water and I slowly "awoke." The prankster had something else up his sleeve. He carried me over to a nearby fountain and dropped me in. Mind you, this was in downtown Orlando, and I'm certain all of the bums used this fountain to bathe in.

I quickly came to after this and climbed out, soaking wet and sporting one strip of hair down the middle of my head. We snapped a few pictures before someone let me know about my new hairstyle. I let Jerry finish shaving my head while he and everyone else had a good laugh at my expense. Hell, I was laughing at this point. At least until I saw myself in a mirror. All I can say is that I will never be sporting a shaved head again.

JERRY LYNN: When the day came, it was ungodly hot and humid so there weren't too many people. I still had to make it look good, not necessarily for the people but for the welcome-to-the-business chair shot Fritz was about to receive. It sounded like a gunshot, and Coach's jaw just about bounced off the table. Fritz took it like a champ and later tried to no-sell it to the best of his ability. When we went through the table, it was eerily silent. (It had to have been silent heat. I swear.) It was sick! It sounded like a train wreck, especially my ass colliding with the concrete. But I'm proud to say I took care of Fritz. Coach had the same look on his face as any first timer at an ECW show. He was suffering from severe culture shock. I then had the honor of shaving Fritz's head. I thought I did him a favor by leaving a Mohawk, but he wasn't too fond of it. Then, without Fritz's prior knowledge, I proceeded to throw him into the fountain, to rinse off all that hair, of course. All in a day's work.

Jerry Lynn, Dickerman, B. Randall Myers and Fritz

Every once in a while, I pull out the tape and watch this shining moment and wonder what I was thinking. Dickerman still believes I was crazy to ever do it. But sometimes, there are just stupid things you feel compelled to do, and this was one I was lucky enough to live to tell about.

ECW

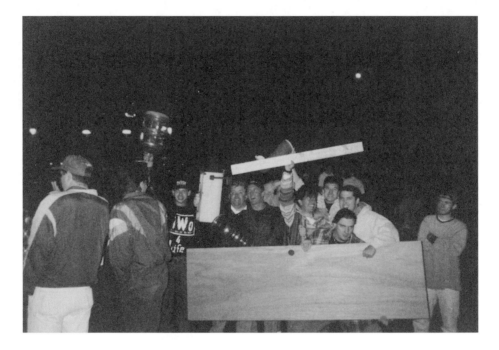

Hardcore BTR!

Chapter 10

Professional wrestling in a bingo hall wouldn't generate excitement even in the most ardent wrestling fan, unless it was produced by Extreme Championship Wrestling. With the national powerhouses in a stagnant depression, in the mid-90s a tiny promotion in South Philadelphia initiated a wrestling renaissance. Little did any of the hardcore fans, crammed into a dilapidated building on the corner of Swanson and Ritner Streets, realize that their darling promotion would help transform a dying business and blossom into a legitimate national operation.

Before ECW became "extreme," there was Eastern Championship Wrestling, a NWA affiliate run by local jewelry store owner, Tod Gordon. Eddie Gilbert, known to wrestling fans as "Hot Stuff" from his work in WCW, handled the booking of the promotion's matches, offering product radically different than what the WWF and WCW showcased nationally. Blending a hardcore, violent style with a strong in-ring product, early ECW mirrored successful Japanese promotions that had become the standard for first-class wrestling while the American business wallowed in the doldrums. ECW became the independent hot spot for a motley crew of performers: past-their-prime national stars (Terry Funk, Don Muraco, and Jimmy Snuka), talent that wasn't pushed in the national companies (Shane Douglas and Gilbert himself), and unknown newcomers hoping for a break (The Public Enemy, Tommy Dreamer, and The Tazmaniac).

Gilbert and Gordon had a falling out in September 1993, forcing Gordon to bring in Paul Heyman, who had been fired from his $250,000 per year managerial and commentating position in WCW

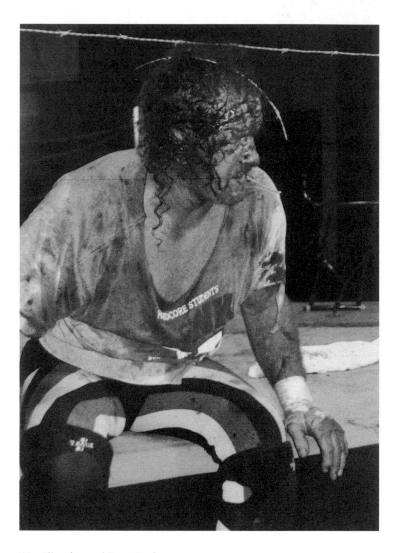

Wrestling legend Terry Funk

in a cost-cutting maneuver. Heyman handled the creative for ECW, including the weekly television program on the local SportsChannel affiliate in Philadelphia, and the monthly events at the bingo parlor, dubbed the ECW Arena.

Eastern Championship Wrestling plugged along as a run-of-the-mill independent group until one match at the ECW Arena made wrestling fans around the country take notice of the happenings in South Philadelphia. Dubbed "The Night The Line Was Crossed," a sold-out crowd of about 1,000 fans witnessed a Three-Way Dance — a rarity in U.S. wrestling at the time — between Terry Funk, Sabu, and Shane Douglas on February 5, 1994. The three men battled and brawled for one hour to a time-limit draw that put fans on their feet for a lengthy standing ovation after the bell. Many called it the greatest match they had ever seen. Regardless of where it ranked in the annals of history, this one match put ECW on the map as a legitimate wrestling organization.

> **SHANE DOUGLAS:** The first match that I recall ever feeling good about was The Night The Line Was Crossed. I remember coming back to the back and thinking to myself, "I don't know how we did it, but somehow that was a pretty damn good match." It was like riding a bike without training wheels. The first couple of times, you fall down, but once you finally do it, it's like taking a breath.

Later in the year, the company truly set itself apart in a gutsy and controversial move that demonstrated the renegade mindset of those in charge. A one-night single elimination tournament for the vacant NWA World Heavyweight Title was held at the August 27 ECW Arena event. Heyman and Gordon negotiated with the NWA Board of Directors, in particular rival New Jersey member Dennis Coraluzzo, to book ECW's top heel, Shane Douglas, as the tournament winner and NWA Champion before dropping the title down the line to Chris Benoit. With everything in place, the tournament proceeded without a hitch, as Douglas defeated Too Cold Scorpio in the finals. The championship presentation that followed, however, became the story of the night.

With the NWA belt in his hand, Douglas launched into a classic tirade against the National Wrestling Alliance, labeling it an ancient organization that had been dead in the minds of wrestling fans for years. He followed by throwing the NWA belt to the ground and proclaiming himself the first ECW World Heavyweight Champion. The entire incident had been a carefully constructed real-life double-cross by Gordon and Heyman, designed to disassociate themselves from the tradition of the NWA in favor of a new rebellious attitude. Gordon renamed his organization Extreme Championship Wrestling, and the sport would never be the same.

SHANE DOUGLAS: Paul came to me and said he had an idea that he thought would help elevate ECW. It was something I didn't need to think about very long before I said yes. My dad, when I was growing up, always said, "You can walk with everybody else and be the same and just another face in the crowd or you can take chances and elevate you and set yourself apart from everybody." This was the first time in my life I ever recall as a man being able to put that philosophy into practice. The NWA had been an organization that was really breathing its last breaths at the time, and ECW was sucking in its first deep breaths. It was a question of "Do I facilitate the NWA, who had showed no loyalty to me or to our fans, or do I do what's right for me, our company, and our fans?" When Paul Heyman came and said, "I've got this idea. What do you think? When you win the tournament, throw the belt down and elevate ours to world title status." Clearly, it was the defining moment for my career. It was the initial step toward ECW's future greatness and I'm real proud of that. Coraluzzo was completely in the dark.

Chapter 11

Extreme Championship Wrestling's plans broadened beyond the Northeast for the first time. The company purchased airtime on different regional sports television networks — including the MSG Network in New York, the Sunshine Network in Florida, and Prime Sports Networks in the Midwest — to expose its product to new markets before running live events. ECW slowly evolved into the most talented collection of performers from around the wrestling world. Cactus Jack had left WCW months earlier to work independently, and made ECW, where he'd competed on and off already as part of a talent exchange with WCW, a regular stop between tours of Japan. Foley teamed regularly with Mikey Whipwreck, an undersized preliminary wrestler who became a crowd favorite for absorbing

Public Enemy and Chris Jericho with Fritz and Dickerman

beatings night after night, as adversaries for The Public Enemy over the ECW World Tag-Team Titles. "Crippler" Chris Benoit and "Shooter" Dean Malenko, arguably the two most proficient in-ring technicians in the world, and held back in the U.S. only by their size, toured regularly with New Japan Pro Wrestling and called ECW home in the States. ECW regulars Tommy Dreamer, The Sandman, Sabu, The Tazmaniac, and World Champion "The Franchise" Shane Douglas became household names to hardcore fans. But the true star of the promotion may have been Paul Heyman, who concocted storylines and produced television that made his performers appear like stars on par with the WWF and WCW main-eventers.

As much as the talent enjoyed working for ECW, the reality of the situation painted a different picture. Despite the critical acclaim, ECW was a regional promotion that couldn't pay talent commensurate to the national groups. ECW events averaged several hundred fans to one thousand on a good night, making it difficult for talent to earn enough to support their families without a second line of income. Still, the ECW locker room busted their butts out of respect for the fans and respect for the promotion. ECW also represented an opportunity, both for younger, unknown workers hoping to be noticed, and established guys looking for another shot at the big time. While the talent that passed through the doors gave ECW fans everything they had, their tenures often ended at the first call from the WWF or WCW.

In the ring, neither the WWF nor WCW could touch ECW in early 1995. Through Heyman's creative booking prowess, Shane Douglas evolved into a bona fide World Champion in the ring and on the mic. The Public Enemy were heralded as one of the top tag teams in the world for their wild brawls and popular table-breaking matches. The beer-swilling, cane-swinging Sandman became a top guy as an opponent of Cactus Jack and Terry Funk. Newcomer Raven entered the mix, and started a program with Tommy Dreamer that would arc throughout the company's existence. Chris Benoit and Dean Malenko's stock rose every time the bell rang. The Tazmaniac, despite his physical stature at 5'6", began to get over with the fans as a legitimate tough guy. And Sabu, perhaps the man most synonymous with ECW, became the hottest independent performer in the world.

Yet a pattern of losing key talent to the deep-pocketed competition soon began. Sabu, the homicidal, suicidal, genocidal maniac hailing from India, became the first to walk out of ECW, opting to work on the April 8, 1995, New Japan Pro Wrestling event overseas for more than five times the money, rather than honor a verbal commitment to work in the main event at the ECW Arena the same night. Paul Heyman took a unique approach by apologizing to the live audience before the show began and publicly firing Sabu. The crowd respected the gesture, and cursed-out Sabu for essentially spitting in the face of his fellow wrestlers.

The following week saw more controversy, this time involving Shane Douglas. The April 15 event saw the first Extreme Championship Wrestling World Title change as Douglas dropped the belt to The Sandman. After the match, Douglas donned a *Monday Night Raw* T-shirt and claimed to be headed to the WWF. He stuck around for a few months to play up the angle before joining the WWF as Dean Douglas, a spin on his real life schoolteacher position outside of the ring. The same ECW Arena event featured an infamous scene, with Terry Funk attacking Cactus Jack with a flaming branding iron, which cemented ECW's reputation among its loyal fans as the most hardcore and violent wrestling promotion in the world.

The summer of '95 featured awesome in-ring action combined with chaotic hardcore matches that made ECW a must-see attraction for the small percentage of wrestling fans in the know. Eddie Guerrero and Dean Malenko engaged in a series of wars over the ECW Television Title, many two-out-of-three falls ending in a draw. The Public Enemy and The Pitbulls battled in bloody dog-collar bouts for the ECW Tag-Team Titles. The Sandman's ECW World Title reign continued, including a barbed-wire match victory over Cactus Jack.

But by the fall, the talent defections had struck again as Chris Benoit, Eddie Guerrero, and Dean Malenko signed deals with World Championship Wrestling, which had been adding fresh talent before the launch of *Nitro* on Monday nights. While the WWF also demonstrated some interest in all three, WCW's talent relationship agreement with New Japan Pro Wrestling became the deciding factor. All three could continue participating in Japanese tours while working for WCW on $150,000 per year deals.

> **EDDIE GUERRERO:** Paul has a great mind. Yeah, you could give him credit. He is the first one who saw us and gave us an opportunity.

To replace the loss of the technical wrestling triumvirate, Paul Heyman looked outside of the United States again, this time south of the border. Mexican "lucha libre" wrestling had gained a strong foothold in the United States, namely on the West Coast of the country, with its unique, high-flying action a stark contrast to the plodding, slow-paced style proffered by the WWF and WCW. ECW introduced lucha libre to the rest of the country, and made acrobatic luchadors Rey Mysterio Jr., Juventud Guerrera, Psicosis, and La Parka into stars. "Extreme lucha libre," as the company called it, got over not just fans, but with rival organizations. WCW President Eric Bischoff again noticed the success of the new talents, and figured lucha libre would get over on a national scale as well. In early 1996, Mysterio, Guerrera, and several other Mexican wrestlers joined WCW to bolster the cruiserweight division and became instant stars through their revolutionary style — but only after being nationally spotlighted in the United States by ECW.

The stream of talent didn't always flow from ECW to WCW. While Eric Bischoff and company wisely scooped up Benoit, Guerrero, and the Mexican cruiserweights, his eye wasn't infallible. In the fall of 1995, Bischoff fired Steve Austin over the telephone while Austin was recuperating from a torn triceps injury. At an annual salary of $500,000, the WCW braintrust felt Austin could never be marketed as a money-drawing character. Obviously, Bischoff's decision would turn out to be pure folly years later, but the WWF initially didn't have Austin on their radar. Fortunately for Austin, Paul Heyman did. Austin and Heyman were paired together at times in WCW. He couldn't wrestle at the time due to the injury, but Heyman wanted to bring in Austin at $500 per night to cut interviews. The ECW promos displayed Austin's verbal abilities, a skill never fully exploited in WCW, as he parodied Eric Bischoff, Hulk Hogan, and other WCW personalities he believed led to his downfall.

> **STEVE AUSTIN:** It was a deal where Paul Heyman gave me a call and said, "Steve, what are you doing?" I said, "Nothing." He goes, "How about coming to work?" I said, "Well, I got a busted arm. My triceps is still healing up." He goes, "Hey, just come down and cut promos. I'll give you 'X' number of dollars per week to cut promos." Sounds good to me. I wasn't making any money. I was hurt. So I went there and cut promos. It was really the first time I had ever been given a platform. Me and Brian [Pillman] had a couple of promos, but not real heavy angles, and it was splitting the mic time. When we starting doing the promos between four and five in the morning, because they had one camera there for everybody's promos, Paul E. said, "Just tell your story. Just start talking about the things that happened down there." That's how it all started. I said, "Let's start doing some impersonations," and we did Bischoff and we got Hogan and that's how all that stuff came about. But I credit Paul a big part and Brian Pillman being a big influence in my promos with ECW.

Once his health permitted it, Austin returned to the ring and worked with new ECW Champion Mikey Whipwreck — who won the strap from The Sandman in an October 1995 ladder match at the ECW Arena — and willingly put over the champion despite plans in the works to crown Austin.

> **MIKEY WHIPWRECK:** Basically when I first started, I would just get beat up. I took the stupid bumps and bumped real hard. When you're nineteen, twenty years old, your body can take it. You bounce right back. As I got older, it started to take its toll, and working with The Sandman for three to four months physically did me in. But finally Paul gave me the shot. People were behind me, and by the grace of God, they got behind me enough and Paul put the strap on me.

Austin's straight-shooting style finally caught the attention of the WWF, particularly Jim Ross, who watched the performer's antics weekly on the ECW television program. The offer finally came and Austin moved on to become, first, The Ringmaster, and eventually Stone Cold Steve Austin, arguably the biggest attraction in the history of the sport.

Austin's former tag-team partner in WCW, Brian Pillman, made several ECW appearances following Austin's departure, ironically while still working for WCW. Pillman, a former linebacker and special teams player for the NFL's Cincinnati Bengals, became a top attraction as a high-flying cruiserweight well before the style was in vogue in the States. Like Austin, Pillman's career languished in WCW upon the arrival of Hulk Hogan, Randy Savage, and friends. He wanted to try something unique, and devised a "Loose Cannon" character in which he acted unpredictably on and off television. In early 1996, Pillman appeared to have walked out on WCW, and only Pillman and Bischoff knew it was a storyline. Pillman convinced management to issue him a legitimate termination notice. To further the idea, Bischoff allowed Pillman to work shows for ECW. He continued the Loose Cannon persona with crazy interviews and stunts, including once attempting to urinate in the middle of an ECW ring. The stint ended following a disagreement between Heyman and Pillman, but Pillman's antics made him a popular figure among fans, which he parlayed into a bidding war for his services between WCW and the WWF, which was won out by Vince McMahon, who offered a rare guaranteed contract offer.

Austin and Pillman would be joined in the WWF by another former WCW and ECW star, Cactus Jack. After a couple of years toiling on the U.S. and Japanese independent circuits, where he abused his body in sickeningly sadistic matches in front of few people for little money, Mick Foley received the call from the WWF to play a toned-down version of Cactus Jack called Mankind. In ECW, Jack's promo work overshadowed his in-ring labor at times, particularly his anti-hardcore interviews, in which he denounced the ECW fans for demanding tables, weapons, and bloodshed every night while pretending to idolize former boss Eric Bischoff and WCW. The segments turned ECW television into can't-miss programming. Jack's final nights in ECW turned out to be an interesting story, based on the polarized crowd reactions during the *Big Ass Extreme Bash* weekend. In Queens, New York, on March 8, 1996, Cactus lost to Chris Jericho and gave a farewell speech amidst boos, profanity, and chants of "You Sold Out!" The next night, in front of the ECW Arena faithful in Philadelphia, Jack received a lengthy standing ovation before and after his victory over Mikey Whipwreck. The reactions reflected the good and bad of the ECW product and its audience — fans who respected the hard work and dedication of the performers and those who clamored only for blood and guts.

> **CHRIS JERICHO:** It was the first time I ever appeared on a worldwide stage in the States, and it really gave me great exposure to the wrestling fans over here who pretty much knew who I was anyway just through my work in Japan. The fans in ECW were very smart. They traded tapes and the moment I walked through the ECW Arena doors the first time, I had people who knew who I was and that was really cool for me. It was the first time I could show what I really could do in the spotlight of the U.S.

Chapter 12

Despite all the departing talent, ECW continued to grow in 1996. Shane Douglas and Sabu both returned to the fold. Newcomer Rob Van Dam, with a quasi martial-arts style, debuted and slowly got over as a fan favorite. The company had firmly established itself as the number three promotion in the land, with eyes on national expansion.

Both the WWF and WCW had been fully cognizant of the happenings at the bingo hall. WCW, on the strength of their nWo invasion angle after the arrivals of Scott Hall and Kevin Nash from the WWF, had pulled ahead in the wrestling war. The WWF struggled to find a storyline to compete with the nWo and attempted to fabricate their own version of it. Instead of creating a worked outsider faction, the WWF talked with ECW. Most wrestling fans were still unfamiliar with the renegade organization, but they would soon get a very brief taste.

The WWF ventured into ECW's backyard for its September 22, 1996, *In Your House: Mind Games* pay-per-view. In a closely guarded secret, McMahon and Heyman worked out an agreement for an ECW presence on the show. In the opening match between Savio Vega and Justin Hawk Bradshaw, an ECW threesome — Heyman, The Sandman, and Tommy Dreamer — sat in the front row. When the action spilled to the floor, The Sandman spit beer in Vega's face. Security escorted the ECW contingent out of the building while fans chanted "ECW, ECW" and the announcers acknowledged their presence. The next night on *Raw*, ECW popped up again. Taz and manager Bill Alfonso hopped the rail during a match carrying

ECW World Champion Taz

a large sign boasting, "Sabu Fears Taz," based on the ongoing ECW feud. Fans cheered for Taz while the show abruptly went to commercial. Days later, Paul Heyman placed a call to *Livewire*, the WWF's Saturday morning talk show, claiming the WWF stole its ideas and talent from ECW. The angle died down, but ECW would later return to WWF programming.

In the interim, ECW strategized for its biggest venture to date — pay-per-view. Fans beyond the eastern seaboard would be able to sample a live ECW event on television for the first time. The extreme movement would finally receive national attention. But negotiations with the two major pay-per-view providers, Request TV and Viewer's Choice, did not run smoothly. Both carriers became leery of the product, fearing a backlash similar to the one faced by the Ultimate Fighting Championship and other no holds barred fighting groups. The style that had made ECW a cult phenomenon became an albatross in its quest to promote pay-per-view events.

The pay-per-view companies, Viewer's Choice in particular, worried about conducting business with ECW after performing due diligence about the product. Living up to its extreme name, ECW booked several controversial angles in 1996, starting with a lesbian make-out session between valets Kimona Wanalaya and Beulah McGillicutty at the ECW Arena. Criticism over the incident cost the company many of its syndicated television affiliates. Later that year, also at the ECW Arena, the company went through with an angle involving ECW World Champion Raven and The Sandman. Following a beatdown by Raven and his flock, the group tied the bloody Sandman to a large wooden cross and placed a crown of barbed wire on his head in a mock crucifixion scene. Even ECW apologists were offended, forcing Raven to appear out of character after the show to apologize for the incident. The footage never aired on ECW television. As luck would have it, Olympic gold medalist Kurt Angle, who was considering the possibility of working for ECW down the line, was in attendance but walked out in disgust following the crucifixion. The Sandman–Raven program also featured The Sandman's wife, Lori, and 8-year-old son, Tyler, aligning themselves with Raven.

But the worst incident came at a November 23 house show in Revere, Massachusetts. One of the ECW regulars, Axl Rotten, could not make the spot show, leaving D-Von Dudley without a partner for his tag-team match against The Gangstas. Erich Kulas, an aspiring independent wrestler, attended the show with some local midget wrestlers with the hope of getting booking on the undercard. Kulas weighed 400 pounds and performed a Ralph Kramden–type character called Mass Transit. He cajoled his way into the tag-team match, claiming to be 19 and a student at Killer Kowalski's wrestling school. Unbeknownst to Paul Heyman, Kulas hadn't yet reached his eighteenth birthday.

Putting a haphazardly trained person in an ECW ring could be a recipe for disaster. Putting a haphazardly trained *minor* in an ECW ring guaranteed it. The tag-team match deteriorated into a trademark ECW brawl, involving weapons ranging from crutches to toasters. As part of the match, Kulas was required to "blade," a common wrestling practice of cutting one's forehead to draw blood and add dramatic effect to the match. Being a novice, Kulas didn't know how to perform the technique and instead asked New Jack of The Gangstas to carry out the mutilating task with an X-acto knife. In the heat of the moment, New Jack's overzealousness led to more than just a prick on the forehead. Blood poured out from ear to ear faster than water from a faucet. The horrific scene left fans sick and lakes of blood all over the ring. Paramedics arrived to stretcher the kid to the hospital after the building ran out of towels trying to stop the profuse bleeding. Kulas survived and would later file charges, but the incident caused more pressing troubles for ECW. A tape hit the black market and eventually reached the offices of Request TV.

Viewer's Choice had decided independently against airing ECW even before learning of the Kulas incident. But Request TV seemed interested until viewing the match in Revere. Just days before Christmas 1996, Request axed ECW from its schedule. Shut out of approximately twenty-five million homes of the pay-per-view universe, ECW returned to the drawing board. The company continued to court Request TV by agreeing to tone down the violent aspects of its shows and submit to regulations set forth by Request. By the end of January, ECW's dreams finally came true. On April 13, 1997, at 9pm eastern, ECW *Barely Legal* would air live on pay-per-view from the ECW Arena for $19.95.

The loyal ECW audience pledged to tune in for the historic event. Pay-per-view advertisements from the carriers would help locate new buyers. But the company needed additional publicity to ensure success and got back into bed with the WWF. With the majority of the WWF's roster booked on an overseas tour, the live

Dickerman, Stevie Richards and Fritz

Raw on February 24, 1997, from the Manhattan Center needed some juice. In came ECW. Jerry Lawler played the heel for the feud, dubbing the organization as "Extremely Crappy Wrestling." Paul Heyman led a contingent of ECW stars into New York City for three ECW matches on *Raw*, including Taz over Mikey Whipwreck and Tommy Dreamer over D-Von Dudley. Heyman consistently plugged *Barely Legal* on commentary, before nearly coming to blows with Lawler to end the angle.

Would it be enough? The bingo hall underwent a full overhaul for the big night, including a fresh coat of paint, new ECW banners, and upgraded lighting grids. Aesthetically, the production couldn't hold a candle to the WWF or WCW. But between the ropes, few shows from the "big two" could compete with *Barely Legal*. The undercard featured The Eliminators regaining the ECW Tag-Team Titles from The Dudleys, "The Franchise" Shane Douglas retaining the ECW Television Title against Pitbull #2, and a hot six-man tag featuring light heavyweights from Japan's Michinoku Pro Wrestling. Taz submitted Sabu in their long-awaited grudge match, but was laid out by Rob Van Dam, Sabu, and ex-manager Bill Alfonso afterwards. In the main event, Terry Funk won a Three-Way Dance against The

Sandman and Stevie Richards, leading to an ECW World Title match against Raven. With help from protégé Tommy Dreamer, the fifty-two-year-old Funk cradled Raven to capture the title in a truly emotional moment. In what was perhaps an omen of good fortune, twenty seconds after the live pay-per-view broadcast concluded, the power failed in the building. Had it happened seconds earlier, it would have killed the show and possibly ECW's future.

Barely Legal drew respectably on pay-per-view, but with limited clearance and the later start time, the company lost money. Still, over 40,000 buys and a 0.26 buyrate gave ECW a sense of optimism that Viewer's Choice and other small providers would pick up future events. ECW scheduled August 17, 1997, for its second pay-per-view, *Hardcore Heaven '97*.

Between the two shows, ECW underwent several changes. Despite the buoyancy following *Barely Legal*, the talent defections continued, as Raven jumped to WCW. In his last match, Tommy Dreamer finally pinned Raven to culminate their nearly three-year feud. Stevie Richards soon followed Raven to Atlanta.

> **BUH BUH RAY DUDLEY:** If somebody wanted to leave, it was like this: If you're dating a chick and she doesn't want to be with you anymore, screw her and let her leave. She doesn't want to be here. Too bad. It was definitely an us-against-them mentality, especially WCW. We kind of always knew that Paul was in bed with Vince [McMahon], but we knew Paul hated Bischoff. We knew there was all this bad blood there. ECW truly was a revolution. It was legit. It was a wrestling revolution. ECW changed the face of pro wrestling. If some dude decided to up and out for the money or for whatever reason, it definitely left a bad taste in the locker-room's mouth.

The ECW-WWF program restarted. Jerry Lawler brought Rob Van Dam, referring to himself as "Mr. Monday Night," to *Raw*. Other ECW wrestlers appeared and wrestled on WWF programming, but the WWF never allowed its talent to lose. The angle went further on the ECW end, with Jerry Lawler appearing at the ECW Arena. Lawler, Sabu, and Van Dam regularly laid out the ECW babyfaces to build heat for the blowoff on ECW's next pay-per-view.

PAUL HEYMAN: The sentiment from a lot of people in ECW, they really, really hated Lawler. But at the same time, when Lawler came into our dressing room, we had to sneak him in. We went through all of these security measures to get him into the building secretly and safely. But when the guys saw him in the locker room, the first thing the guys said to each other was, "Wow, this is going to get us a lot of notoriety" and, "Wow, this is going to be a great angle" and, "Wow, this is going to attract a lot of attention" and, "Wow, this is going to draw more money, so how can we help?" Remember, in his first night at the ECW arena, it was Lawler, Sabu, Rob Van Dam, and Bill Alfonso that laid out our entire locker room.

Fort Lauderdale, Florida, hosted *Hardcore Heaven '97*. The event turned out to be the exact opposite of *Barely Legal*. Weak production values made the show difficult to watch. In the ring, the work was also a step down from April. Jerry Lawler battled Tommy Dreamer in an overbooked match featuring run-ins by Jake "The Snake" Roberts and the WWF's Sunny, before Dreamer pinned Lawler with a DDT. The main event crowned Shane Douglas the new ECW World Champion with a victory over Sabu and Terry Funk in a Three-Way Dance in a decent main event.

Still without clearance on Viewer's Choice, Cablevision, and other outlets, *Hardcore Heaven* dropped slightly to a 0.21 buyrate, but this event managed to turn a small profit.

Chapter 13

The positive ECW mojo was halted by Labor Day '97, when a clandestine plot to destroy the company became public. Rumors swirled of a mole within the organization trying to orchestrate a mass exodus of talent to WCW. The investigation uncovered an unlikely perpetrator, the man who had created ECW and spearheaded the extreme revolution, Tod Gordon. While his role had decreased within the organization since selling the majority of the company stock to Heyman, Gordon had remained a public ECW figure. But behind the scenes, Gordon allegedly maneuvered to cripple ECW by jumping to WCW for a version of an invasion with as many as ten top performers. Gordon negotiated with Terry Taylor of WCW talent relations, and discussed the names of Rob Van Dam, Sabu, Bill Alfonso, Shane Douglas, The Dudleys, The Pitbulls, and others. Big money offers were extended — as much as $300,000 for some — as WCW looked to bolster its roster with the addition of the *Thunder* television program. Several wrestlers hesitated to make the move and began whispering Gordon's plan to others. Paul Heyman caught wind of the scenario and went so far as to hack into Gordon's voice-mail to hear messages from WCW officials and ECW talent about the plot. While the raid never materialized, Gordon's involvement with the company he had built ended.

ECW's first pay-per-view without Gordon, *November To Remember '97*, emanated from the Golden Dome outside of Pittsburgh, Pennsylvania, on November 30. For the first time, Viewer's Choice agreed to carry the show, albeit on a secondary pay channel not available in every home. Time Warner and Cablevision in New

York remained the only holdouts. The event ended up as a major success live, with 4,600 fans in attendance for a $100,000 gate, both company records. The show itself turned out to be closer to *Hardcore Heaven* than *Barely Legal*. Several WWF performers — Doug Furnas, Phil LaFon, and Brakus — appeared to aid Rob Van Dam in a WWF vs. ECW flag match against Tommy Dreamer. Hometown hero Shane Douglas retained the ECW World Title against Bam Bam Bigelow in the main event. However, the show was marred by a disastrous Tables and Ladders match between Sabu and The Sandman, a candidate for worst match of the year. On pay-per-view, *November To Remember* garnered a 0.20 buyrate, in the same neighborhood as the first two shows and, impressively, half what the WWF drew the following week for its *In Your House: Degeneration X* event.

The growth of Extreme Championship Wrestling would become a significant story in 1998. For the first pay-per-view of the year, *Living Dangerously*, on March 1 from the Asbury Park Convention Center in New Jersey, Time Warner Cable of New York relented and carried the event for its subscribers. The pay-per-view industry also moved the show up two hours to the traditional 7pm EST starting time. The event ended up being memorable for the creative spot of Taz and Bam Bam Bigelow crashing through the ring during their Television Title match, won by Bigelow in his hometown. Al Snow, on loan from the WWF, teamed with Lance Storm to defeat Shane Douglas and Chris Candido in the main event. The show drew over 3,500 fans and did a 0.19 buyrate on pay-per-view. With added clearances, the buys topped well over 50,000.

Prior to the May *WrestlePalooza '98*, their next pay-per-view event, Rob Van Dam won the ECW Television Title from Bam Bam Bigelow at an April television taping in Buffalo, New York. Van Dam would hold onto the title into the next millennium. Heading into *WrestlePalooza* from Marietta, Georgia, the company received good news, as Cablevision finally agreed to air all ECW events. Viewer's Choice also moved the company's pay-per-view to its main pay channel, meaning ECW would be available to the entire pay-per-view universe for the first time. But the injury bug hit before the show, wrecking the original lineup. Taz's match was scrapped due to a deep cut on his shin. Shane Douglas was booked to defend the ECW Title against Al Snow in the main event, but needed to be hospitalized two days before the match with a severe sinus infection, and was in need of major elbow surgery. Douglas gutted out the match and retained the title, despite an expected six-month layoff. Overall, the show came off poorly, due to bad matches and a minor league facility, but still managed a 0.23 buyrate for 75,000 purchases with the entire pay-per-view universe accessible for the first time.

With the ECW Champion sidelined indefinitely, Paul Heyman decided to try something new. He planned to build around Taz as his top babyface and eventual heir to Douglas. Without a major title to focus on, Heyman created the "Fuck The World" Title for Taz. More a symbol than an actual championship, Taz's FTW belt epitomized his bad-ass no-nonsense attitude. Taz defended the title regularly, with Heyman building toward a Taz vs. Douglas showdown.

The fourth pay-per-view of 1998, *Heatwave '98* on August 2, became the first ECW show to live up to the high standards set by *Barely Legal*. The company booked its biggest venue ever, the Hara Arena in Dayton, Ohio. Nearly 4,500 packed the building to the tune of a $110,000 gate, another company record. On top, Taz successfully defended his FTW Title against Bam Bam Bigelow, while The Sandman, Tommy Dreamer, and Spike Dudley defeated Buh Buh Ray, D-Von, and Big Dick Dudley in a bloody brawl. But it was the undercard that made the show, with Justin Credible and Jerry Lynn, both future ECW Champions, and Masato Tanaka and Mike Awesome from Japan stealing the show.

Yet the outlook for ECW took a turn for the worse as the autumn leaves turned brown. The company lost its television outlet on Channel 31 in New York City, its biggest market, and struggled to find a replacement. More importantly, the company lost its most popular performer, The Sandman, to WCW in September. The company had averted disaster with the Tod Gordon fiasco one year earlier, but it couldn't prevent The Sandman from accepting a three-year offer at a big increase over his $156,000 guaranteed ECW salary.

THE SANDMAN: My character was a guy who you would meet in any corner bar on a Friday afternoon that wants to play you in a game of pool, and the game is for a drink or who wants to buy the next round, the guy who wants to fight with you after he loses. That's my guy. Everyone can relate to that character.

I was getting paid a great deal of money by WCW. I got a $10,000 signing bonus. They signed me for $245,000 for three years. Pay me and I know I signed my career away. I consider myself lucky.

The defections continued just prior to *November To Remember '98*, as Bam Bam Bigelow jumped ship for a lucrative WCW contract. With ECW growing, the "big two" took notice once again, prompting a feeder-system mentality and establishing ECW as a distant third in the wrestling pecking order.

With morale down, *November To Remember* was nothing memorable. From the Lakefront Arena on the campus of the University of New Orleans on November 1, the event drew an ECW record of 5,800 fans, 4,700 of which had paid for tickets. But those in attendance and viewers at home were treated to a poor show filled with bad matches up and down the card, including the main event of Taz, Sabu, and Rob Van Dam defeating Shane Douglas, Chris Candido, and the departing Bam Bam Bigelow, with Sabu pinning the ECW Champion.

1999 would be a make-or-break year for ECW. Buyrates had steadied, while live attendance remained strong week after week. After almost a full year of total pay-per-view clearance, the next logical step in expansion would be to national television. Syndication worked well, but the costs and hassles involved often proved troublesome. Both the WWF and WCW dominated cable television ratings every week, making ECW's search for a national home slightly easier.

Chapter 14

The new year kicked off with the long-awaited title change, as Taz choked-out Shane Douglas in the main event of ECW *Guilty as Charged* in Kissimmee, Florida, on January 10, 1999, to become ECW World Heavyweight Champion. The show also featured the ECW debut of Sid Vicious. Six days later, at the ECW Arena, The Public Enemy returned after several unproductive years in WCW.

But the big story in early 1999 would not be in the ring, but rather the fiscal future of the organization. Throughout February, a rash of bounced checks to wrestlers and creditors raised suspicions about the financial well-being of the company. Despite successful house shows in new markets, namely the Carolinas and Michigan region, the costs of running live events and paying for television slots chewed up the bulk of the revenues. Without the ancillary income that the WWF and WCW earned, the lengthy turnaround in receiving pay-per-view revenue — a minimum of three months for the company's largest revenue stream — made life difficult between events.

SHANE DOUGLAS: It's no secret that ECW has been under great financial duress. It's not bankrupt. I can't speak exactly what the balances of the company are because I don't get that in-depth with it. But I can tell you the company in the past has had trouble making payments to the wrestlers and it's caused quite a bit of concern. Keep in mind, we have bills to pay. As much as we would love to contribute to the company in whatever way we can, and put off being paid our total amount of money for a prolonged period of time, it reaches a point where you have to say you can't do it without substantial amount of pay soon. If you make ten bucks, you're used to living on ten bucks. If you make a thousand dollars, you're used to living on that. A millionaire can't live on ten bucks. We get used to a certain lifestyle and we spend a ton of money on the road. Hotel rooms are 150 bucks a night. Rental cars aren't cheap. Airfares aren't cheap. You can only hold out so long without getting any pay.

To ease the financial crunch, ECW finalized several business deals to ensure solvency, at least temporarily. On top of a private loan for three-quarters of a million dollars, the company inked a marketing agreement with Buena Vista Television. As part of the deal, Buena Vista agreed to cover expenses for each pay-per-view, approximately $250,000, and spend an additional $100,000 to advertise each event, in exchange for first dibs on the revenues from the pay-per-views and a healthy cut of any increase above the 0.24 buyrate *Guilty as Charged* drew. ECW also cleared availability on Viewer's Choice Canada for the first time to capitalize on the fertile Canadian wrestling market.

With its financial woes behind it for the time being, ECW presented *Living Dangerously* on March 21, 1999, from the Asbury Park Convention Center for the second consecutive year. The building sold out easily, to the tune of 3,900 fans paying $100,000. The main event saw Taz defeat Sabu to unify the ECW and FTW Titles, the latter belt won by Sabu previously at the ECW Arena. Perhaps the highlight of the night was Rob Van Dam's Television Title defense against Jerry Lynn, which required overtime to decide. This inaugural Van Dam vs. Lynn battle would start a feud that would continue in ECW for the remainder of its existence.

> **ROB VAN DAM:** It was a kick-ass match the first time I wrestled him. There was a lot of pressure riding on it. I was extremely happy with the competition between myself and Jerry Lynn. I was looking forward to this match like I haven't looked forward to any other match. During the match and afterwards, I felt like it was great. . . . When you watch me versus Jerry Lynn, then you get to see what I like about wrestling.

But the annual theme of financial instability again reared its ugly head on the eve of the May 16 *Hardcore Heaven '99* event in

Poughkeepsie, New York. This time, it cost the company several key pieces of talent. Former ECW World Champion, "The Franchise" Shane Douglas no-showed the event over a dispute with Heyman, mainly about $100,000 in money owed to him, and never worked for ECW again.

> **SHANE DOUGLAS:** I started seeing signs with ECW that maybe I better begin exploring other options. With wrestling being so hot, I'm at that awkward age where I'm at the peak of my career and I'm really doing the best wrestling I've ever done, yet I'm in a smaller company and I don't want to miss the big boat. I'm very proud of the accomplishments that ECW has attained and what I've done in ECW. Unfortunately for ECW, I'm hearing these salaries of the other places, and I had a discussion with one of the top wrestlers in another company and his words to me were, "You've done all you can in ECW. Don't miss the boat. This is where the money is." And when you've been busted up as much as I've been busted up, you start to look at things differently. Your priorities change. My priority for the first eighteen years of my career was always the veracity of the sport, the legacy that "The Franchise" would be remembered as. And suddenly, I'm looking at it thinking whatever money I'm making, I've got to make enough to retire on because retirement is sooner than later for me.

Sid Vicious fluctuated in and out of the mix after a series of bounced checks before ultimately jumping to WCW. Chris Candido and wife Tammy "Sunny" Sytch were fired after the pay-per-view, despite Candido being owed $80,000 for company airline tickets bought on his personal credit cards. Amidst a lot of uncertainty, *Hardcore Heaven* took place, headlined by two successful ECW Title defenses by Taz against Candido and Buh Buh Ray Dudley. But Jerry Lynn and Rob Van Dam stole the show once again, despite Lynn being knocked unconscious early in the proceedings. Van Dam went over after twenty-six minutes to retain the Television Title.

ECW needed an injection of good fortune to boost sagging morale and help increase revenue. Their savior, or so it seemed, was The Nashville Network, which agreed to air a one-hour ECW television program at 8pm eastern on Friday nights starting in the fall, as part of a new sports and adventure weekly block. The two sides structured the deal in favor of TNN, with ECW paying the weekly production costs, the network keeping all advertising revenue save for five minutes, and TNN earning a percentage of any increase above the promotion's $11 million in annual revenue. The deal wasn't perfect, but ECW banked on the national television outlet bumping up pay-per-view, live event, and merchandise revenues. TNN also aired in Canada, which would give ECW free television penetration north of the border for the first time.

> **ROB VAN DAM:** Everybody's got a very positive outlook on this. Everybody's looking forward to finally getting a chance to be compensated for all the hard work and time they've put into ECW. I've been with ECW almost three and a half years now and all along I've had people say, "Rob are you going to WWF? Is it true you're going to WCW? Why don't you leave? You're too good for ECW." When we get on TNN and the whole nation gets to experience ECW wrestling, everybody will see why I didn't leave. They're going to understand why I stuck it out with ECW.

The company also finalized licensing agreements with Acclaim for a video game, and Pioneer Home Video for VHS and DVD releases. Earlier in the year, the *ECW Magazine* hit newsstands. A CD compilation of ECW wrestler theme songs had been released by CMC International the previous year. With national television forthcoming, optimism reached an all-time high.

> **JOEY STYLES:** When you pick up a WWF CD, Steve Austin's face is on the cover. When you pick up a WWF video game, Steve Austin's face is on the cover. If Steve Austin were to drop dead tomorrow, you could flush that whole thing. With ECW, everything we do has the company logo and every ECW personality on the cover. Look at our album. When our video game comes out, there's not going to one person on the cover, it's going to be all the stars of ECW with the company logo. So if one person leaves or two people leave, or three performers leaves, the company will go on because Paul Heyman, the executive producer, talent coordinator, owner of ECW, is

smart enough to market the company that way. It's the product, not the individual performers, so that way he's never held hostage by one individual performer.

The *Heatwave '99* pay-per-view came off as a transitional show back at the Hara Arena in Dayton, Ohio. Fans paid an ECW record $125,000 gate for what turned out to be an average show. Taz retained the ECW World Title against Yoshihiro Tajiri, while Rob Van Dam and Jerry Lynn teamed to defeat Justin Credible and Lance Storm, collectively called The Impact Players, in the main event. The company's grand long-term plans remained on hold in anticipation of the *ECW On TNN* debut.

Chapter 15

On the eve of the company's biggest venture, national television in prime time, as if on cue, another calamity struck. The ECW World Heavyweight Champion and the ECW World Tag-Team Champions prepared to debut on national cable television — but not for ECW. Taz and The Dudleys had negotiated contracts with the WWF. Despite the friendly relations between the two companies, the WWF operated in an acquisition mode over the summer in preparation for the launch of its two-hour *Smackdown* show. With constant question marks surrounding ECW's stability, all three men would have had a difficult time passing up more money, given the fear of bounced checks, or worse, their employer going under.

Despite asking for only a one-dollar raise to stay, The Dudleys signed contracts with the WWF after Paul Heyman refused the request, realizing he could never compete monetarily with the "big two" for talent, perhaps a damning sign for the future of the company.

BUH BUH RAY DUDLEY: I always knew in the back of mind that something was up. I always knew that this was the Triple-A affiliate of WWE. This was the breeding ground where they cultivated all their talent. And it's true. Go back and look. Everybody who's anybody passed through those doors. When we finally got a call and they wanted to sit down and talk to us, we went to Paul. It was the night of the last pay-per-view we were on where I went crazy on that girl and her mother. That night, we sat down with Paul and told him what the deal was. He said, "I can't get into a bidding war with them." I said, "We don't even know what they have to offer. Give us a dollar more right now. Tell us something and we will stay." Because we did not want to go. I believed in ECW so much. That was like my family's company. I was involved with that company behind the scenes. I did more behind the scenes than I did in the ring. I had no reason to leave. I was one of those people that had pride in what I did and a love for ECW. I told Paul to step up to the plate here just a little bit and he said he couldn't. When he said that, that's when I knew. They already called him and said, "We want the Dudleys and that's final." And that's the way it was.

On their last night, The Dudleys won the ECW Tag-Team Titles from Balls Mahoney and Spike Dudley at the beginning of a TNN taping in Queens, teased presenting the belts to Vince McMahon, and then lost them at the end of the night to Tommy Dreamer and the returning Raven, who came home to ECW after walking out of his big-money WCW deal for half the guaranteed salary. Raven's surprising return temporarily eased the loss of Buh Buh Ray and D-Von.

The ongoing problems became masked by the debut of *ECW On TNN* on August 27, 1999. The one-hour broadcast featured highlights of the best of ECW, showcasing the wrestlers and their recent storylines, with Joey Styles and Joel Gertner on commentary. The rating came in at a 0.94, about half of the 1.9 rating TNN had promised to advertisers. However, ECW's show far outdrew the other TNN programs in the Friday night sports block.

But just days after the debut show, word leaked out that ECW World Champion Taz had been in covert negotiations with the WWF. One month earlier, ECW publicly announced that Taz inked a three-year deal for $300,000 per year to stay. But before the signatures, Taz and Heyman had had a falling out, leading to the champion deciding to join the WWF. Because he still held the belt, all sides agreed to have Taz drop the strap at the September 19 *Anarchy Rulz* pay-per-view.

TAZ: I never thought I would be leaving ECW. Never. I had checks bouncing while my wife was eight months pregnant for so many weeks in a row, and I never even contemplated leaving ECW. I didn't do anything to go ahead with trying to get out of the company because I figured things would clear up. I can't leave Paul now. He's in a really bad position and I have to stick by him. Just like all the other guys in the locker room did. Everybody stuck by Paul, and he stuck by all of the guys. We had a good family bond. I never thought I would leave the company, but this is a good deal for me. My deal that I was going to have in ECW just wasn't happening the way it was supposed to happen. I did what I had to do.

Whether it was the exposure on TNN or a testament to the Chicago wrestling market, ECW drew its biggest house for *Anarchy Rulz* at the Odeum Theater in Villa Park, Illinois. Almost 6,000 fans paid $208,000 — both new company records — as Taz wrestled Masato Tanaka and Mike Awesome in a Three-Way Dance. In a shocker, Taz lasted less than a minute before being eliminated. The crowd serenaded the champion with boos and catcalls during his entrance, but applauded him with a classy ovation upon his departure. Tanaka and Awesome battled on for the next twelve minutes, with Awesome going over to win the ECW World Title.

TAZ: I had issues with Paul. He had issues with me. Not only did Mike Awesome beat me, I handed him the belt and shook his hand. I don't want to sound conceited, but the character Taz in ECW was an over son of a gun, and that character endorsed this new champion and Taz never endorsed anyone. I didn't do it because I liked Mike. One of the reasons I did was because Paul needed Mike to beat me. I felt like it would help Paul's business for my character to endorse Mike. I didn't want to hurt ECW by leaving. I knew I wouldn't. No one could hurt Paul's company by leaving, because people come to see ECW. I knew by me leaving, it wasn't going to kill ECW. But I did know that I was pushed as a very credible world champion, so by me leaving and passing the belt to Mike Awesome, who was on the sidelines for so long with a knee injury, could have hurt Paul's belt. I have a lot of pride in the ECW World Heavyweight belt and I didn't want to see that happen. So I endorsed Mike the right way and Mike accepted it the right way, and we had a long talk after the match in Chicago and it was great. It was real cool.

ECW On TNN showed signs of life after early declines. Ratings in September fell into the low 0.70's before bouncing back as high as

1.20 in October. The pay-per-views stagnated around 70,000 buys, but with the television deal and new clearance on pay-per-view in Canada, *Anarchy Rulz* peaked at a record 85,000 buys, a 0.23 buyrate.

The worm turned for ECW fans with a surprise return to the company at the October 23 ECW Arena event. Despite leaving ECW on bad terms, The Sandman returned from a nondescript stint in WCW as Hardcore Hak. Released in a cost-cutting maneuver, Heyman brought back The Sandman as a babyface alongside Tommy Dreamer and Raven. His return to the ring came at *November To Remember '99* on the November 7 at the Bert Flickenger Center in Buffalo, New York. The Sandman, Dreamer, and Raven fell to Justin Credible, Lance Storm, and Rhino in the main event. The big story of the show was Taz's final ECW match — a loss to new top star Rob Van Dam in a Television Title match. Meanwhile, ECW World Champion Mike Awesome retained his title in a singles rematch with Masato Tanaka.

November went on to be a strong month for the company, with the announcement of a new investor. Acclaim finalized its video game deal with ECW, called *Hardcore Revolution*, and took a fifteen percent equity interest in the company. The infusion of funds helped solidify the shaky financial situation. The company also did well at the gate during the month, drawing 4,000 fans at a November 18 television taping in Chicago. Two nights later, the company received some valuable publicity with an angle at a Limp Bizkit concert in Peoria, Illinois. In front of a sold-out crowd, Steve Corino interrupted the show with a heel promo running down the band and the crowd. Balls Mahoney and Axl Rotten appeared to save the day with a pair of wicked chairshots for Corino, to the delight of the rock fans. ECW wisely aired the footage on TNN, and also received airplay on MTV.

> **STEVE CORINO:** I think it would have been cooler if I knew exactly who they were at the time. I'm not a big fan of that type of music, so I had no idea who they were. I just knew that this group must be something good. I saw 12,000 people there and thought maybe I should start listening to their music more often.

Fritz and "The American Dream" Dusty Rhodes

"The American Dream" Dusty Rhodes, who had been let go as a WCW color commentator, joined ECW at the December 2 TNN taping in Atlanta, Georgia, to initiate a program with Corino. Later in the month, to generate interest in the TNN shows on Christmas and New Year's Eves, Heyman flip-flopped the ECW World Title. Masato Tanaka won the gold at the December 17 taping in Nashville, Tennessee, to air seven days later, but dropped it back to Awesome on the December 23 tapings in White Plains, New York, which aired eight nights later. The idea worked, as the ratings held up on both holidays, 1.1 and 0.9, respectively.

PAUL HEYMAN: We started getting the phone calls going into the Christmas Eve and New Year's Eve shows, saying why don't you just send recap shows because you know that you are going to be doing a 0.3 or a 0.4, which is what *RollerJam* was doing. So we said, no we're not going to lose our audience at all because it's destination programming, and people are going to watch it. We didn't lose any viewers on Christmas Eve or New Year's Eve. We had our audience.

The January 9, 2000, *Guilty as Charged* pay-per-view in Birmingham, Alabama, kicked off the new year, highlighted by The Impact Players winning the Tag-Team Titles from Raven and Dreamer. Dusty Rhodes continued to appear, working angles with Corino and Rhino. *ECW On TNN* drew its highest rating, 1.24, on the January 21 show built around Rob Van Dam's chase for the ECW World Title. But all long-term plans went out the window when Van Dam broke his ankle and fibula at a January 29 house show in Orlando, Florida. The freak injury occurred while performing a routine baseball slide. Headed for an extended trip to the disabled list, Van Dam forfeited the ECW Television Title, ending his record two-year reign.

Chapter 16

The major angle on television revolved around ECW rebelling against TNN, portrayed as heels in the storyline by Cyrus, the former pay-per-view color commentator with Joey Styles. Ironically, there was an element of truth to the narrative as TNN's parent company, Viacom, publicly announced intentions to negotiate with the WWF to shift its uber-popular cable wrestling package from the USA Network to TNN, a deal which would leave ECW homeless.

The March 12 *Living Dangerously* pay-per-view took place in Danbury, Connecticut, with Super Crazy winning the vacant Television Title in the tournament finals over Rhino, and Dusty Rhodes pinning Steve Corino in a bloody bullrope match.

Yet again, any ECW momentum was stopped dead in its tracks by perhaps their most problematic talent defection ever. Without notice, reigning ECW Champion Mike Awesome walked out of the promotion with the belt without notice, then appeared on the April 10 edition of WCW *Monday Nitro*. Awesome, however, had a legally binding three-year contract with ECW at approximately $200,000 per year. ECW and WCW had negotiated a deal to allow Awesome to leave in exchange for a six-figure payment to ECW and a promise Awesome would return to drop the title. But the sudden jump destroyed plans for Awesome to eventually drop the belt to Rob Van Dam. Heyman and ECW were left in the lurch, not knowing how to handle the title situation, which would go down at a special television taping on April 13 in Indianapolis.

JOEY STYLES: I know Mike Awesome had a signed contract, because I saw it. I've read an interview online where he said, "I have a three-year deal." I have an audio interview in my possession that he did for *ECWwrestling.com* out at Acclaim's world headquarters where he said, "I just signed my new three-year deal." I hadn't spoken to Mike. Mike was always very nice, very soft-spoken, and a gentleman at every show I saw him at. I really liked Mike Awesome. I thought he was a phenomenal worker. I don't know what he feels gave him the right to pretty much break his contract. The fact of the matter is, the ECW legal team was working around the clock, and they stopped him and they paid us for Mike Awesome and that's it. In Mike's case, he really sold out because his intention was to go on TV and trash our company publicly. He must have been pretty angry.

The predicament led to a historic match in which a WCW wrestler fought a WWF wrestler for an ECW title in an ECW ring. Heyman arranged with the WWF for Taz to return for a brief period to beat Awesome in one minute for the ECW Title in Indianapolis. The footage aired the next night on TNN.

TAZ: I was completely shocked. I never, ever expected that. I wasn't really into it up until I landed. When I was on the plane, I wasn't crazy about it, but I figured it would be cool and get a good buzz going and no one would expect it. When I got to Indianapolis and I saw all of the guys I used to work with in ECW, it was really cool. Then, going to show, it was like, "This is pretty cool." It got building better and better. And then going out there and facing Awesome, it was really, really cool.

The following week, Tazz (the WWF spelling) appeared on *Raw* and *Smackdown* wearing the ECW Title. However, he was questionably booked to lose to Triple H, the WWF Champion, in a non-title match in ECW's home market, Philadelphia, on *Smackdown*. Theoretically, the match could have killed the value of the ECW championship. The entire plan culminated in Taz returning to the ECW Arena on April 22 to drop the title.

The *Cyberslam* event at the ECW Arena came off with a confusing series of title changes. Taz lost the ECW Title to Tommy

Dreamer, who actually never wanted to win the title. In the post-match celebration, Justin Credible hit the ring, threw down his half of the tag-team titles, and challenged the new champion. Credible went over to capture the title, ending Dreamer's brief reign and instantly ascending to the top spot he had been destined for since he debuted.

Once the chaos settled, ECW presented *Hardcore Heaven* on May 14, 2000, from Milwaukee, Wisconsin. Credible retained the ECW World Title against his former partner, Lance Storm, who left the company shortly thereafter to sign a three-year deal with WCW.

> **LANCE STORM:** Paul wanted to negotiate a new long-term deal. I told him I was more than willing to, but I wanted to look at my options. Paul gave me his pitch on what ECW could offer me. I heard WCW was interested. I managed to get in touch with them fairly easily. I met with them and they pitched what they were willing to offer me. They were offering me, what I thought, was a bigger opportunity and I joined their team.
>
> It was very hard to leave the people I was working with, because I really, really enjoyed it. But when it comes right down to it, you have to look at it from a business end. You sit down and you look at dates, opportunity, and money, and you look at it more on a point and counterpoint thing and do what mathematically adds up to a better decision for you and your family.

Also at *Hardcore Heaven*, Rhino, who'd won the ECW Television Title from Tajiri at *Cyberslam*, retained the gold against The Sandman. Perhaps most importantly, Rob Van Dam and Jerry Lynn both returned from lengthy injuries to wrestle each other, with Lynn going over.

The approaching summer would end up determining the future of ECW. A battle between Viacom, the USA Network, and the WWF would be settled in court to resolve the future of wrestling programming on TNN. Internally, Paul Heyman predicted he would be done with TNN and continued his part-shoot/part-work anti-TNN angle to spite the network. He refused to invest any special production into the TNN tapings, believing the network had reneged on promises and gone behind ECW's back to flirt with the WWF. ECW's ratings had slowly declined since their peak earlier in the year, from the low 1.0's to 0.8's and even into the 0.7's.

> **JOEY STYLES:** Did you realize that we're the highest rated series on TNN and we average a 1.0? The average rating of the entire network is a 0.6. CBS Cable owns it and you would never know. FOX does such a fantastic job of using the synergies between FOX, the FOX News Channel, FX, FOX Sports. They co-promote on other channels. CNBC is now going to be showing the PGA Senior Tour. They're going to be promoting the hell out of it during NBC Sports and on MSNBC. You would think CBS, during football games, during a golf tournament, during whatever sports they're showing, would say, "Thursday nights on TNN, our network, you can see live arena football," or, "While you're watching Falcone, you're watching guys get whacked, you can watch guys get whacked with steels chairs Friday nights with wrestling." With every one of the stories I've read in the AP, *Variety*, the *New York Post*, the *LA Times* that talk about CBS wanting to get into the wrestling business and CBS wanting to buy ten percent of the WWF for $100 million, there's already wrestling on TNN. There's absolutely no synergy between CBS and TNN. And you can bet that if Vince McMahon gets on the network, they will completely rename the network, redesign the network, and push WWF programming on CBS as network. You'll be reading about it everywhere. They kind of leave us out there on the network that nobody watches, they give us no help, and everyone takes shots at us.

Heyman's premonition proved accurate when a Delaware court ruled in favor of the WWF and Viacom, which facilitated the move of *Raw*, cable's number one show, to TNN. The network wasted no time in canceling ECW effective September 22, three days before *Raw*'s debut, citing that "ECW has failed to meet some of the criteria of the agreement, including ratings performance targets."

Chapter 17

With its television and overall future in doubt, ECW ventured west for the first time to the Grand Olympic Auditorium in Los Angeles for *Heatwave* on July 16. The show, however, was marred by a local knockoff independent group, Xtreme Pro Wrestling, attempting to disrupt the event. Several XPW personalities sat ringside and instigated a shoving match with Francine and Tommy Dreamer just prior to the pay-per-view main event. The commotion, which could not be seen on television, escalated later outside the building, where a brawl erupted between ECW and XPW talent, with ECW greatly outnumbering their opposition, until the XPW talent fled in a limousine. The events seriously hurt the show, which saw Credible retain the ECW World Title in a barbed wire ladder match against Tommy Dreamer.

> **SIMON DIAMOND:** I wouldn't know any of their people or the guy who runs it if he stood next to me in an elevator. The last time I checked, there were three wrestling promotions in the United States — WWF, WCW and ECW. We run six pay-per-views a year, we have national syndication, and we have a national cable television program shown weekly in every market in the United States. With that, I ask you again, who are these people?

The company continued producing its lame-duck TNN program while searching for a new television home. Heyman talked extensively with the USA Network, which would be losing its seventeen-year wrestling franchise, about a Saturday late-night show, combining elements of ECW and MTV's reality TV lifestyle show, *The Real World.*

The expected final tapings for TNN took place during a back-to-back sold out stay at the Hammerstein Ballroom in New York City on August 25 and 26. Ironically, despite its murky future, the company received publicity on the front page of the *New York Daily News*. The first night featured a one-night tournament for the ECW Tag-Team Titles — vacated since Credible threw his belt down and Storm left for WCW — won by Mikey Whipwreck and Yoshihiro Tajiri, managed by The Sinister Minister, over Jerry Lynn and Tommy Dreamer as well as Simon Diamond and Swinger in a Three-Way Dance. The next night, Little Guido and Tony Mamaluke, a.k.a. The F.B.I., won the belts from the new champions. Also, Justin Credible defeated Steve Corino in a great ECW Title match, while Kid Kash defeated Rhino to win the ECW Television Title following a wild brawl after Cyrus "cancelled" *ECW On TNN*.

The company debuted in Canada on September 8 in Mississauga, Ontario, a suburb of Toronto, in front of a sold-out crowd of more than 5,000, a testament to the hot Canadian wrestling market. Despite the big house show successes in New York and Mississauga, payroll problems crept up again, with multiple wrestlers several weeks behind on checks. The company got an unexpected boost when Vince McMahon waived his exclusivity clause and allowed ECW to remain on TNN through the end of the year. Heyman, a brilliant wrestling mind but a terrible businessman, needed to pull off a new television deal or face extinction.

With his company's future in the balance, Heyman switched to monthly pay-per-view events to boost revenues and keep money flowing into the organization. The first such show, ECW *Anarchy Rulz*, took place on October 1, 2000, from St. Paul, Minnesota, with Jerry Lynn, in his hometown, winning the ECW World Title from Justin Credible.

> **JERRY LYNN:** I think I'm still in shock because everyone keeps asking me, "How does it feel?" Well, I still feel the same. The more I think about it, it's so surrealistic, it was almost like a dream. It was the biggest night of my career. I think I'm still in shock.

But the company's fortunes took another downturn when

despite McMahon's stay of execution, TNN abruptly cancelled the Friday night ECW show on October 17 after the two sides failed to agree on an extension through the end of the year. The company could rely on its syndicated show, *ECW Hardcore TV*, but it needed a national deal to survive. Heyman entered into a strategic alliance with Farmclub.com, which aired a music show on USA Network, but couldn't finalize a deal for his own show on the ex-WWF television home.

> **PAUL HEYMAN:** We were scheduled to sign papers with USA, through the president of USA, Steven Chao. We were ready to jump. We were there. The president of USA, Steven Chao, was signing us on, and at the very last minute — I mean right before the official announcements that we were going on USA, and they were buying into the company. Then Barry Diller, who was the chairman at USA, decided that he wanted to take the network in a different direction, and the decision was made not to put any more wrestling on. We were out. That was it.

The monthly pay-per-view events continued with *November To Remember* on November 5 from Chicago with Steve Corino winning his first ECW World Title from Jerry Lynn, Justin Credible, and The Sandman in a Double Jeopardy match.

> **CYRUS:** I wasn't surprised that he got the strap. Had you asked me six months ago or a year ago did I think Steve Corino was going to get the title in the next year, I wouldn't have thought it was possible. I, of all people, realize that size is not the most important thing. What really gets people over is talking ability and charisma, and Steve has lots of both. There were probably a half-dozen other guys I would have bet on before I would have picked Steve Corino six months ago. Having said that, Steve has worked very hard.

Rob Van Dam didn't work the event due to a prior movie commitment, and with the money situation worsening, soon filed for breach of contract, being more than thirty days behind on pay. At the same time, Heyman brought in Scott Hall, formerly of WCW, to work a handful of house shows.

By December, the financial situation had reached dire straits. A house show swing in Texas was cancelled. Wrestlers fell behind as much as six weeks in pay heading into the December 3 *Massacre On 34th Street* pay-per-view in New York City. The show drew a sellout crowd and came off well, with Steve Corino retaining the ECW World Title over Justin Credible and Jerry Lynn in a Three-Way Dance. Later in the month, the company sold out its television tapings in Queens with appearances from The Dudleys and Tazz, in a surprise homecoming, another goodwill gesture from the WWF.

The turn of the new year changed little, as most regulars remained seven weeks behind in pay. The company lost its biggest syndicated outlet, MSG Network, after missing payments of $4,000 per week for the airtime. ECW produced another pay-per-view at the Hammerstein Ballroom, *Guilty as Changed*, in front of a sold out crowd, built around Rob Van Dam's surprise one-night return for a main event match with Jerry Lynn. The ECW World Title changed hands twice, with The Sandman winning the belt in a four-way Tables, Ladders, Chairs and Canes match before losing an immediate impromptu match with Rhino, who ended the night as champion.

> **LITTLE GUIDO MARITATO:** I've been here since '96, so I've been on this roller coaster for a long time and it did have its ups and downs. I guess it is hard to stay patient, but I think it's going to work out in the long run if I do stay patient. Paul E gave me my chance back in 1996 when I got home from Japan, and I feel obligated to him. He did dig us out of the hole one time with TNN, and TNN really didn't do the right thing with us and they kind of put us back in the hole. The chips are down now. It makes it worth more to you when the chips are down and when you break out of it. It makes you appreciate it more.

The company ran two house shows, basically because the rights were sold to local promoters ahead of time, in out-of-the-way markets — Poplar Bluff and Pine Bluff, Missouri — using a skeleton crew. The final match of the second night on January 13, 2001, saw The Sandman defeat Justin Credible. Realizing the inevitable, the locker room emptied into the ring to celebrate and say goodbye on the night the "extreme revolution" died.

Chapter 18

The little flicker of faith for ECW's survival extinguished as many of the company's top stars signed elsewhere. Justin Credible started the exodus in early February by signing with the WWF. Jerry Lynn and ECW World Champion Rhino followed. WCW, also on its last legs, expressed interest in several talents as well. Heyman then cancelled a March 11 pay-per-view date that most never expected to materialize anyway.

Fritz and Justin Credible

PAUL HEYMAN: The fact of the matter is this. If you look at it objectively, if we had scored a network, then we would have gotten our pay-per-view money, and we would have survived. If we could have just gotten our pay-per-view money, we could have survived without a network for a long long time, because we could have marketed ourselves in many different ways and survived off the royalties of the DVDs, and off the CDs, and other things. That doesn't mean that we would have kept all of our talent, we might have gone down to bare bones again. But we would have stayed in business. The little neon light that flashes "ECW, ECW" would have stayed on. Without the network, and Dan York at In Demand's decision not to give us our money, we're out of business. It's that simple. It can't be any more simplistic than that.

The final nail in the ECW coffin came on the March 1 edition of WWF *Raw*. Paul Heyman, wearing an ECW baseball cap, was introduced as the new color commentator, replacing Jerry Lawler alongside Jim Ross, ironically on TNN. Heyman had signed a five-year contract with the WWF, signaling the official end of the company that changed the wrestling landscape out of a South Philadelphia bingo hall.

NOVA: I guess that was the hallmark that things were never going to be the way they were. It was good and it was bad. It's good at one point that I'm glad to see Paul do something, because he has so much to offer wrestling still. But it was bad because it was a hallmark that things and the way they were will never be the same.

Despite promising to avoid bankruptcy, to at least leave a glimmer of hope for the wrestlers to collect money owed to them, Heyman filed Chapter 11 on April 4 for HHG Corporation, the parent company for Extreme Championship Wrestling. He also filed for personal bankruptcy. The paperwork revealed $7.5 million in company debt, with creditors ranking from Richard Heyman, Paul's father, at $3.8 million, Acclaim at $1 million, FarmClub.com at $300,000, MSG Network at $240,000, and various legal and accounting firms at $190,000 total. Producer Steve Karel was owed more than $170,000 in personal and business debts. The filing also revealed the money owed to the talent roster, including Rob Van Dam ($150,000), Tommy Dreamer ($100,000), announcer Joey Styles ($50,480), Rhino ($50,000), Shane Douglas ($48,000), and Francine ($47,275), among others.

> **ROB VAN DAM:** I'm sure a lot of the guys don't expect to see any of their money. On the flip side, I'm sure a lot of guys expected them to declare bankruptcy. It did take a long time. It wasn't like we just started having problems and then quit running either. Even over the past few years, from some checks bouncing and then checks getting behind, to getting paid every other week, to the point where it was forget about those other checks. At the same time, everyone was happy, even with all of this going on. As long as they were able to get by, they were willing to stay with ECW and to hopefully make it out of the hole as a team with everybody. That is what everybody held on to for a long, long time. We had some good times there.

The most interesting creditor listed was the World Wrestling Federation, owed $587,500. The information confirmed rumors for years that the WWF and ECW had secretly collaborated to help each other. The ECW appearances on *Raw*, and clandestine funding helped keep ECW going. In return, the WWF sent wrestlers to ECW for grooming, such as Al Snow and Vic Grimes. McMahon rationalized the pilfering of ECW talent and creative ideas, which helped turn his company around, by putting HHG Corporation on the monthly payroll. Yet many of McMahon's strategic decisions — from signing away Taz and the Dudleys just before ECW started on TNN, to having Triple H pin interim ECW Champion Taz in Philadelphia on *Smackdown* — contributed to the company's ultimate demise.

While ECW lay dead and buried as a wrestling promotion, the brand name was revived on WWF television in the summer of 2001. To aid the floundering WCW invasion storyline, ECW rose from the ashes to align with WCW against the WWF. Paul Heyman led the ex-ECW wrestlers on the WWF roster, including newly signed Rob Van Dam and Tommy Dreamer, with Stephanie McMahon acting as owner of the group. Shoddy booking doomed the WCW/ECW Alliance angle, which ended in a winner-take-all match against Team WWF at the *Survivor Series* four months later.

> **MIKE AWESOME:** Actually, when they turned to ECW, I thought it was going to work. I don't know if you were at any of the arena shows but any time they did something with ECW, everyone there was chanting "E-C-W." That only lasted for a few TVs and somebody squashed that idea. You can't have a WWF arena and everyone chanting "E-C-W" the whole time. If they would have just let ECW go against the WWF, it would have worked. The fans like to scream for ECW.

Short of a smattering of "E-C-W" chants at occasional live events, the brand collected dust until late 2004. WWE, having purchased the ECW intellectual property rights and video library for $1.9 million, released *The Rise and Fall of ECW* on DVD, a three-hour compilation of the history of the organization. The award-winning documentary sold more than 100,000 units, the second most of any wrestling DVD in history at the time.

> **PAUL HEYMAN:** Well, you know the funniest thing was at first I was kind of pissed off that they were even coming out with it, because I quite frankly didn't think they would do it any justice. I didn't think they could do it any justice, and I didn't think they would do it any justice. And when it first came out, I didn't even watch it when the preview copies came out in the studio. It took Rob Van Dam and Tazz and the Dudleys and Tommy Dreamer and even Tommy Dreamer's wife, who was known as Beulah McGillicutty, all these people got on the phone with me and said basically you got to watch this because they actually did us justice, and when I watched it I was beyond pleasantly surprised at the fact that they did do us justice. You could only expect so much to be told of the seven-year history in only three hours. They made the most of those three hours, and it's pretty much the most comprehensive look at who we were and what we did and what happened to us that I've seen so far.

The unexpected DVD success led to a revival of the brand for one night only on pay-per-view. The Hammerstein Ballroom in

New York City, a regular ECW touring stop, hosted *One Night Stand* on June 12, 2005, with former ECW wrestlers, those under WWE contract, and many outsiders going back in time to relive the company's glory days in front of many of ECW's regular fans.

> **BUH BUH RAY DUDLEY:** ECW is Vince's whore. Whenever he wants to send his whore back out onto the street to make him some money, he will. That whore made him a nice little payday for *One Night Stand*. He's got that whore in his back pocket for whenever he wants to use it. And I don't say "whore" is a bad word: it's a moneymaker for Vince.

But a WWE-produced ECW event couldn't capture the true legacy of Extreme Championship Wrestling — the men and women who busted their butts weekly for little money in front of small crowds in even smaller buildings, and the showcase of first-class wrestling talent, most of which was raided by WCW, and innovative, novel ideas, many of them lifted for the WWF's "attitude" era, that excited cult fans who traveled long distances to partake in the hardcore action. But ultimately, ECW's bid to outgrow its underground reputation landed them in wrestling purgatory. By the end, ECW became too big to be small, and too small to compete with the big boys. Yet the legacy has lived on for the promotion that forever changed the sport by taking professional wrestling to the extreme.

PART III

Fritz, Jim Cornette and "Beautiful" Bobby Eaton

One of the most intelligent and articulate individuals you will ever speak with, regardless of profession, is Mick Foley. I respect the hell out of the guy for what he has done in the ring, but he is amazing when it comes to his creativity and the talented way that he can tell stories. Plus, he possesses a great sense of humor. To be able to package that with his generosity is simply something special.

I had always heard stories about this brilliant person disguised as a crazy, wild-eyed maniac who would enter the squared circle under the name Cactus Jack, but I never really believed it. That is, until I had the opportunity to interview him. It was several weeks after his infamous "I Quit" match against The Rock at the 1999 WWF *Royal Rumble*. Mick took an unbelievable beating, with his hands being handcuffed behind his back, followed by close to a dozen unprotected chair-shots to the head. When I watched that pounding, it left me with a sick feeling in my gut. This was a real beating that man was taking, and it was literally mind-boggling for both him and wrestling fans.

The WWF booked Mick on a radio tour to promote the next pay-per-view, which included a rematch between the two super-stars in a Last Man Standing match. He had already done several interviews that morning to promote the event, but they were conducted by people who knew little about wrestling. We didn't have that problem, and luckily Mick caught on right away that we were fans and followed the sport.

"Every one else has asked what a Last Man Standing match is, or why I wear a mask," said Mick. "You guys really know your stuff.

This is great." It was quite the compliment coming from the "Hardcore Legend." It was a thrill for Dickerman and I to speak with one of our all-time favorites.

Since then, it seems like I have bumped into Mick every time he visits Central Florida. About a year after our first interview with him, he became a best-selling author on the success of his first autobiography. During that book tour, Dickerman and I met him at a book signing, which was held at a car show of all places. In fact, I had to pull myself out of bed because I had been sick all week, but it was well worth the trip.

It wasn't too long after that when Mick made an appearance between periods at a local minor league hockey game. I was covering the game for the radio station and figured I could get a few words with Mick once he came off the ice. Well, a few words were about all he had time for, since he needed to leave immediately to catch a flight home. So, we taped an interview during the walk from inside the building to his car, which lasted a whopping sixty-six seconds. Ah yes, what an in-depth profile of the legendary Mick Foley! Actually, it was good enough for the time we had, considering that Mick had just had one of the greatest matches of his career, reprising the Cactus Jack character in a street fight against Triple H at the 2000 *Royal Rumble*. Plus, rumors swirled that he was on the verge of retirement, which he explained during my probing interview.

Another time, Mick was throwing out the first pitch at a minor league baseball game in nearby Melbourne, and I helped spread the word about his appearance as a favor to a friend who worked with the team. I watched the game from the press box, while Mick was in the front row. In the seventh inning, I decided to use the restroom and, of course, that is when he decided to come looking for me. Timing has never been my best quality. Anyway, we caught up and he shared a few minutes after the game.

Luckily, Mick has always been generous with his time over the years, and we have enjoyed some good discussions and laughs with him. His best quality has to be how generous he has been, not just with all of his fans, but also with the charities he supports, especially when it comes to helping various children's causes. You

*Fritz and "Hardcore Legend"/*NY Times *bestselling author Mick Foley*

wouldn't know it to look at the guy, but Mick Foley is a modern-day Renaissance man.

> **MICK FOLEY:** I have had the pleasure of appearing on *Between the Ropes* on several occasions. On each occasion, I warn them that I will only be on for a few minutes, and on each occasion, I end up talking for an hour. Therein lies the secret of the show. The guys make the wrestlers want to talk.

* * *

I cannot think of any person that has appeared on the show more than "The Franchise" Shane Douglas. He is another great speaker, never shy about sharing his opinions on wrestling, politics, sports, or anything else that comes to mind.

I became acquainted with Shane back in ECW, and we have stayed in touch through the good and the bad of his career. When

I say bad, I mean the tough times in World Championship Wrestling. Anyone that worked in WCW during its final years suffers from lingering emotional problems thanks to the constant turmoil. And Shane definitely went through some frustrations there.

At the time, I wrote a regular wrestling column for *The Orlando Sentinel*, and could always count on Shane for a juicy quote. I can remember him ranting about various things as we spoke off the record, and then, out of nowhere, he would say, "All right, back on the record. What did you want to ask me about again?" Good times.

Going back to his days in ECW, the two of us had an encounter before we knew one another at a live event in Central Florida. I was seated in the front row along with Dickerman and our friend Pat Lynch. The promotion used to pack people into a building in Kissimmee, so we were literally pushed right up against the guardrail. During the show, Jerry Lynn wrestled with "The Franchise," who was accompanied to the ring by his valet Francine. Sometimes, it was very difficult to watch the action and not watch Francine, who was, as usual, wearing one of her revealing outfits at ringside. At one point in the match, the action spilled outside the ring. Francine walked near us and I decided to take that moment to enjoy a little eye candy. I had only taken my eyes off the match for a few seconds when it happened. Wham! Shane had whipped Jerry into the guardrail, which I was up against, shooting the top of the rail right into my chin!

"Whoa!" the crowd yelled out as I sat there holding my face in pain. I stood up and spit out the blood that had filled up my mouth. Meanwhile, Shane stayed right in heel mode and laughed at me!

I thought I had easily lost a couple of teeth, but somehow all thirty-two were still in place. Since it was ECW, I got a little bag of ice to go with the little sympathy from the promotion about my aching mouth.

Shane is a great storyteller and well-respected by his peers in the wrestling business. I know of many guys who enjoy having him in the locker room, not only for the wisdom he offers from his experiences in wrestling, but because he's also good for some laughs. And he is always giddy once he gets his Starbucks cappuccino with an extra shot.

SHANE DOUGLAS: In the world that is professional wrestling, there are a multitude of so-called journalists. Some of these pundits actually DO know what they're talking about. Most DO NOT. With the advent of the internet (my career actually predates the internet — wow, I've really dated myself, haven't I?), these so-called experts have come out of the woodwork. Any and every fan with a computer feels they have the insight and intelligence to qualify what is a good match or bad. Most of these "experts" have never been closer to a ring than the first row, yet they inundate the net with their dribble about why a certain match or performer should have, or shouldn't have, done this or that. Now don't get me wrong, I feel every fan does have a right to their opinions. However, most of these "journalists" postulate their opinions as THE final word on judging the quality of the performance and/or performer. In this sea of pseudoexperts there are, actually, a relative few who do know their shit, and present their critiques as an opinion rather than fact. Brian Fritz is one of those people.

I have appeared many times on his radio show called *Between the Ropes*, a show he has cohosted since its inception in 1998. There are literally dozens (that I know of, and have guested on) of these types of shows, on both mainstream and internet media. Some of these programs are good. Most are not! Oftentimes, when you go on these programs, you are met with some of the "experts" I mentioned above. These are the types that are simply "marks" that "mark out" because they are talking to one of their wrestling heroes. On these shows, you are met with questions and interviews that are reminiscent of the Chris Farley character from *Saturday Night Live*: "Remember that time you threw down the NWA title . . . that was great." The questions are about as deep as a child's wading pool or as pertinent as a condom at a convent. Brian Fritz, however, is one of those legitimate journalists that is both knowledgeable and well-prepared. When he's interviewing you, you get the feeling that this is a fan that has done his homework. Because of its very nature, it is difficult to invoke such phrases as "highbrow" when discussing pro-rasslin'. Yet Brian's show does bring a certain level of legitimacy to the sports entertainment so many of us love.

* * *

One of my favorite all-time guests, especially during the early years of the show, was Tazz. He was everything you could ask for out of a guest

— smart, well-spoken and very honest about what he believed. He was never short on opinions either, and always shared them on the air.

The first time we had Tazz on the show was before his match against Shane Douglas at the *ECW: Guilty as Charged* pay-per-view in Kissimmee, where he won the ECW World Heavyweight Title. Following that show, I met him briefly at a Dennys next to the hotel he was staying at. It was the middle of night, and he was there along with his wife, Joey Styles, Francine, and Tommy Dreamer. What a scene it was, too. Tazz introduced me to everyone as Dreamer sat at a booth by himself filled with several finished plates of food and about a half-dozen milkshakes he had already sucked down. The first words Dreamer said were, "I'm Tommy. That is Francine. Her boob fell out tonight on TV." Nice introduction.

Tazz ended up being a semi-regular guest on the show, and I also helped him with audio commentaries on his Web site. I always enjoyed the conversations we had when we weren't taping, mostly talking about a variety of things, from wrestling, to sports, to our families.

Fritz and Tazz

Later, Tazz ended up leaving ECW for the WWE, which was a great move for him. It looked like he was going to get a big push there, but instead he ended up having a short run as a wrestler, and has since become a very good color commentator. I think he was more than happy to stop taking bumps and hang up his boots to work at the announcer's table. I have a feeling he will be calling matches in WWE for many years to come.

* * *

The most common question I hear from listeners is: "What has been your favorite interview?" To be honest, I can't really pinpoint one, because I've enjoyed having so many amazing people on over the years. But if I had to pick, one interview really stands out.

In the summer of 1999, the wrestling war between WCW and the WWF reached full throttle. In WCW, the nWo was running wild and Bill Goldberg was squashing opponents left and right. But many of the mid-card guys were stealing the show nightly with their outstanding work in the ring. They were dying for more of an opportunity, something management was reluctant to give them.

One such person was Chris Jericho, who had really started to come into his own in WCW. Jericho was the blueprint for a wrestling superstar. He possessed a charismatic, engaging personality and evolved into one of the best talkers in wrestling. He had a unique look, and could more than carry his own in the ring.

WCW booked Jericho in a variety of mid-card storylines, and he was wildly entertaining in all of them. As a heel, while feuding with the "Man of 1000 Holds" Dean Malenko, Jericho played off him and dubbed himself the "Man of 1004 Holds," calling out the different wrestling maneuvers he used during his matches. Jericho adopted a cocky, smarmy character, intentionally calling his opponents by the wrong name. Dean Malenko became "Stinko Malenko." Rey Mysterio was now known as "Ron Mysterio." Even announcer Mean Gene Okerlund felt Jericho's wrath as "Scheme Gene."

Even when he was set up to fail by WCW, Jericho found a way to make things work. Such was the case when the promotion saddled him with an old, out-of-shape company truck driver named

Ralphus. The guy literally looked like a bum you would find face-first in a ditch somewhere. But Jericho found a way to make it work, and the pair were definitely entertaining.

Regardless, Jericho became tired of the backstage politics permeating WCW. He was set to have a major feud with Goldberg, but it was squashed before it had any chance to take off, due to Big Bill's reluctance to work with a lower-card wrester. Jericho wanted a bigger role in the company, and felt he deserved it. Management didn't see it that way.

When his contract came up in the summer of '99, Jericho had options, and more importantly, leverage. He was a free agent during one of the hottest times in wrestling history and his services were in demand. While he could easily have returned to WCW for big money, Jericho made headlines when he jumped to the WWF.

Well before the official announcement, devoted wrestling fans knew Jericho had indeed signed on with Vince McMahon's promotion. It became one of the top stories of the year, and I desperately wanted to have Chris as a guest on the show.

Both Dickerman and I had met Chris earlier that year, when he appeared at a local promotional event with Real Rock 101.1, our sister station and Dickerman's full-time employer. Jericho and Dickerman really hit it off talking music, especially when it came to Jericho's specialty, '80s rock. Naturally, I barged in a little bit and introduced myself. Just a few weeks later, Jericho filled in as a guest host for another radio station down the hall from us. Since I knew he was going to be there, I decided to pop in for a quick moment. Well, Jericho decided he would like to have someone with him in studio so I sat in on the show for the next three hours. He nicknamed me "Fritz the Historian," and urged people to call in and stump me with wrestling trivia. Luckily, Chris backed me up and no one was able to get one past us.

I grew to know Chris a bit, and he was a great guy. He gave me his contact information and said he would happy to come on the wrestling show sometime. When the time was right and I knew he was making the jump to the WWF, I decided to try and cash in on that promise. At the same time, I didn't want to bother the guy and drive him away. So, every Monday for a month, I would send Chris an e-mail asking him to call in to the show that week. I also left him phone messages with the hope that he would join us on the air sometime.

Dickerman, B. Randall, and I were into the second segment of the July 20, 1999, show when B. Randall had a strange look on his face and began pointing wildly at the call screener. I was almost shocked when I looked over and saw: CHRIS JERICHO. Finally, my persistence had paid off.

Chris was driving back to his Florida home after playing some hockey with his friends, and decided to give us a call and share his thoughts on his time with WCW, why he decided to leave the promotion, and how much he was looking forward to the opportunities ahead for him in the WWF.

"You can't believe I took time out of my ridiculously busy schedule to call you?" he chuckled on the air. Of course we didn't, and we were more than happy to have him on with us.

He explained that he was never going to get any chances to move up the ladder in WCW, and felt he was being held down by management. He detailed the problems he had with Goldberg and said he knew that once that storyline got derailed, he wanted out of the promotion.

> **CHRIS JERICHO:** I've found over the years that of all of the radio shows I've done, Fritz and Dickerman are the most professional and most importantly, the most fun for me to do. They never ask the same old stock questions, which enables me to not have to give the same old stock answers, which makes my job so much easier. It also makes for a much more entertaining interview. Isn't that what it's all about?
>
> These two guys are very informed and knowledgeable about what they speak about, and as a result, I find them to be two of the best guys to talk with in the wrestling radio business.

The Chris Jericho interview proved to be very big for the growth of the show. The hottest free agent in wrestling was speaking for the first time about his problems with WCW and why he had signed a contract with the WWF. We got the full scoop on our show straight from the man himself.

The next day, we sent out a detailed recap of the interview with Jericho, which quickly popped up on every known wrestling Web site. Our Web site received a huge amount of traffic as people tuned in for an archive of the show. The Jericho interview really put us on the map and made people aware of *Between the Ropes*.

Fritz and Dickerman rock with Chris Jericho's band Fozzy

WWF/WWE

Back: Dickerman and B. Randall Myers; Front: Jeff Jarrett, Fritz, Debra and the late Owen Hart

Chapter 19

"Anything can happen in the World Wrestling Federation."

That was the ironic mid-'90s motto of the WWF product, which often exhibited all the flash and sizzle of the senior's golf tour. But before long, Vince McMahon's adage would prove true time and time again. For better or for worse, the World Wrestling Federation rarely experienced a dull moment as the decade drew to a close. The roller-coaster ride from record-low business and near collapse, to unimaginable highs and entertainment dominance, to another inevitable dip could only be topped by the events that precipitated the rotating cycle. And overseeing the madness was Vince McMahon, the promoting genius who injected his brand of clean-cut wrestling into America's consciousness in the mid-'80s. This time around, he readied a completely opposite approach to do it again, and prove to his naysayers that anything could indeed happen with his product.

By 1995, the McMahon empire had crumbled to a shell of its former self, thanks to a string of controversies and an evolving audience. McMahon had escaped personal disaster the previous summer when a jury of twelve acquitted him of charges of steroid distribution and conspiracy. Several years earlier, the government locked up Dr. George Zahorian, a regular backstage at the WWF's television tapings who prescribed more than just basic medical care to the wrestlers. Twelve counts of illegal steroid allocation put Zahorian behind bars, and the federal government hoped to do the same to McMahon. They believed McMahon conspired with Zahorian to chemically bulk-up WWF superstars. The prosecution paraded ex-

WWF wrestlers who recalled tales of their boss suggesting the use of performance-enhancing drugs. Federal Express receipts from Zahorian to major WWF names furthered the case. But damaging testimony from Hulk Hogan, whose memory suddenly went blank on the witness stand, nearly sunk the prosecution, who felt double-crossed. With evidence and testimony falling apart, and the McMahon defense team running circles around the government lawyers, the jury was left with an easy decision: Not guilty.

McMahon may have saved his hide from years of imprisonment, but he was now was faced with saving his empire. Negative publicity from the steroid allegations pummeled the WWF's bottom line. On top of those charges, claims of sexual harassment perpetrated by male WWF officials on underage ring-crew boys sparked waves of controversy. The media painted a picture of pedophiles and homo-sexuality running rampant through Titan Towers. McMahon fought back with lawsuits for libel and slander, but the barrage of stories had already greatly eroded his fan base. Top attractions from the glory days, namely Hulk Hogan and The Ultimate Warrior, were out of the picture. Other larger-than-life, overly muscular performers were phased out in favor of a new generation of stars. Bret "The Hitman" Hart and Shawn Michaels, both originally tag-team com-petitors, splintered off into the singles ranks and ascended to the top. Former WCW bottom-feeders Vinnie Vegas and The Diamond Studd reincarnated themselves in the WWF as superstars Diesel and Razor Ramon. Company stalwart The Undertaker helped stabilize the fort.

As McMahon and his confederates tried to resurrect their for-tunes, they encountered another obstacle in the form of a newly energized World Championship Wrestling promotion. WCW launched a Monday night wrestling show running head-to-head with WWF *Monday Night Raw*. Hulk Hogan's sabbatical from the sport ended when he joined WCW. "Macho Man" Randy Savage jumped as well. The WWF attempted to create new stars, but out-side of the aforementioned names, had little success. The top stars had trouble drawing fans, as the entire industry remained in a lull following the earlier scandals.

In 1996, *Monday Night Raw* averaged 2.6 rating for the year. Pay-per-views drew a 0.63 mean buyrate, while paid attendance dropped to just south of 5,000 fans per show. Creatively, Shawn Michaels reached the pinnacle of his career by winning the WWF Championship at *WrestleMania XII* from nemesis Bret Hart, who subsequently went on hiatus to contemplate his wrestling future. With the company's fortunes on his shoulders, "The Heartbreak Kid" proved to be a weak-drawing champion. Michaels' consistently amazing matches failed to spark business. Matters were not helped by the loss of Razor Ramon and Diesel to the competition. Together, they flew south to WCW for big money and guaranteed contracts, a novel concept in wrestling at the time. The duo paid off their contracts tenfold by helping ignite the ultra successful New World Order invasion angle, which propelled WCW and further damaged their previous employer's fortunes.

If anyone felt 1996 had gone poorly, 1997 sent the WWF to new depths of despair. The year started with Michaels regaining the WWF Title for a second time from Psycho Sid at January's *Royal Rumble* in front of an announced crowd of over 60,000 in the Alamo Dome in San Antonio, Texas. But the mammoth crowd was an aberration. Television ratings continued to slide as WCW siphoned away WWF fans and introduced new viewers to wrestling. The WWF hit rock bottom when *WrestleMania 13* rolled around on March 23, 1997. The show failed to sellout the Rosemont Horizon in Chicago, Illinois — the only *Mania* event not to sell every available ticket — and garnered only 237,000 pay-per-view buys, the lowest in the show's history by a wide margin. In fact, *WrestleMania 13* was not the most watched WWF pay-per-view of 1997, the only *Mania* event to lay claim to that dubious distinction.

Despite the lack of paying customers, *WrestleMania 13* offered one memorable moment, and arguably the start of the company's turnaround. Bret "The Hitman" Hart, who had returned to the WWF months earlier with a new twenty-year contract, wrestled "Stone Cold" Steve Austin, a burgeoning star touting a no-nonsense, full-speed-ahead bad attitude, in an "I Quit" match. The two constructed a wrestling masterpiece, won by Hart with his patented

Sharpshooter maneuver. But the actual result did not matter as much as the popularity shift, with Austin turning babyface and Hart going heel in the fans' eyes. The perfectly executed double-turn set the stage for a summer-long program that started to bring eyeballs back to WWF television.

The heel Hart joined forces with brother Owen and brothers-in-law Davey Boy Smith and Jim Neidhart as a Canadian alliance to combat "Stone Cold" Steve Austin. Team Canada presented the foul-mouthed, beer-drinking, finger-gesturing Austin as a symbol, in their mind, of the deterioration of American society. Austin, along with other babyfaces including the red-white-and-blue clad wrestler known as The Patriot, became foils for the Canadians. The nationalistic feud produced entertaining television and energized crowds above and below the U.S.–Canadian border.

The summer of '97 catapulted "Stone Cold" into the top tier of the WWF roster. He won the Intercontinental Title at the August 3 *SummerSlam* event in New Jersey. But the match took on much greater significance when a botched piledriver left Austin temporarily paralyzed and in need of major neck surgery. He would be sidelined until November's *Survivor Series* event in Montreal, Quebec, Canada.

That night changed the entire course of wrestling history, but it had nothing to do with Austin.

Chapter 20

Shawn Michaels and Bret Hart, the WWF's two most popular performers of the mid-'90s, would become the co-stars of the Montreal drama, along with the central figure, owner Vince McMahon. The events leading up to the November 7 pay-per-view started three months earlier at Madison Square Garden. McMahon had approached Hart and asked out of their twenty-year contract, citing "financial peril" as a result of losing the ongoing battle with WCW. McMahon even suggested that Bret try to secure a deal with WCW. A bewildered Hart examined his options, then began negotiations with WCW that resulted in one of the richest guaranteed contracts in wrestling history. Hart was ready to leave the company that for over a decade he had helped build to go to the organization that was hell-bent on destroying it. But there was one problem. Hart was the WWF Heavyweight Champion, and needed to lose the title before departing. To compound matters, word of Hart's departure leaked to the public. The craziness erupted days before the annual *Survivor Series* pay-per-view extravaganza, where Hart was booked to defend against Shawn Michaels.

The easy solution of Hart losing to Michaels at the pay-per-view came apart when Hart refused to go down in front of his Canadian fans. He believed losing in Canada, where he was a legitimate national sports hero, would kill his marketability for his WCW career. Hart's WWF contract stipulated full creative control over the final thirty days of his tenure, so McMahon needed to concoct a different scenario. To Hart's face, McMahon seemed willing to try a different finish, with Hart retaining the title and eventually dropping it several weeks later before heading south. But in his mind, McMahon had no intention of allowing Hart to leave Montreal with the belt, fearing Hart would walk onto WCW *Nitro* as WWF Champion and destroy the credibility of his main championship.

November 7 arrived with tension in the cold Canadian air. Hart and McMahon huddled hours before show time to discuss the evening's plans. Unbeknownst to McMahon, Hart wore a microphone during the closed-door meeting as part of a documentary being shot on "The Hitman's" career. Forever immortalized in the *Hitman Hart: Wrestling with Shadows* film, Hart and McMahon seemingly agreed on a resolution to their title dilemma:

> **HART:** What would you want to do today then?
>
> **McMAHON:** I'm open to anything.
>
> **HART:** I think what I'd like to do is get through today. I think tomorrow I should go in, do my speech, and forfeit the title. I think it allows me to leave with my head up and leave in a nice way. I don't have to beat Shawn. We could have a schmooz or whatever you want.
>
> **McMAHON:** I think it would be a run in type thing. But I'm open to anything. Like I said before, I'm determined that this is going to end up the right way.

Little did Hart know that McMahon had already made up his mind. He believed Shawn Michaels had to win the championship, regardless of whether Hart complied. McMahon and his top aides, along with Michaels, congregated in a hotel room the night before to formulate the step-by-step strategy for the main event. To ensure the success of his plan, McMahon gave up his commentating duties and stood ringside for the match. Hart and Michaels battled for approximately twenty minutes in the Molson Centre. To set up for the finish, referee Earl Hebner was knocked down. As agreed upon, Michaels applied the Sharpshooter, Hart's own finisher, on the champion. Before Hart could counter and interference could arrive for the double-disqualification, Hebner popped up and signaled that Hart had verbally submitted. McMahon rushed to the time-keeper and ordered him to "ring the fucking bell." Michaels feigned frustration, grabbed his newly won title, and was escorted to the locker room through thousands of riled-up fans. Hart realized he had been screwed in front of the world, and, enraged, spit directly in McMahon's face on camera. He followed by destroying the ring-side equipment, including expensive television monitors. Backstage, Hart confronted Michaels, who blatantly lied about his prior knowledge of the double-cross. McMahon then went to Hart's locker room presumably to explain, but left with a black eye courtesy of Hart's right hand.

The screwjob heard around the world left the WWF in a state of utter chaos as the year closed. Financially, 1997 went down as the worst year so far in company history. The fiscal year culminated in $6.5 million in losses off $63.9 million in revenues, with *Raw* averaging a mere 2.7 rating against *Nitro*. But, in one of the few positives of the year, 1997 planted the seeds for rejuvenation thanks to the solidification of "Stone Cold" Steve Austin as the top babyface, and a red-hot heel to counteract Austin — none other than Vince McMahon himself.

> **BRET HART:** Unfortunately, I don't have much of a WWF career. I worked there for fourteen years, and I don't have any access to my career there. I don't have any film footage, I have no archive photos or anything like that. I like to think of it as Cal Ripken or Wayne Gretzky not having a picture of themselves playing. The bottom line for me is that on two different occasions with Vince McMahon, one was the week before that *Survivor Series* we had a discussion about that, was that one of the things I thought was invaluable to me and meant more than money was my career and all the things I accomplished. I wanted to always have some kind of access, some kind of connection with that. He said that would never be a problem. Little did I know that one week later I would get screwed and knock him out and I never got it.

Coming off the *Survivor Series* screwjob, fans began looking at McMahon in a different light. The WWF exploited the controversial Montreal events in an attempt to portray Hart as the bad guy. Instead, the public's ire landed on the mastermind. Fans no longer viewed McMahon as the over-the-top announcer on *Monday Night Raw*, but as the backstabbing, self-serving corporate boss. Ever the astute businessmen, McMahon took the fan sentiment and ran with it. If the people truly hated him, why not transfer that heel heat to his television show? Thus, the evil Mr. McMahon character was born.

Chapter 21

The suit-wearing, high-talking corporate McMahon provided a great foil for the anti-establishment Austin character. "Stone Cold" won the 1998 *Royal Rumble* en route to winning the WWF Heavyweight Title at *WrestleMania XIV* on March 29, 1998, in Boston, Massachusetts. But the event that truly put the WWF back

Fritz and Dickerman at Raw

into the mainstream awareness came on the road to *WrestleMania*. The WWF executed a bold move by investing $3.5 million to hire controversial boxing star Mike Tyson for a guest referee position at the big event. The face-to-face confrontation between Tyson and Austin on the January 19 *Raw* sent shockwaves throughout the media. The footage appeared on news and sports programs across the country and gave Austin mainstream attention for the first time. As part of the storyline, Tyson sided with Shawn Michaels and his Degeneration X troupe leading up to *Mania*. In his role as ringside enforcer, Tyson showed his true colors by counting the pinfall for Austin's title victory. The scene of Tyson raising Austin's arm again put Austin in the national spotlight. Just as important, the Tyson experiment directly impacted business, as *WrestleMania XIV* collected 750,000 buys, better than a 200% increase over the previous year.

WrestleMania XIV marked the end of Shawn Michaels' career for an extended period due to a serious back injury. The new champion needed a heel rival to work with. The talent roster was still thin, so McMahon decided into put himself in the mix. The Austin vs. McMahon chemistry provided magical television week after week. On April 13, 1998, the WWF snapped WCW's eighty-three-week head-to-head Monday night ratings winning streak. The reason? The teased first in-ring confrontation between Austin and McMahon.

> **STEVE AUSTIN:** I got that going for me. Sometimes you don't feel like going to work, but here is what I get to do if I go to work. Yeah, it's a little more inspiration to go to work and beat up the boss.

Since McMahon couldn't become an actual in-ring antagonist, he ushered in opponents to dethrone the champion. Mick Foley, alternating between his Mankind, Cactus Jack, and Dude Love personas, became a main-eventer for the first time through his battles with Austin. Foley's uncanny ability to absorb punishment, as evidenced in matches involving barbed wire, thumbtacks, fire, and C-4 explosives in ECW and Japan, earned him a great deal of respect from hardcore fans. It wouldn't be until a WWF match with The

Undertaker at the 1998 *King of the Ring* pay-per-view that Foley elevated himself to legendary status among the entire wrestling world.

The demonic Hell In A Cell, a larger and enclosed steel cage structure, reared its ugly head for only the second time in WWF history at the June 28, 1998, *King of the Ring* event in Pittsburgh, Pennsylvania. Fans expected a contest full of blood and violence, but even the most sadistic fan could not have predicted what Foley would try. In an attempt to perform something memorable, and top the standards set by the original Hell In A Cell match, Foley and The Undertaker began on top of the cage — sixteen feet above the ground. After exchanging blows, Taker grabbed Foley and launched him off the top of the cage, sending his 300 pound body hurtling through the Mellon Arena air before exploding through the wooden announcers' table onto the cold, concrete floor. Miraculously, Foley avoided serious injury and, after several minutes of medical attention, continued the match by heading back up to the top of the cage. This time, Taker chokeslammed him through the top of the steel onto the hard ring canvas ten feet below, a bump even more dangerous than the first. With his body in shambles, Foley continued on. The insanity culminated with The Undertaker slamming his opponent onto a puddle of thumbtacks before mercifully pinning him. Taker got his hand raised, but the performance promoted Foley to a bona fide superstar, especially after thousands of replays of the bumps aired over and over on future WWF shows.

The Foley–Taker Hell In A Cell classic secured a prominent place in the annals of WWF history, but it also became symbolic as a turning point in the company's creative direction. Since the *Survivor Series* screwjob, the WWF radically shifted its brand of wrestling from a family-friendly, cartoon version of violence, to a raunchy and salacious product no longer suitable for impressionable youths. Foul language, sex, and violence became the norm during every WWF broadcast. "Stone Cold" Steve Austin's vocabulary during interviews routinely involved every indecent word that could pass the network censors. The extended middle finger became his emblem. Degeneration X rose to prominence as a babyface faction, rivaling the popularity of WCW's New World Order group. Triple H, Chyna, X-Pac, and The New Age Outlaws epitomized cool to the WWF audience, with their sophomoric antics and two-word motto — "Suck It!" For eye candy, Sable, a top-heavy blonde who started as a valet for her husband but broke away to become one of the WWF's most popular female attractions, strutted around in little clothing, often wearing only enough fabric to cover her private parts. The era of WWF "Attitude" arrived in full swing, and the public, particularly teenaged and twenty-something males, couldn't get enough.

> **MICHAEL COLE:** I have no problems with the direction of the company. In fact, I've embraced it. Vince McMahon and I were involved in a critics convention, and that question was addressed. . . . I let my oldest son watch *Raw* because he is a teenager, but my younger son I don't allow to watch *Raw*. I think as a responsible parent, it's up to the parents to decide what their kids should watch. I have no problem at all with the current direction of the WWF.

The WWF was back. The success of the new stars — Austin, Foley, and DX — put the company on even ground with WCW as it geared up to break away for good. Austin carried the company as champion into the fall, with programs against The Undertaker and Kane. In the mid-card, another new star slowly blossomed thanks to his improving in-ring work and, more importantly, his microphone work. Dwayne Johnson, a third generation wrestler with a University of Miami football background, anointed himself "The Rock." Few could predict that he would end up competing not just for the WWF Title, but the title of biggest mainstream star in pro wrestling history. His ascent to greatness began two years after his debut, when he won the WWF Championship in a one-night tournament at *Survivor Series '98*. The finals saw The Rock defeat Mick Foley, and then turn heel to join Mr. McMahon's Corporation, which already included Ken Shamrock, Test, The Big Bossman, and son Shane McMahon as a part-time wrestler.

> **THE ROCK:** Did I expect success to come? Yeah, because I grew up in the business as everyone knows, and I was always kept very close to the busi-

ness. . . . I always knew I wanted to get into the business some day as soon as football finished. It was just a matter of working hard. I knew I had something to give to the business and contribute in some way. It just so happened things clicked. I think a lot of things clicked. I got in tune with the character "The Rock," and it's been great ever since.

With catchphrases such as, "Know your role, shut your mouth," The Rock transformed his character into a cocky, arrogant fast-talking antagonist, and fans took to it. Foley and The Rock would be married in the storylines for the next six months, as they traded the WWF Championship back and forth. The first switch came, in hindsight, on the biggest night in the weekly Monday night war with WCW.

Chapter 22

January 4, 1999. The WWF had long since caught WCW in terms of popularity and television ratings. In some people's eyes, the WWF was back on top. If that wasn't the case before January 4, it would quickly become so after. While WCW offered its inexplicable one-finger Nash-to-Hogan WCW World Title change in front of a packed Georgia Dome crowd, the WWF aired a taped *Raw* broadcast from Worcester, Massachusetts, featuring Mick Foley's first WWF Title win, a thrilling milestone for a well-respected performer who'd sacrificed his body for over a decade before achieving his career dream. *Raw* won the close ratings battle, 5.8 to 5.0, but the main event numbers told the true story — 6.2 to 4.1 in favor of Foley.

Foley and The Rock continued their program at the 1999 *Royal Rumble* in an infamous "I Quit" match in Anaheim, California. The Rock literally bashing in Foley's skull with a steel chair — eleven brutal, unprotected shots in all — embodied how violent the WWF product had become, especially after the footage became glorified in the *Beyond the Mat* documentary. The third title switch occurred during halftime of Super Bowl XXXIII. The publicity stunt on the USA Network, called *Halftime Heat*, worked to perfection. Football fans switched to wrestling as Foley and The Rock battled in an empty arena in Tucson, Arizona, for the title. The match set a WWF cable record, with a 6.6 rating for Foley's second championship win. After a draw in their Last Man Standing match at *St. Valentine's Day Massacre*, the fourth and final switch in the series came again on free television. The Rock won a Ladder Match on the

February 15 *Raw* against Foley with help from newcomer, "The Big Show" Paul Wight. In the ratings, the WWF's domination swelled — 5.9 to 3.9 over *Nitro*.

The booming business intensified with *WrestleMania XV* in Philadelphia, where "Stone Cold" Steve Austin and The Rock went head-to-head in a battle of the industry's two biggest stars. Austin won the match and the WWF Title from The Corporation's in-ring general, further advancing the prevailing Austin vs. McMahon theme. The show set the wrestling pay-per-view record at the time, a 2.2 buyrate, or approximately 850,000 buys. To further demonstrate how popular the WWF had again become, four wrestlers adorned *TV Guide* covers to promote *Mania*, Sable's nude pictorial in *Playboy* sold over one million copies, and media outlets from ABC, NBC, FOX News, and ESPN to *The New York Times* and *Entertainment Weekly* produced features on the white-hot sports entertainment phenomenon.

> **SABLE:** The reason that I chose to do *Playboy* is because it's a great opportunity. No one else in this business has ever been offered that. Actually, they contacted me about two years ago and asked me if I would be interested in doing it, and at the time it was not something I wanted to do. We just continued to negotiate and I felt if I was ever going to do it, this was the prime opportunity.

The Monday night war, for all intents and purposes, had long ended by mid-1999. The separation often exceeded two full ratings points, with *Raw* occasionally doubling up its once formidable competition. An unopposed *Raw* on May 10, 1999, put the stamp on the WWF's victory — an 8.1 rating, the second-most-watched wrestling show in cable television history. Already dominating cable, the WWF set its sights on network television. The company had been off the networks for close to a decade, after NBC cancelled the periodic *Saturday Night's Main Event* late night specials. This time, the WWF focused on a prime-time weeknight program, and the struggling UPN network exhibited significant interest. The WWF filmed a two-hour pilot called *Smackdown*, which aired to decent ratings on UPN on April 29, 1999. Desperate for any type of successful programming, UPN issued the green light for a weekly two-hour Thursday night series. Much as WCW faced with the introduction of *Thunder*, the WWF was running the risk of diluting its product by adding two additional hours of weekly television, but the company couldn't pass up the prestige of a network series. By the fall, *Smackdown* had become UPN's "must-see TV."

Seemingly nothing could slow down the WWF machine . . . until one tragic night in Kansas City, Missouri, altered the wrestling world forever. The scene was the Kemper Arena. The date was May 23, 1999. The event was WWF *Over the Edge* on pay-per-view. Several hundred thousand homes spent $29.95 to watch The Undertaker challenge Steve Austin for the WWF Title, and The Rock defeat Triple H via DQ. Instead, less than thirty minutes into the proceedings, tragedy befell the World Wrestling Federation and the entire wrestling community.

As a taped promo by Owen Hart, decked out in his Blue Blazer costume, aired on the video screen in the arena, and on television for home viewers, Hart stood nervously in the rafters of the arena preparing to be lowered to the ring for his Intercontinental Title match with The Godfather. As he began his descent, booked as a comedic spoof of Sting's rappelling entrances in WCW, the quick-release mechanism on his harness opened. In front of a sold-out crowd, Hart's body plummeted dozens of feet through the air, landing sternum first on the corner turnbuckle before flipping into the ring. His body morbidly changed in color from white to grey to blue. The fans stood in shock while the television cameras, after returning from the taped promo, focused away from the ring. Jim Ross uttered the sobering words to the home audience, "This is as real as real gets."

In a decision would be debated for years to come, just minutes after Hart's lifeless body was wheeled out of the Kemper Arena, the pay-per-view continued. Some labeled it callous. Others preached that "the show must go on." But all of the arguing and excuses could not change the outcome. Owen Hart — devoted husband, loving father of two, great friend, and exceptional performer — had died.

The next night, the WWF paid tribute to its fallen star on the live *Raw* broadcast from St. Louis, Missouri. For one night, story-lines moved to the backburner and the raciness of the product, which Owen publicly despised, took a backseat. The show featured quick matches sandwiched between comments from many of the wrestlers, recalling fond memories of their unforgettable friend. In an industry filled with unscrupulous and unsavory individuals, Owen Hart was a flower among the weeds, a true good guy in a world full of bad guys.

> **JIM ROSS:** Owen was probably the most likable, good-natured guy in the whole company as far as wrestlers were considered. I didn't know anybody that didn't like Owen Hart, because he probably played a practical joke on each and every one of them. He played plenty on me. I have yet to go back and look at the night that he died from that accident when he fell from the rafters. The King and I were sitting fifteen to twenty feet from the ring where Owen landed. I had seen it all, I thought, until that night. I was not prepared for that, and to have to go back on the air with about thirty seconds to prepare to tell the world this wonderful human being had died and that it was not part of the storyline. We're not performing here. This is real. It was a night I'll never forget. I have yet to go back and look at the tape, but someday, when I write my auto-biography, I'm going to have to go back to look at it and get those feelings back of that night. I'll never forget that night in Kansas City. He was a wonderful, wonderful guy and it was just so heartbreaking to see that happen.

Little changed in the aftermath of the Owen Hart tragedy and the unprecedented whirlwind of media coverage it brought. Predictions of the demise of the WWF proved incorrect. In fact, business jumped, with ratings for *Raw* regularly hitting the high 6.0's. Perhaps to deflect the controversy, the WWF traveled the celebrity route once again. For this occasion, the decision was political, literally.

Prior to the Hart tragedy, pro wrestling had only garnered front-page headlines for the shocking gubernatorial victory by former wrestler and commentator, Jesse "The Body" Ventura. Running as an independent in Minnesota, Ventura's straight-shooting style resonated with voters, particularly the young segment of the population, who had tired of the traditional bureaucratic attitude. The coup for the WWF came at a six-figure expense, but proved to be well worth it in publicity. Ventura returned to the WWF for the first time in seven years to work as guest referee in the main event of the August 22, 1999, *SummerSlam* pay-per-view at the Target Center in his governing state.

Indifferent to the media backlash surrounding his involvement in a WWF event, Governor Ventura counted the fall for Mick Foley over Triple H and WWF Heavyweight Champion "Stone Cold" Steve Austin in a Triple Threat Match. Foley's championship run barely reached twenty-four hours, as Triple H won the title from him the next night on *Raw*. The win marked the arrival of the next major WWF superstar.

Triple H's first night as top dog came on the inaugural edition of WWF *Smackdown* on UPN. Similar to *Raw*, *Smackdown* capitalized on the WWF's momentum and drew solid ratings, this time network ratings against the most-watched television programs in the country. The debut on Thursday, August 26, amidst a great deal of promotion, drew a 4.1 network rating, by far the highest rated UPN show of the week. The ratings steadied in the low 4.0's for the remainder of the year, peaking with a record 5.0 for the November 11 show featuring an appearance by Arnold Schwarzenegger.

The addition of *Smackdown* may have resulted in fiscal success for the WWF, but creatively, the company bore the brunt of producing two additional hours of weekly television. Within one month, the first casualties fell. Vince Russo and Ed Ferrara, the company's lead writers during its resurgence, abruptly resigned in early October. The wear and tear of the demanding WWF schedule had sapped their artistic juices. The duo had also believed the WWF had peaked in popularity and sought a new challenge. They found one in WCW, walking out on Vince McMahon for huge contracts to rescue Turner's sinking ship. Their departure stung briefly, but the WWF marched on undeterred.

ED FERRARA: I was happy with it to begin with. At one point, I did quit after I had been there for about nine months. I went to Vince McMahon and

I basically said thank your for the opportunity and thank you for bringing me on board here, but I think this is where I need to say my goodbyes. He asked me why, and I told him the travel schedule was getting to me. It wasn't so much the travel, but it was relentless. I was with them twenty-four hours, seven days a week and you can only be creative with a gun to your head so frequently.

Vince Russo called him from a payphone that night rather than hitting him with it at the absolutely last moment, which would have been not showing up the next morning or calling him the next morning. He called him that night so Vince knew. I wanted to speak with Vince McMahon as well, but he said to call him in the morning and let him just deal with this. So, out of respect to Russo, I did that and I called the next morning and caught him on his cell phone. He was in his car driving there. It was a very quiet phone call. I could tell he felt a little hurt, a little abandoned and probably a little sideswlped by the whole thing.

Russo and Ferrara proved to be replaceable cogs in the WWF machine, but the next loss would be more difficult to recover from. "Stone Cold" Steve Austin was hurting. The company had ridden its workhorse hard for two great years, and Austin's body had paid the price. Problems with his spinal cord, stemming from the tombstone piledriver gone awry at *SummerSlam '97*, worsened. With his spinal column narrowing, Austin faced major neck surgery before he could even consider returning to the wrestling ring. Austin on the shelf put the WWF in a quandary. Their biggest star since Hulk Hogan, and a legitimate money magnet, had been indefinitely sidelined. With The Rock catching on as an Austin-level babyface, the onus fell on Triple H to carry the ball as a heel champion.

Chapter 23

Austin's nebulous future forced major modifications to the WWF's storyline plans heading into 2000. At the same time, significant changes took place in the business arena. Back to back years of incredible revenues and profits convinced Vince McMahon to open up the family business. For the first time, fans could own of a piece of the wrestling empire. Projections of hundreds of millions in additional revenue lured McMahon to wrestle Wall Street in an initial public offering of company stock.

After an extraordinary $56 million in profit for fiscal 1999, the WWF decided to offer 17% of the company in $137 million of common stock. The IPO price of $17 per share skyrocketed to $32 when the NASDAQ market opened for business on Tuesday, October 19, 1999. wwf closed at 25 1/4 on its first day on the big board, putting the company's value on paper at over $1.2 billion. After years of fighting tooth and nail with billionaire Ted Turner's WCW, McMahon had finally achieved the same esteemed plateau.

> **VINCE MCMAHON:** I think the future is very, very bright. Again, I think we have our fingers on the pulse of the marketplace. There's nothing we won't do to entertain our audience. That's what we're all about. We're not just about grabbing the money, some billionaire's money, and going through the paces and walking and talking. We're about performing. We perform. We love to perform for our audience. So, I think the future is extremely bright for the World Wrestling Federation.

The decision to go public brought a new set of responsibilities to the company, namely to the investors who had poured their money into the WWF. No longer could McMahon deal with business issues behind closed doors, without fear of stockholder response. The first crisis for World Wrestling Entertainment Inc. (renamed from Titan Sports Inc. as part of the IPO) came from a morality watchdog group disgusted with the scandalous content of *Smackdown*. The deceptively named Parents Television Council had a history of interfering with network television programs it deemed ill-suited for prime time. Their strategy focused on targeting advertisers, hoping to cripple the show and the network's major revenue stream. The brains behind the operation was L. Brent Bozell III, son of a former speechwriter for controversial Senator Joseph McCarthy, who achieved notoriety for spearheading an outrageous witchhunt for communist sympathizers in the U.S. during the 1950s. The PTC courted legitimacy with the general public through celebrity spokespeople, including 2000 vice-presidential candidate Joseph Lieberman, and legendary actor and comedian Steve Allen. Perhaps recalling his father's involvement in the "Big Lie," Bozell set his sights on *Smackdown*.

> **KEVIN KELLY:** Hell, we cross the line every week! We've trampled the line. We don't want to offend people. We want to challenge their thoughts. We want to drive their emotions and push the right buttons within them. Any time you challenge people in a thought-provoking way, you're going to get critiques. People out there are narrow-minded. They have a certain set of values and beliefs they take into doing anything in their life. If you do something different, something that stirs them inside, their first reaction is going to be to protest.

The first advertiser domino to fall from PTC pressure was Coca-Cola beverages, a significant sponsor across the WWF television network. With the taste of success on his lips, Bozell upped the ferocity of his attack. Picking out scenes from *Smackdown* storylines suggesting rape, attempted murder, excessive sexual innuendo, vulgar language, and heavy violence, Bozell contacted the WWF's roster of advertisers to question their corporate values. The response was swift. Afraid of negative publicity for being associated with lowbrow wrestling, AT&T, M&M/Mars, and the U.S. Army, Navy, and Air Force each withdrew their advertising dollars from *Smackdown*, despite the show's strong demographics among the coveted young male category. Publicly, the WWF tried to sooth the controversy by announcing plans to tone down the UPN show. Privately, the company labeled Bozell and his group as public enemy number one.

After several weeks of lying low to gauge the new TV-PG version of *Smackdown*, the PTC wasn't satisfied. The "advertiser education campaign" resumed, and the battle with the WWF heated up considerably. From a business standpoint, the PTC's efforts didn't injure the WWF to any significant degree. The amazing ratings and demos for WWF programming enabled them to find replacements with ease. RC Cola, for example, jumped right in once Coca-Cola pulled out. However, the media criticism against the WWF following the PTC's reports made life difficult for the sales team to recruit more high-profile sponsors. WWF stock also took a tumble as Wall Street read the negative stories.

Inside the squared circle, the effort continued to cement Triple H as a legitimate top guy and viable WWF Champion. The classic wrestling blueprint calls for an established main-eventer to work with a rising star and eventually lose to that up-and-comer to endow him with a sense of legitimacy in the audience's eyes. Traditionally, egos and selfishness prevent the formula from succeeding. But luckily for the WWF, the man tapped to put over Triple H realized whose time had come and whose time had passed.

Mick Foley's career had been winding down. Years of punishing his body before he made it to the big time had shortened his prime years. His Mankind character had transitioned to a comedic babyface role based around a sock puppet, Mr. Socko, and skits involving his best-selling autobiography, *Have A Nice Day: A Tale of Blood and Sweatsocks*. With Austin out of the picture, Foley had agreed to stick around to work with Triple H. The stage was set for the January 23, 2000, *Royal Rumble* from New York's Madison Square Garden. Foley reverted to his Cactus Jack persona for his feud with Triple H and brought with it the violent, hardcore style that personified the character. The *Rumble* showdown for the WWF Title was booked as a street fight, utilizing barbed wire and thumbtacks as the two brawled throughout the Garden. Triple H retained, with a dangerous Pedigree onto the sharp tacks.

> **MICK FOLEY:** I thought that was up there in my top five of all time. It was a good one. It was nice to be able to show people I could still get to that level. I think Triple H had one of the best matches of his career also.

Foley wasn't finished, and wanted a rematch. This time, he put his career on the line for a shot at the belt at *No Way Out* in the specialty match he put on the map — Hell In A Cell. But the outcome proved to be the same as the previous encounter. February 27, 2000, at the Hartford Civic Center in Connecticut would be Foley's last match — or so they said — in another classic consisting of a flaming barbed-wire baseball bat and another memorable fall, albeit much more protected, from the top of the enclosed cage and through the ring below. The daredevil stunt was a fitting symbol to conclude an influential career.

With Austin gone and Foley retired, the WWF received a much-needed talent boost with the addition of four top WCW stars — Chris Benoit, Eddie Guerrero, Perry Saturn, and Dean Malenko — following their dispute with their former employer's management. The defections only underlined the notion that the wrestling war had ended. In particular, Benoit left WCW as reigning World Champion. All four would have a role in the upcoming *WrestleMania 2000* event.

The sixteenth installment of *WrestleMania* emanated from the Arrowhead Pond in Anaheim, California. More than 18,000 fans crammed the venue to the tune of $1.3 million in gate receipts to witness a Fatal Four-Way main event for the WWF Title. As part of the build-up, each competitor had a member of the McMahon family in his corner — Triple H with storyline wife Stephanie, The Rock with Vince, The Big Show with Shane, and Linda McMahon's representative . . . Mick Foley. Just one month after "retiring," Foley returned to headline *Mania* for the first time.

MICK FOLEY: Actually, I was kind of happy the way things turned out in February. So, I wasn't as up for *Wrestlemania* as I should have been. I thought I did a pretty good job in it. Really, a lot of guys were all over my case for saying I retired and coming back. It wasn't like I planned it that way. I was met with some of the biggest responses of my career, so I have to accept that most of the people protesting and yelling the loudest wouldn't be able to say no to Vince McMahon if he asked them to cut his lawn, let alone main event at *Wrestlemania*. So I can't worry myself too much about it.

The battle came down to Triple H and The Rock. For the first time in *Mania* history, the heel went over in the main event, as Triple H retained the WWF Title with help from Vince McMahon, who made storyline peace with his daughter and son-in-law. The show failed to live up to high *WrestleMania* aesthetic standards, but drew impressive pay-per-view numbers, a 2.1 buyrate, translating to 820,000 buys.

Chapter 24

With no end to the popularity surge in sight, the WWF decided to expand outside of the wrestling business. It wasn't their first attempt. In the early '90s, Vince McMahon had tried to impart his marketing genius on professional bodybuilding with the creation of the World Bodybuilding Federation. Despite a weekend morning program on the USA Network and a decision to sign competitors to big money contracts, including Lou Ferrigno of *The Incredible Hulk* fame and WCW wrestler Lex Luger, the WBF lasted exactly one pay-per-view competition. Other keen ideas, including the ICO-PRO nutritional supplement, met the same fate. But McMahon believed this new push would be different. After all, his core business was experiencing more success than ever before. With profits pouring in, the WWF had money to burn and diversification represented a solid business decision.

The first project dealt with the hospitality industry. Initially, the company purchased a 193-room hotel and casino in Las Vegas, Nevada — the former Debbie Reynolds Hotel and Casino — to be renovated in a WWF motif. The plan never panned out, and the company resold the property to focus on New York City. The old Paramount Theater in the heart of Times Square became the site of WWF New York, a theme restaurant and retail shop. Embedded in the busiest section of the country, the restaurant indicated what most people already knew — the World Wrestling Federation had become a true slice of Americana.

WWF New York represented a major business endeavor, still it was a blip on the radar screen compared to McMahon's master plan

The genius behind the XFL, Vincent Kennedy McMahon Jr. and Fritz

— his own professional football league. Never a sports fanatic, McMahon still believed he could transfer his Midas touch with professional wrestling to the gridiron. The NFL had garnered the reputation of being soft and McMahon felt he could return the sport to the smashmouth days of Dick Butkus and "Mean" Joe Green, with a little WWF entertainment flare mixed in. The announcement of the formation of the XFL came on February 3, 2000, one year to the day before opening kickoff.

Despite the overwhelmingly long odds of even modest success, the XFL's chances grew brighter when NBC joined the party. Dick Ebersol, President of NBC Sports who worked with McMahon on *Saturday Night's Main Event* specials in the 1980s, believed in the McMahon hype. He convinced the network brass not just to air XFL games on Saturday nights in prime time, but to also join in as partners in the league. With NBC owning a fifty percent equity stake, the XFL went from laughing stock to potential success in one press conference, but still faced the daunting task of attracting the football fan after the Super Bowl, something the United States Football League, World League of American Football, Arena Football League, and NFL Europe could never do.

> **VINCE McMAHON:** The legitimacy issue is only an issue as far as the media is concerned. It's not an issue as far as fans are concerned. Football is football, no matter who is presenting it. We've done other sports. We've done boxing and a few other things. NBC, the network of the Olympics, certainly brings a lot of credibility to the XFL, but I don't think it would have mattered one way or another as far as fans are concerned.

The preparation for the XFL occupied most of Vince McMahon's plate in 2000, but he still managed to consummate a blockbuster business deal that would change the WWF's fortunes and swell their piggybank to new levels. The WWF ventured into a five-year broad strategic alliance with CBS/Viacom, primarily to move the five hours of highly rated WWF cable programming off the USA Network and onto Viacom-owned TNN and MTV for a whopping $28 million per year. But the Viacom deal included other far-reaching provisions, such as television coverage for the XFL, and other special wrestling programming, a publishing deal with Simon & Schuster, radio specials on Infinity Broadcasting stations, billboard advertisements, and a $30 million investment in WWF stock. But the rights to *Raw*, which averaged an incredible 6.1 rating in 1999 against weekly WCW competition, was the focal point. Viacom hoped to rebrand TNN, originally The Nashville Network, around the WWF franchise. USA Network fought to block the move by filing a lawsuit based on their contractual right to first refusal. But the courts felt that USA, despite matching the television aspects of the deal, could not fulfill the ancillary perks in the Viacom proposition. The seventeen-year relationship between the WWF and USA came to a close, and a new chapter in WWF history was set to commence.

VINCE MCMAHON: It's been a pretty big turnaround for us. There's no question about that. There're some bumps and all of that along the way, as we've always had in this business. Any business does. Right now, we've been able to amass a number of broadcast partners — NBC for the XFL, as well as Viacom/CBS for WWF and XFL. So with those two powerhouse conglomerates combined with the mentality of the World Wrestling Federation, we're enjoying quite a bit of success.

The nice part about the Viacom/CBS deal is the people we're doing business with are really, really great people. They're not elitist in any way. They're real down to earth. They understand a good deal and understand the power in the World Wrestling Federation and want to be associated with the WWF and its fans. It's nice to be welcomed somewhere, and those are two important aspects of Viacom.

As the WWF prepared for a September launch on TNN, the Triple H era, paired with TV wife Stephanie McMahon-Helmsley, dominated WWF television through WWF Title programs against The Rock, The Undertaker, and Kane. Ironically, the belt changed hands when The Rock pinned Vince McMahon in a six-man tag at the 2000 *King of the Ring*, in which the WWF Championship was up for grabs. The company attempted to inject some new blood into the top mix by booking main events to include Chris Benoit, Chris Jericho, and Olympic gold medalist Kurt Angle, who had only been on the main roster for a few months but had progressed into a main-event caliber performer in record time. Angle began to segue into a program with Triple H over an infatuation with Stephanie. The love triangle would become the predominant WWF storyline heading into the fall, attracting female viewers to the set as well.

Cable television's highest-rated show, WWF *Raw*, debuted on TNN on September 25, 2000, off the *Unforgiven* pay-per-view. In addition to the first Triple H vs. Angle bout, which saw Triple H win in a questionable booking decision that deterred the hot storyline, "Stone Cold" Steve Austin returned to the full-time roster. Austin made a cameo earlier in the year at April's *Backlash* event, and drew a monstrous 600,000 buys for the B-level event. His return to free television on the TNN *Raw*, along with a loaded lineup of matches, helped the debut show draw a 5.4 rating, slightly lower than recent USA numbers, but tremendous for the struggling TNN.

The return of Austin, along with current main-eventers Triple H, Angle, The Rock, and Benoit, helped continue the strong business and even stronger in-ring action. Outside the ring, activity percolated. The controversy stirred by the Owen Hart tragedy finally received some degree of closure when the WWF and lawyers for widow Martha Hart settled the wrongful death lawsuit. The WWF took a $17 million hit, although insurance covered the majority of the settlement. The substantial sum would help fund Oje and Athena Hart's formative years, but could never truly ease the pain of losing their father.

With the legal albatross removed from the company's neck, McMahon turned his attention back to his nemesis, the Parents Television Council. In recent months, another handful of advertisers had bowed to PTC pressure and pulled advertisements from *Smackdown*, including Dr. Pepper/Seven-Up and ConAgra Foods. McMahon's response was twofold. He publicly ridiculed the organization on his television shows by creating a heel group dubbed The Right To Censor. Led by mid-card wrestler Steven Richards, the group included diva Ivory, storyline pimp The Godfather, and porn star character Val Venis as converts from their lewd and lascivious pasts. McMahon's second move was much more threatening — a $55 million lawsuit. In the suit, the WWF asserted that the PTC maliciously used lies and misleading statements to persuade advertisers to pull sponsorship from *Smackdown*. According to the WWF, the PTC disingenuously claimed forty sponsors had abandoned WWF programming. In reality, less than ten advertisers withdrew their ad dollars as a result of PTC pressure. More importantly, the WWF lashed out at the PTC's claim that its wrestling shows, specifically *Smackdown*, were responsible for four recent deaths.

The most publicized case involved twelve-year-old Lionel Tate murdering four-year-old Tiffany Eunick while play-fighting at the girl's home. While Tate admitted he understood pro wrestling violence was fake in trial interviews, and a defense strategy involving diminished capacity had been thrown out of court, the PTC continued to use the story and similar deaths in its promotional material against *Smackdown*.

Bozell refuted the charges initially by referring to the lawsuit as "one of the most malicious and dishonest pleadings ever placed before a court." Ironically, it would be Bozell who would ultimately admit to deceitfulness after the two sides reached an out-of-court settlement twenty months later. Perhaps fearing an adverse judgment would bankrupt the organization, the PTC agreed to pay $3.5 million to the WWF, to publicly apologize to Vince McMahon, and to cease meddling in WWF business. Bozell's act of contrition noted that, "the WWF was within its right to be angry at the MRC, PTC, their spokespersons, and I for contacting WWF's advertisers, to go beyond complaining about WWF content by passing along accusations which we now know are false."

The latter part of 2000 saw the WWF in full control of the wrestling war. The October 8 Monday night battle, for example, underlined the state of affairs — *Raw* crushed *Nitro*, 5.4 to 2.5. But the war had ended much earlier, when it became evident that Vince Russo and Ed Ferrara couldn't save the sinking WCW ship. Rumors swirled of dissatisfaction among Time Warner hierarchy, and impending changes in the works for WCW, either in the form of a new owner or a complete shutdown. With his rival ripe for a takeover, Vince McMahon couldn't help but inquire about buying it himself.

Meetings in October 2000 included cursory negotiations. For McMahon, purchasing World Championship Wrestling would hand him a guaranteed moneymaking storyline pitting WCW talent vs. the WWF in elusive dream matches. McMahon would also get the ego boost of buying out his competition and beating his archrival, "Billionaire" Ted. But talks hit a snag which involved neither Time Warner nor the WWF. Viacom stepped into the mix, making it clear that the WWF could not produce wrestling programming for a competing cable network. Had the WWF and Time Warner reached an agreement, McMahon planned to run WCW as a separate entity, keeping *Nitro* and *Thunder* on TNT and TBS, respectively. For $28 million annually in rights fees, Viacom demanded exclusivity, and the WWF was forced to pull out of negotiations for the time being.

The year 2000 closed with Kurt Angle on top of the mountain as WWF Heavyweight Champion. Fiscal 2000 proved to be another record-breaking year for WWF, with $280 million in revenues and a whopping $86 million in profit. Almost two and a half million people attended live events during the year. Pay-per-views averaged a 1.25 buyrate. The WWF's momentum showed no signs of letting up. But 2001 would mark a dip into unchartered waters. Major changes to the whole wrestling industry were in store, along with the debut of the WWF's brand of pro football. Could McMahon juggle both?

Chapter 25

February 3, 2001. You never get a second chance to make a first impression. The old adage was never more apropos than for the debut of the XFL. The hype, rumors, stories, and controversy of the past twelve months would mean little once the opening whistle blew. The eight XFL teams — ranging from major markets (New York, Chicago, and Los Angeles) to mid-sized cities (Birmingham and Memphis) — were filled with NFL washouts, has-beens, and many others who simply never were. Advertisers had cautiously spent their dollars on promises of a 4.5 weekly rating on Saturday nights on NBC, a 3.0 rating on Sunday nights on UPN, and a 2.5 rating on Sunday afternoons on TNN. Unlike most start-up sports leagues, the marketing prowess of McMahon and the crossover promotional opportunities during NBC events guaranteed interest in the first week. It was now up to the league to deliver a satisfactory product to bring those viewers back.

Despite the partnership with NBC, the peacock's top sports commentators refused to participate in the XFL project. Instead of legendary sportscasters Bob Costas and Dick Enberg calling the action, journeyman play-by-play broadcaster Matt Vasgersian got the nod. Joining him in the booth would be an unexpected color commentator, Minnesota Governor Jesse Ventura, who admittedly had more experience commentating on wrestling than football. But McMahon built the league on bucking conventional trends (see the human ball-scramble replacing the traditional opening coin toss to determine possession), and Ventura's blunt personality fit the XFL mold. The wrestling connection grew larger, with WWF announcers Jim Ross and Jerry Lawler handling NBC duties for the "B" game.

"This is the XXXXXFFFLLL!!!" bellowed McMahon on the 50-yard line of Sam Boyd Stadium, where the Law Vegas Outlaws prepared to host the New York Hitmen on NBC. The next three hours would ultimately determine the success or failure of the league. And more important than the final scores would be the television ratings. After week one, there was plenty of room for optimism. NBC drew a 9.5 rating for the opening night, well above the 4.5 projections, and more than double the network's average Saturday night audience. But a closer look at the ratings pattern tempered the enthusiasm. Throughout the three-hour telecast, the audience consistently dropped off, at an alarming rate of nearly forty percent. Viewers sampled the league, found it unimpressive, and moved on. It was a discouraging sign, but if the league could maintain half the debut rating over the long haul, there was hope.

> **JIM ROSS:** I've always loved football, and broadcasted Falcons football back in the early '90s. I officiated a lot of football in my younger years. I had a great time. I'm a football fan, and it was fun to be a part of the ballgame, fun to be part of the excitement. Where the announcers are out here in the open, around the fans, you can really feed off their adrenaline.
>
> I think if you're a real football fan and haven't had the opportunity to be on the field, or someone that hasn't had the opportunity to play the game, it's fun to hear what's being said there. The NFL protects its players as far as the verbiage is concerned. The team box is sacred ground, and here there's nothing sacred. Cameras and microphones everywhere, all the time. I think it really gives the fan at home a real unique perspective of what's going on in a football game.

Week two would tell the real tale. NBC headed west to broadcast professional football's return to the city of Los Angeles. From the very beginning, it was clear this would not be the XFL's night. A power generator exploded at the Los Angeles Coliseum, knocking the telecast off the air and delaying the game more than thirty minutes. Viewers were treated to the "B" game until the

Chicago Enforcers and Los Angeles Xtreme finally took the field. But the problems continued to mount. Octavious Bishop of the Xtreme broke his leg in the third quarter, delaying the proceedings another fifteen minutes. The programming schedule called for games to conclude by 11 p.m. eastern in time for the late local news and *Saturday Night Live*. It was especially imperative to keep to schedule on this night, with music and acting sensation Jennifer Lopez hosting the sketch comedy show and expectations for a record rating.

When 11:35 p.m. arrived, J-Lo was still in her dressing room. The Enforcers and Xtreme had gone into overtime. If that wasn't bad enough, the teams went on to double overtime. By the time the Xtreme secured the victory, it was Sunday on the east coast. *SNL* started at 12:15 p.m. and, not surprisingly, drew its lowest rating of the year. Executive producer Lorne Michaels, who nearly cancelled the live broadcast out of anger, stormed into NBC the next day demanding safeguards to prevent a repeat incident. The outside sports and entertainment world already had it in for the XFL, and now the league was feeling the heat internally from NBC.

If Saturday night was a storm, Sunday morning was a full-blown monsoon when the Nielsen ratings arrived at 30 Rockefeller Plaza. Week two of the XFL garnered a 4.6 rating on NBC, a downright scary plunge of 52% from the debut. The UPN game experienced a similar freefall. Attendance dropped across the board. Most pundits had predicted such problems, but even the harshest could not have expected them this soon. With ratings already below promised levels, the XFL needed to stage a miraculous comeback to get back in the game.

Coach McMahon drew up a new strategy for the league. Trying to appeal more to the wrestling fan, Jim Ross replaced Matt Vasgersian as play-by-play man on the "A" game. McMahon also tried to stir up some controversy by instructing Jesse Ventura to disparage the performance of New York Hitmen's head coach Rusty Tillman, hoping to ignite a wrestling-style on-air feud. Tillman wouldn't bite. In another of many embarrassing moments, color commentator Jerry Lawler quit the WWF and XFL just a few weeks into the season, forcing an ill-prepared Dick Butkus to transition from league spokesman to the broadcast booth. Nothing helped, as week five on NBC scored a hopeless 2.3 rating, just short of the lowest prime-time number in television history on a major network. The desperation hit a new low for the March 10 game, with a sleazy promotion built around cameras in the cheerleaders' locker room at halftime. The grand scheme included a poorly contrived dream sequence featuring a Rodney Dangerfield cameo at the end. The hype brought the league up only three-tenths of a ratings point on the night.

The wrestling approach failed miserably, so the focus again shifted. This time, the target became the traditional football fan. Matt Vasgersian returned to his original position. The goofy skits involving the cheerleaders disappeared. The wacky camera angles, including the behind-the-QB cam and overhead X-Cam, were tabled in favor of the normal sideline view. Rules changed weekly to liven up play, which actually improved as the season continued.

But it was already too late. Wrestling and football fans had long departed for other forms of Saturday night entertainment. The March 17 NBC game between Birmingham and Las Vegas set the record for the lowest prime-time television rating on a major network, 1.9. UPN games ended up below the 1.0 level on Sunday nights. TNN numbers on cable were half that. The league tried to place the blame on the media for its demise. The finger-pointing followed from all sides, with excuses flying like errant passes. The end was near.

Chapter 26

While the week-by-week shenanigans of the XFL dominated wrestling headlines, the entire industry was changing in a manner no one could have predicted. The sale of World Championship Wrestling seemed to be complete. Eric Bischoff amassed a group of investors to purchase the company from the merged AOL–Time Warner corporation. Despite the public announcement, the deal died once Jamie Kellner took over as head of Turner Broadcasting and cancelled all wrestling shows on TNT and TBS. Without the television exposure, the company's value didn't amount to much. The only buyer who could benefit now was McMahon. The television exclusivity clause would no longer act as a dealbreaker. The WWF could acquire the WCW brand name, its vast video library, and cherry-pick talent of its choice to facilitate the dream WWF vs. WCW program. The WWF couldn't pass up the opportunity to control the entire North American wrestling landscape and struck a deal to purchase the remnants of World Championship Wrestling for a bargain-basement $2.5 million, ending the bitter thirteen-year wrestling war.

As the WWF finalized its biggest wrestling acquisition, the only other national outfit closed its doors for good. Extreme Championship Wrestling's tenuous future collapsed under the weight of heavy debt and the absence of a national television deal, lost once the WWF moved to TNN. The symbolic end arrived when ECW owner Paul Heyman surprised many, including his own employees, by strutting out on *Raw* to replace Jerry Lawler as color commentator. The WWF would seek to acquire the ECW assets in bankruptcy court to bolster its monopoly on professional wrestling.

At least on the surface, the WWF intended to maintain a semblance of competition by operating WCW as a separate brand. As part of the buyout, the WWF assumed the contracts of twenty-four WCW performers, mostly lower-paid, younger mid-card talent such as Lance Storm, Mike Awesome, Billy Kidman, and Stacy Keibler. AOL–Time Warner remained responsible for the high-priced top-level talent the WWF opted to pass on. Reports swirled of a WCW branded television program on TNN, either in a late-night Saturday slot or replacing *Raw* on Monday night while the WWF roster took *Smackdown* on Thursday. The hope would be to run two completely distinct brands, ideally with the goal of doubling wrestling revenues, before eventually booking interpromotional matches. With the way the WCW brand had been bastardized in its last few years, the WWF faced a major uphill battle to restore luster to a group it had attempted to bury for a decade.

As if the company's plate wasn't full enough with the XFL, WCW, and ECW, *WrestleMania X-7* rolled around on April 1, 2001, from the Reliant Astrodome in Houston, Texas. On a day known for practical jokes, *WrestleMania* was anything but. Financially and critically, *WrestleMania* hit a mammoth home run, ironically in a venue not conducive to giving up the long ball during baseball season. More than 67,000 fans filled the stadium, with a gate over $3.5 million, a North American record for pro wrestling. The attendance trailed only *WrestleMania III* in Pontiac, Michigan, and *SummerSlam '92* at Wembley Stadium in England as company records. Over one million dollars in merchandise was moved in one night. On pay-per-view, more than one million homes spent $39.95 for the show, a record for a non-boxing pay-per-view event. Those viewers were not disappointed in what turned out to be the greatest *WrestleMania* extravaganza, headlined by The Rock vs. "Stone Cold" Steve Austin in a babyface vs. babyface WWF Title showdown. Austin won the championship, but turned heel in the process, joining up with archenemy Vince McMahon in a dubious creative decision. McMahon wrestled earlier in the night, losing a street fight to son Shane. Kurt Angle pinned Chris Benoit in a technical masterpiece, while Edge and Christian won the WWF Tag-

Team Titles in the second-ever Tables, Ladders, and Chairs match against The Hardy Boyz and The Dudleys.

> **JEFF HARDY:** Just doing the swanton every night, I'm just knocking bumps off my bump card. It's shortening my career. Night after night, I feel it. You can't do that forever. It's just gradually slowing down. It's time for some other young dude to come up and start jumping off twenty-foot ladders and stuff.

In hindsight, *WrestleMania X-7* culminated a five-year wrestling boom that took the sport to unparalleled heights. The business had peaked, and with WCW and ECW dead as legitimate rivals, the future of pro wrestling lied in the hands of one person. History indicated that wouldn't necessarily be a good thing.

The post-*WrestleMania* challenges for the WWF differed from previous years, thanks to the additional workload involving the relaunch of WCW. The albatross known as the XFL wrapped up its inaugural season in virtual anonymity. The final two weeks of the regular season set prime-time television record lows with 1.5 ratings. The Los Angeles Xtreme became a footnote in trivia history as winner of the April 21 Million Dollar Game, the league's championship game where the winning squad split the seven-figure amount. Minutes after the final play, the league's future turned dark. NBC refused to air games for a second season, and planned to extricate itself from the partnership by any means necessary. McMahon hoped to continue with UPN and TNN airing games in traditional Sunday afternoon football timeslots. But UPN asked for concessions, including cutting a half-hour off *Smackdown* to air an original series, in exchange for a second XFL season. McMahon balked at injuring his wrestling empire, and realized his dream of conquering professional football was over. A conciliatory McMahon, along with Dick Ebersol, announced the demise of the league, both wishing they had taken more time before debuting. The few bright spots — the emergence of Tommy Maddox and Rod "He Hate Me" Smart who both achieved notoriety in the NFL thereafter — couldn't wash away the bad taste of the final outcome. In the end, the XFL earned its place as the biggest flop in the annals of sports and television history for the price of $100 million, split between the two companies and proving their fallibility in front of a snickering nation.

Fresh off the failure of the XFL, the WWF took pains to avoid a similar fate with the new WCW. After all, football had been foreign to Vince McMahon, and a failure, based on his track record, was hardly unexpected. But wrestling was his bread and butter, and there would be no excuses if this business didn't pan out. The WCW relaunch took several months to organize, including multiple postponements of the proposed start dates while the WWF amassed an entirely new talent roster and front office. Ultimately, the goal was to get it right, no matter how much time and energy it took.

On the WWF side, problems surfaced slowly. The Rock began transitioning to Hollywood, taking the summer off to shoot his first starring role in *The Scorpion King*. The heel turn of Steve Austin quickly proved to be a tactical error. Fans enjoyed cheering Austin in his battles with Vince McMahon, not seeing them pal around as the top bad guys. More than anything, the television ratings following *WrestleMania* told the story. In theory, the absence of competition from WCW should have boosted the WWF's numbers, but instead, ratings fell week after week — from 5.7 on April 2, to 5.1 on April 23 and a 4.2 on May 21. The precipitous drop confirmed that the glory days were over and treacherous times awaited.

To compound troubles, a debilitating injury sidelined one of the company's top performers. Triple H had dominated the heel side of the company for the previous twenty months. Now aligned with Austin in a heel team, the company planned to focus on them before an inevitable breakup and feud. But all the long-term planning went out the window when Triple H tore his quadriceps in a WWF Tag-Team Titles match with Austin against Chris Benoit and Chris Jericho on the May 21 *Raw*. The match was booked to elevate Benoit and Jericho into top positions because of a shortage on the babyface side. But the freak injury threw all plans out of whack.

Chapter 27

One of the pending changes in the aftermath of the Triple H injury involved the launch of World Championship Wrestling. The idea of running WCW as a separate brand had waned based on the inability to lock up enough talent for a full roster and the disadvantages of the late weekend timeslot. The latest idea involved integrating WCW talent into WWF programs, allowing fans to familiarize themselves with the new wrestlers before revisiting the original plan.

The assimilation began with appearances by Lance Storm, Stacy Keibler, Booker T, and Diamond Dallas Page (the latter two accepted buyouts of their AOL–Time Warner contracts at fifty cents on the dollar) on *Raw* and *Smackdown*. Shane McMahon had been installed as figurehead leader of WCW after outsmarting his father to buy the company in the storyline. The idea was to build toward the July pay-per-view, renamed *Invasion*, with a WWF vs. WCW main event. To get the ball rolling, the company took a calculated risk. They booked the final half-hour of the July 2 *Raw* from Tacoma, Washington, as WCW *Raw*. The look, feel, and sound would be totally different. Booker T and Buff Bagwell were put in the position of WCW flag-bearers as the participants in this crucial match. Much like with the XFL, the first impression meant everything.

If any differences existed between the debut of the XFL and the new WCW, it would be that the football league had at least one good week. The brief glimpse of WCW *Raw* proved disastrous on every level. Fans immediately turned on the product, booing Bagwell and Booker out of the building. In a sense, it wasn't unexpected. WWF fans had been conditioned for years to despise WCW. Now they were being asked to cheer the brand, long after it had been considered cool by even its own supporters. The fiasco left the WWF seriously rethinking the prospects of an equal WCW brand.

> **BUFF BAGWELL:** Me and Booker T have had good matches and good chemistry before. What I believe happened was several things. One, Pat Patterson does the main events up there. Keep in mind, this was a new thing for everyone. Well, Pat Patterson doesn't know Buff Bagwell and my moves. He doesn't know Booker T's moves. We don't know how things work in the WWF. WCW style is different than WWF style. Of course, we don't know that, so we're we wondering why we are wrestling in Tacoma and next week the show will be in Atlanta. That's why I think I was singled out a little bit. Why wouldn't you wait for a babyface match for a main event, which I shouldn't be in, especially in my debut? Then it's in a WWF town. I don't understand. We got booed out of the building. It was set up to fail. They brought out WCW announcers and they were booing even before we came out. Then me and Booker went out there and blew it. We had a horrible match.

It didn't take long for the vision to change again. Feeling WCW couldn't cut it on its own, the WWF resurrected ECW from the ashes to join forces with WCW. As per the storyline, Stephanie McMahon purchased ECW and aligned with her brother and Paul Heyman to destroy the WWF in the latest interpromotional concept. Former ECW mainstays Rob Van Dam and Tommy Dreamer were signed to join the ECW crew, with wrestlers already on the roster. The wholesale changes led to a WWF vs. WCW/ECW Alliance ten-man tag at the July 22 *Invasion* pay-per-view in Cleveland, Ohio.

Still operating without the top stars from WCW's heyday, the decision was made to switch one of the WWF's stars to balance the sides. The *Invasion* main event saw Booker T, Diamond Dallas Page, Rhyno, and The Dudley Boyz defeat "Stone Cold" Steve Austin, Kurt Angle, Chris Jericho, The Undertaker, and Kane after Austin, the WWF Champion, turned heel and joined The Alliance. As an isolated event, *Invasion* became a colossal success, with 775,000 pay-per-view buys, the largest non-*WrestleMania* figure in wrestling history. The single event paid for the WCW purchase many times over. But as an attempt to put steam into the interpromotional feud, *Invasion* fizzled out.

The Rock's return helped spark business briefly, particularly at *SummerSlam*, which did 565,000 buys built around him winning the WCW World Title from Booker T, The Undertaker and Kane unifying the WWF and WCW Tag-Team Titles by beating Diamond Dallas Page and Kanyon, and Kurt Angle defeating Austin via disqualification in the WWF Title bout. But the overall booking of the show did nothing to turn the program around. Even with Austin, fans didn't accept The Alliance as a legitimate threat. Losing all three top matches, and six of eight overall at *SummerSlam*, hammered the nail deeper.

With ratings for *Raw* now hovering in the mid-4.0's, including a three-year low 3.9 on October 22, and business showing no signs of a turnaround, the WWF essentially threw in the towel on WCW. For the November 18 *Survivor Series* event, the main event would be the coup de grace — the WWF vs. the WCW/ECW Alliance in a winner-take-all match. The losing side, including whichever McMahon owners, would theoretically head for the unemployment line. Just a couple of years earlier, the notion of the WWF vs. WCW for control of the business would have had fans drooling a river. At worst, the interpromotional storyline would have provided material for a couple of years at minimum, with a handful of big money shows along the way. Yet less than six months after the first WCW angle on WWF programming, the anticipated greatest program in wrestling history needed to be euthanized to save the floundering business. Whether it was ignorance or ego-driven booking, despite the initial interest shown by the mammoth *Invasion* buyrate even without the top WCW stars, the basic creative ideas needed to make WCW appear dangerous and the WWF appear vulnerable never materialized.

To no one's surprise, at the *Survivor Series*, Team WWF with The Rock, The Undertaker, Kane, Chris Jericho, and The Big Show finished off the WCW/ECW Alliance of Steve Austin, Kurt Angle,

Shane McMahon, Rob Van Dam, and Booker T. Angle had turned heel along the way, becoming Austin's comedy sidekick in a move that did little to bolster either man's career. Portrayed as a geek after coming out as the loser in the Stephanie McMahon love triangle the year prior, Angle lost further steam as a serious, top-level performer. The ten-man tag match itself offered more excitement than the actual invasion, with The Rock pinning Austin to allow the WCW and ECW brands to finally rest in peace.

The follies of the XFL and the decimation of the WWF's business hit home when the company was forced to hand pink slips to nine percent of its front office. Ratings still registered in the low 4.0's and the *Survivor Series*, expected to draw interest for "the end of an era," culled merely 450,000 buys. The final interpromotional showdown managed 325,000 fewer buys than the inaugural battle four months earlier, the clearest example of the WWF's failure to capitalize on its biggest opportunity.

Ironically, one night after the end of WCW, the WWF brought in the one person who could have generated at least some interest in the invasion — "Nature Boy" Ric Flair. The man synonymous with WCW entered the WWF storyline after Shane and Stephanie sold their stock to his consortium. The latest strategy called for Flair and McMahon to butt heads as partners before splitting the company in two, thereby creating the separate brands the company had been striving toward.

In the ring, Steve Austin's heel turn began to slow down. His run as a villain, while a borderline disaster for business, became memorable for the popularity of his new catchphrase. What? His new catchphrase. What? One of the last great catchphrases of the WWF's glory period. What? More annoying for other wrestlers than entertaining for the fans, Austin chanted "What?" during his own interviews and the fans followed in unison, not only during Austin's promos, but during nearly every in-ring promo for the next year.

With two major championships appearing in the aftermath of WCW's collapse, the company booked a four-man tournament to create a singular world champion. Chris Jericho made history by winning singles matches over both The Rock and Steve Austin in one night at December 9's *Vengeance* to unify the WWF and WCW Championships. The heel Jericho earned his first major WWF push as wrestling's Undisputed Champion.

> **JIM ROSS:** I think that Chris Jericho has great untapped potential. Jericho reminds me more of a Ric Flair–like wrestler when Flair was regarded to be beatable in the old territory days of the NWA. When Flair would go to Dallas and you just knew as a fan that Kerry Von Erich was going to beat Flair. I think Jericho has some of those same advantages in his style. He's physically gifted, but he's not so physically dominating that you wouldn't believe he could lose.

Jericho's reign would be overshadowed by the return of Triple H, after an eight-month absence. His recovery from a torn quad made him a sympathetic babyface, and the fans gleamed at his return to win the 2002 *Royal Rumble*.

But even Triple H would take a back seat to McMahon's latest attempt to inject life into the WWF product. He'd failed when trying to incorporate the WCW brand name. This time, McMahon went back to the well for one of the few WCW ideas that had drawn big money, the New World Order. To do so, McMahon signed the original nWo members — Kevin Nash, Scott Hall, and Hulk Hogan. The move raised a lot of eyebrows both in and outside the business. All three, Nash and Hogan in particular, deserved some level of blame, whether it was through selfishness, unprofessional behavior, or downright indifference toward the well-being of the company, for the demise of WCW. With the WWF floundering, the risks appeared to outweigh the rewards. On top of that, if the trio was worth the money and potential headaches, bringing them aboard eight months earlier would have greatly helped the WCW invasion angle. The depression of the business since that point likely spurred McMahon to find a quick fix to the malaise.

The grand homecoming of three of the biggest stars of the past decade came in Milwaukee, Wisconsin, at the February 17, 2002, *No Way Out* pay-per-view. Sporting the vintage nWo black-and-white colors, the three received thunderous cheers despite being positioned as heels. They ended the night costing babyface Steve Austin the Undisputed Title. The next night, on *Raw* from Chicago, the nWo set their sights on the other top babyface, The Rock. Hogan and The Rock engaged in a memorable in-ring interview to set the stage for a dream match at *WrestleMania X-8*. The nWo had helped provide some interest and a short-term bump for business, with *Raw* back into the high 4.0's and *No Way Out* generating an above-average 575,000 buys.

The well-hyped legend vs. legend bout between The Rock and Hogan headlined *WrestleMania X-8* on March 17 at the SkyDome in Toronto. Despite the soft business numbers, *Mania* set new attendance and gate records thanks to the rabid Canadian fanbase — 68,237 patrons paid $3.8 million in American dollars to watch The Rock pin Hulk Hogan (despite the crowd support for the legendary Hulkster), Steve Austin dispose of Scott Hall, and Triple H win the Undisputed Title from Chris Jericho. Pay-per-view also turned out to be a triumph, with buyrates trailing only *Mania X-7* to that point in history. The return of Hogan, more so than Hall and Nash, brought plenty of casual interest back to the WWF. If history proved to be a guide, that nostalgia would quickly fade.

The fallout from *Mania* resulted in the biggest *Raw* rating of the year the next night, 5.3, for a show that saw Hogan officially turn babyface and team with The Rock in the main event against his former nWo mates. But historically, the show will be best remembered for the announcement of the long-awaited brand extension. The WWF would split the roster via a draft into two groups — *Raw*, headed by Ric Flair, and *Smackdown*, led by Vince McMahon. Only the WWF Champion and Women's Champion could appear on both brands. All other performers would be exclusive to either Monday nights or Thursday nights, thereby forcing viewers to watch both shows to catch all of their favorite superstars, and slow down storyline progression with two hours per brand per week instead of four hours for the entire roster. The split would also help elevate new stars, with the current headliners now appearing on television only once each per week.

JIM ROSS: I think brand extension is a good thing in the long haul. I think we've taken a couple of steps back to take several steps forward. Hopefully, in the long run, it's going to give guys opportunities they might not have gotten so quickly, because the rosters have been separated and divided in half. I think we've taken steps backward in this brand separation. But I think in the long haul, I think it's the right thing to do by creating our own competition, so to speak. But I do know it gives more guys opportunities to live their dream. Somebody is going to be the next Rock or the next Stone Cold or the next Hogan, and some are not. At least we're giving them the at-bats to see what they got.

The campus of Penn State University hosted the momentous draft on March 25 on *Raw*. By virtue of a coin flip, McMahon's *Smackdown* owned the number one selection and drafted The Rock. Flair's first pick became The Undertaker. The two sides alternated choices of Kurt Angle, the entire nWo faction, Chris Benoit, Kane, Hulk Hogan, Rob Van Dam, WWF Tag-Team Champions Billy and Chuck, Booker T, Edge, The Big Show, Rikishi, Bubba Ray Dudley, D-Von Dudley, and newcomer Brock Lesnar. One name conspicuously left undrafted was "Stone Cold" Steve Austin, who had walked out on the company following *WrestleMania* citing creative differences with management. The brief hiatus ended with Austin returning to television on April 1 and joining the *Raw* roster as originally planned.

The Hogan wave continued at the April 21 *Backlash* event in Kansas City, with a victory over Triple H to capture the WWF Championship for a sixth time, the first since 1993. Interestingly, arguably the most popular WWF Champion of all time would also turn out to be the last.

Chapter 28

For two decades, the World Wildlife Fund had hated the confusion over the WWF initials, for which it owned the trademark. The wrestling company and charitable nature organization entered into an agreement in 1994 that permitted McMahon and company to use the initials only within the United States border. But the popularity of the Federation already had an international scope, and they occasionally toured throughout the world under the WWF banner. By the late '90s, the emergence of the internet created a new method of marketing the WWF initials, which precipitated a lawsuit from the Fund. An English High Court examined the 1994 document and interpreted the case as a cut and dry breach. Despite multiple appeals, the World Wrestling Federation was forced to change its name to World Wrestling Entertainment. Along with reimbursing $1 million in legal fees to the World Wildlife Fund, the wrestling promotion abandoned the widely popular WWF.com website and modified its familiar scratch logo. To publicize the switch to WWE, the company embarked on a clever advertising campaign at a self-labeled cost of $50 million to rebrand, urging people to "get the F out."

Hulk Hogan's reign as WWE Champion ended up being merely transitional. The excitement surrounding Hogan's return to WWE dissipated as most fans tired quickly of a 48-year-old champion following prime performers like Austin, The Rock, Jericho, and Triple H. Inspired by a shocking record-low 2.9 rating for the May 2 *Smackdown* featuring Hogan vs. Jericho for the belt, McMahon swapped the championship for the third consecutive pay-per-view.

The Undertaker regained the title for the first time in three years at the May 19 *Judgment Day* event.

Excluding the brief surge surrounding the arrival of the nWo and *WrestleMania* in general, little had improved. *Raw* and *Smackdown* ratings, pay-per-view buyrates, and attendance all reached their lowest points since WWE took off in 1998. In a period where the company needed stability, June 10 turned everything upside down. The biggest star on *Raw*, perhaps in the entire company, Steve Austin, walked out of WWE with no intention of returning. Fed up with the creative direction of the past several months, coupled with serious nagging injuries and personal issues, Austin left the Phillips Arena prior to the live *Raw* in Atlanta and boarded a plane back to Texas.

> **STEVE AUSTIN:** For every action, there's a reaction. Me leaving the company was a huge deal. I don't think it was a case of Vince going to get on the TV and say, "Stone Cold's left." Of course, he was going to hammer me and say exactly what he thought. People were wondering if this was storyline or if it was real. That wasn't any storyline. He hammered me pretty good. By the same token, as frustrated as he was, I was at the house watching all this stuff and I was frustrated when I left and frustrated when I was watching it.

Panicking at the loss of his biggest draw, McMahon booked himself in the main event of *Raw* against counterpart Ric Flair, with the winner gaining full control of WWE, rendering the brand extension useless in a storyline context. McMahon went over with help from rookie Brock Lesnar, but the rushed nature of the events took the edge off what could have been a money angle and match down the road.

The promotion entered a standby mode for the next month. The lone highlight involved the continued push of Brock Lesnar, who won the annual *King of the Ring* tournament. With Austin gone and The Rock transitioning into a full-time movie career while sporadically wrestling, ratings plummeted for both shows. McMahon's next attempt to energize the product came on the July 15 *Raw* from the Meadowlands in New Jersey. To strengthen the brand extension, a general manager was appointed for *Raw* and *Smackdown*. In a complete shock to fans and wresters alike, Eric Bischoff joined WWE as the storyline *Raw* GM, the same Bischoff who had vowed to put WWE out of business while he presided over WCW. The most hated man for years within WWE circles was now gainfully employed by the McMahons. Once again, had the two sides made peace twelve months earlier, chances are the WCW brand would still be alive and kicking.

> **ERIC BISCHOFF:** It was different. It some ways, it really did feel like I was in the enemy camp, so to speak. That's a very unique and strange feeling. But at the same time, I felt like I belonged there in a strange sense because our business is sports entertainment and our platform is that ring. It's our stage. It's our Broadway, so to speak. And having been out of the business for a couple of years, there was a lot of things about the business that I missed, and having the opportunity to kind of step back out in front of a live crowd and do what we do for a living, in a sense, I felt like I was coming home again and that I belonged there. Not so much that I belonged in WWE, but I belonged in the business. I belonged in that ring.

On the *Smackdown* side, Stephanie McMahon, no longer married to Triple H on television, took control as general manager. With the dueling GMs, the product had established a genuinely competitive vibe between *Raw* and *Smackdown* for the first time.

> **PAUL HEYMAN:** I wish that I could contribute more in regards to making legitimate competition between *Raw* and *Smackdown* because Raw had their writers, and I was the lead writer of *Smackdown* and it was balls to the wall. It was let's see who had the better show, and we blew them away. We blew them away quality wise and we blew them away in terms of ratings. It was the first time that *Smackdown* pretty much became the "A" show and *Raw*, simply by the definition of losing in the competition, was becoming the "B" show. I would love for that to be the case again.

Following a period of roster jumps to freshen each show, the summer focused on a star from the past and a star for the future.

Shawn Michaels returned to the ring after a four and a half year hiatus recovering from back surgery. Looking as if he hadn't missed a beat, Michaels defeated former DX ally Triple H at the 2002 *SummerSlam* from Long Island, New York.

> **SHAWN MICHAELS:** I've always loved this line of work, and I didn't want to come back if I wasn't good at it. I wanted to try to at least bow out gracefully. But my body has held up tremendously. I feel awesome. I try to tell people without hammering them over the head with it, that it's a bona fide miracle in my life. I feel great to be back and be able to contribute far and above the expectations that people set for me, and that I set for me.

But *SummerSlam* would mark the crowning of a new superstar in Brock Lesnar, who became the youngest WWE Champion in history by defeating The Rock. With Paul Heyman as his mouthpiece, the former NCAA heavyweight wrestling champion had been groomed for stardom since he signed with WWE out of college. In addition to winning the *King of the Ring*, Lesnar scored a clean victory over Hulk Hogan on *Smackdown*. With Lesnar vs. The Rock on top, *SummerSlam* drew a sellout crowd and 520,000 buys, both rarities at the time.

The luster of Lesnar's big win waned the following week through no fault of his own. With Lesnar being a *Smackdown* talent, the top star on *Raw*, Triple H, felt his brand should also have a champion. Behind the scenes, Triple H had gained considerable power after proposing to Stephanie McMahon, not only the boss's daughter but the head writer on the creative team. Feeling the Intercontinental Title was beneath him, Triple H pushed for and received a championship for *Raw*, the World Heavyweight Title.

> **JIM ROSS:** We do not have a harder-working guy on our roster than Triple H, on *Raw* or *Smackdown*. The fact that he's engaged to Vince McMahon's daughter, in my view, has zero to do with my perception of him as a professional wrestler. What he does in his private time and the fact that he's going to get married, I wish them all the happiness. What they do in their private time is their business and should remain that way. He's the hardest working guy as we have on either roster. He is a lifelong student of the game. . . . I think

the guy gets a lot of undue criticism. A lot of guys have beat him. He's beaten a lot of guys. He's at the house shows. He works hard. Anybody who pays their money to go to a live event sees that he's there. He busts his ass. He's worked through injuries. All of this comes about because of his social standing and who he is engaged to, and I think it's unfair. I think it's terribly unfair.

Without winning a match, Triple H was given the title by *Raw* GM Eric Bischoff on the September 2 show. The physical belt resembled the old WCW World Title. Each brand now possessed its own major title — Brock Lesnar as WWE Champion on *Smackdown* and Triple H as World Heavyweight Champion on *Raw*. Instead of an emphasis on one champion, the dual titles served to devalue the prestige of each belt. Critics pinpointed Triple H's ego as the reason for the unnecessary changes that indirectly stifled Lesnar's momentum as champion, something which would become a recurring motif over the next few years.

CHRIS JERICHO: I'll tell Vince this to his face. I thought it was a very WCW move where you just handed the belt to someone. Maybe they wanted to get the heat out of it, and maybe they have an overall plan where it is going to play out somehow. I'm not going to say that they don't because we don't know. I hope they do because just handing the belt, I don't care if it's Triple H or Chris Jericho or whether it's Sho Funaki, you don't just give a belt to someone, because that takes away all the credibility of a belt in the first place. You can't just hand the belt to somebody.

With ratings still in the tank, WWE went back to the shock TV approach, but took controversy to a new level. On *Smackdown*, Billy and Chuck, a tag team exhibiting homosexual tendencies, staged an engagement designed to lead to a gay wedding on *Smackdown*, which angered many gay and lesbian activists when it was revealed in the storyline that neither man was gay, and the event was just a publicity stunt.

BILLY GUNN: That was one those things people go, "How did you ever do the Chuck and Billy thing?" To me, I thought it was great. I loved it more than the DX thing. It was something different. It was something everybody talked about. When was the last time there was something that people actually talked about? We pulled something off that people never thought we could. It went from people thinking it was absolutely ridiculous, to when me and Chuck came out, and Chuck did that silly-ass dance he did, people went crazy.

While *Smackdown* was featuring gay men, *Raw* introduced Hot Lesbian Action, or HLA, with multiple segments of near-naked women kissing and caressing in the middle of the ring. Complaints poured into TNN headquarters. Taking the cake, however, was a pro wrestling first — necrophilia. As part of the buildup for a Triple H vs. Kane World Title bout, the heel champion accused Kane of murdering an ex-girlfriend, the imaginary Katie Vick, and engaging in sexual intercourse with her corpse. To illustrate his point, Triple H filmed a mock funeral where he dressed as Kane and violated a life-sized doll in a coffin. Those who didn't immediately tune out found few redeeming qualities in the perverse and disgusting storyline.

Chapter 29

The WWE's desperation tactics debunked the myth of "controversy equals cash." By the end of 2002, ratings for *Raw* and *Smackdown* averaged in the high 3.0's and mid 3.0's, respectively. Attendance declined to close to fifty percent of the levels earlier in the year. In fact, August through October 2002 marked the company's first money-losing quarter, XFL notwithstanding, in five years. Business was in the toilet compared to just a few years earlier. But McMahon remained committed to the brand extension, figuring they'd take one step back before taking two steps forward.

With the brand extension doing little to create new stars outside of Brock Lesnar, the company dipped into the free agent market and brought another ex-WCW star into the fold: "Big Poppa Pump" Scott Steiner. His impressive physique and verbal skills made him a formidable challenger for Triple H on the *Raw* side, but injuries diminished his once undeniable in-ring ability. The excitement fizzled out after Steiner's first match, and he went from main-eventer to mid-carder in a flash.

With *WrestleMania* approaching, there were only a couple of marketable matches on top. To prevent a *Mania* disaster, the company went back to the well. Proving time heals all wounds, Steve Austin settled his differences with WWE, fixed his personal life following domestic violence charges, and returned to action.

STEVE AUSTIN: It's a deal where they've really got you mixed in storylines. They're depending on you to draw houses. They're depending on you for a lot of things. They don't take into account the serious nature of your injuries. Even the guys in the company didn't exactly know what I was going through from a medical standpoint. And then for everything good that I've done, for them to be crapping on me from a creative end. When you have someone like myself, when you have someone like a Hulk Hogan, when you have someone like a Ric Flair that can draw huge money, you just don't all of a sudden start crapping on them in storylines. You maintain them. You protect them and you build them and you look out for them. My health was going downhill. I was trying to compete with guys that were ninety or one hundred percent healthy where I was barely running on fifty percent. Each time I stepped in the ring, I was facing a pretty good case of something really bad going on with my neck. Enough was enough. I did what I did. When I came back to the company, I pulled a lot of people of aside, and talked to a lot of people, and explained what was going on and buried the hatchet with a lot of people pretty much across the board. If someone still continues to dislike me or hold a grudge for what I did, I really don't give a rat's ass.

The Rock, with a break in his movie schedule, came back from Hollywood to perform on the stage that made him a household name for a final showdown with "Stone Cold." After a dispute months earlier, Hulk Hogan also came back for a showdown twenty years in the making with Vince McMahon. The full-time performers would headline the night, with *Smackdown*'s Kurt Angle defending the WWE Title against Brock Lesnar in a battle of NCAA amateur wrestling champions, and *Raw*'s Booker T challenging Triple H for the World Heavyweight Title.

WWE needed a strong *WrestleMania* after a disastrous business quarter from November to January, in which the company had posted its biggest three-month loss in history, $26.6 million, thanks mainly to the closing of its Times Square establishment, since renamed The World. Three years of restaurant operations resulted in an XFL-level bloodletting of $53 million, continuing the string of nonwrestling business failures for Vince McMahon. The demise of The World forced a greater emphasis on the success of *WrestleMania*.

The nineteenth annual extravaganza originated from Safeco

Field, home of baseball's Seattle Mariners. The event set a stadium attendance record of 54,097 fans paying $2.76 million. The Rock and Hogan scored pinfalls in their returns. Triple H retained his championship, while Brock Lesnar won his second WWE Title in the main event. On pay-per-view, the event flopped with only 560,000 buys, by far the lowest *Mania* total since the dark days of *WrestleMania 13*.

If that news didn't scare the company, the injury report following the event certainly would. While not publicly acknowledged, Steve Austin's match with The Rock would end up being his last. Austin made the decision to retire from the ring prior to the show due to recurring spinal troubles and the need for spinal fusion surgery. The possibility of life-threatening injuries from wrestling against medical advice sent Austin to the emergency room the day before the show, but he checked out the next morning to deliver one final match and succeeded with a four-star battle. Also facing spinal fusion surgery was Kurt Angle, who'd suffered a neck injury several months earlier but held off the procedure in order to wrestle Lesnar at *Mania*, despite the high risk of paralysis. Angle survived, but eschewed full vertebrae fusion for a minimally invasive operation that would fix the discs in his spine, enabling a much quicker recovery. Instead of a full year, Angle hoped to return to the ring in a couple of months.

With talent thin on top of the card, WWE finally signed Bill Goldberg, one of the last ex-WCW stars to come aboard since the purchase two years earlier, at a hefty $1.5 million price tag. Goldberg immediately worked on *Raw* with The Rock, who had pushed for the company to sign the former WCW Champion. With The Rock headed back to Hollywood to shoot his next feature film, Goldberg pinned him at the April 27 *Backlash* event. But the creative team, which had failed to construct captivating storylines, made similar mistakes with Goldberg. Instead of following WCW's formula of presenting Goldberg as an unstoppable, unbeatable monster, Goldberg became just another wrestler, beaten and laid-out far too often. Fans who'd worshipped Goldberg in WCW reacted with apathy to the toned-down WWE version. The numbers painted the picture, as *Backlash* drew only 350,000 buys for the Goldberg vs. The Rock dream match that would have set business records had it happened just two years earlier.

Despite there being no signs of a turnaround, WWE embarked on a bold decision to run single brand pay-per-views. The company had just announced its worst business year in history, with $19.2 million in losses for fiscal 2003, but proceeded with a plan that would ultimately lead to more pay-per-view events per year. Beginning with June's *Bad Blood* show, only the big four events — *WrestleMania*, *SummerSlam*, the *Royal Rumble*, and *Survivor Series* — would showcase talent from both brands. The remaining eight monthly events would alternate as *Raw*-only and *Smackdown*-only ventures. Ideally, the schedule would expand to include two pay-per-views per month, one from each group, in those eight months. The risky proposition would ultimately make or break the dual brand system.

The summer of '03 featured two major title quests. On *Smackdown*, Kurt Angle made his return to continue feuding with Brock Lesnar, winning the WWE Title back at *Vengeance* in July. The duo followed on free television with a sixty-minute Iron Man match on *Smackdown*'s season premiere, with Lesnar regaining the strap. Goldberg's journey toward the World Heavyweight Title took some questionable turns before he pinned Triple H at September's *Unforgiven*. Perhaps the most eye-catching program pitted Vince McMahon against one-legged wrestler Zach Gowan, an aspiring early-twenties performer who'd lost his leg to childhood cancer. But none of the pairings could boost business, as ratings and buyrates remained at their lowest points in years.

Outside the ring, Triple H happily finished his courtship of Stephanie McMahon by wedding the wrestling heiress on October 25, 2003, technically making him part-owner of WWE and husband of the head creative writer. Already a main scapegoat for the problems on *Raw*, the criticism would only intensify.

Fritz and WWE creative head Stephanie McMahon

BILLY GUNN: Hunter will walk up to you and look you in the eye and go, "Man, you're so good." And soon as you turn the corner, he'll go, "Vince, that guy sucks."

Chapter 30

The backbone of every wrestling promotion lies in its ability to create new stars to which fans establish an emotional attachment. Not until the rise of Steve Austin, The Rock, and Mick Foley did WWE again become a powerhouse. Since the boom period of 1998–2000 subsided, WWE had managed to produce only two successful main-event talents — Kurt Angle and Brock Lesnar. The dearth of fresh faces in the top mix helped trigger the ongoing drought.

But as 2003 closed, optimism reigned with potential breakout stars for 2004. Not since Brock Lesnar in mid-2002 had WWE churned out a money-drawing performer. Hoping for "the next big thing" once again, the company put its energy behind some new faces and a couple of familiar ones. On *Raw*, third-generation wrestler Randy Orton opened eyeballs with his good looks, impressive physique, and sold in-ring and speaking ability. Since day one, the company pegged him for superstardom and facilitated the plans by aligning him with Triple H and "Nature Boy" Ric Flair.

JERRY LAWLER: Randy Orton is pretty impressive all the way around. He's a great-looking kid. He's got a good attitude all around. You can check his pedigree. He comes from a long line of very successful wrestlers in this business. I don't think you can expect anything other than that from Randy. Of his predecessors and of his ancestors, he's got the most physical attributes of any of the three, and maybe the best all-around look so far. If he just gets his head on right and avoids the injury bug, I think he's got a huge future ahead of him.

A fourth member, Batista, a jacked-up 300-pound behemoth, rounded out the foursome known as Evolution. Orton, dubbed "The Legend Killer," received the most attention by taking out stars from the past and popular talent on the current roster. On *Smackdown*, Chris Benoit and Eddie Guerrero's years of hard work and incredible matches began to pay dividends. Benoit finally received a main event push commensurate to his ability, while Latino fans helped elevate Guerrero into a top position for the first time in WWE. Hardly anyone figured those two would shine brightest on WWE's biggest stage.

Benoit's journey led him to the 2004 *Royal Rumble* in Philadelphia, where he entered the thirty-man battle royal as number one and survived over one hour to win a chance to wrestle in the main event of *WrestleMania XX*. Guerrero's popularity earned him a date with WWE Champion Brock Lesnar at February's *No Way Out* pay-per-view in San Francisco, California. A heavy hispanic flavor filled the Cow Palace to see Guerrero upset the champion and win his first major heavyweight championship.

> **JIM ROSS:** Eddie had some problems with drug and alcohol abuse, and we sent him to rehabilitation and we took care of his family while he was there. We took care of the rehabilitation. We had to start over with Eddie after he got out and we've taken it a day at a time. But I'm very proud of Eddie. Eddie's a changed man. He's stepping firmly on the wagon. I pray to God that he always steps there for his and his family's sake. There's nobody on the roster that deserves the opportunity to be in their role more than Eddie Guerrero. Size wise and pound for pound, he's as good as anybody in the business. He's only going to get better.

Guerrero's best friend's destiny — the World Heavyweight Title on *Raw* — awaited at *Mania*.

As home to the first and tenth *WrestleMania* extravaganzas, Madison Square Garden could be the only host for *WrestleMania XX* on March 14, 2004. The commemorative nature of the event resulted in a blockbuster lineup, with five matches that could headline any show in any city at any time. After a five-month absence, The

Undertaker reverted to his original "Deadman" gimmick to enormous fan excitement to defeat Kane. Randy Orton's megapush continued with a pinfall victory over Mick Foley in a handicap match with Batista and Ric Flair against Foley and The Rock. Steve Austin acted as guest referee for a Goldberg vs. Lesnar dream match, which admittedly would have felt more significant prior to Goldberg's WWE debut. Ironically, it would be the final match for both men in WWE. Goldberg's one-year contract expired after the show, and neither side had any interest in continuing the relationship. Lesnar became fed up with the difficult WWE travel schedule and quit wrestling to try professional football. Despite not playing competitively since high school, his notoriety earned him an invitation to Minnesota Vikings training camp, but his work ethic could carry him only so far as a defensive-end prospect. Along the way, he burned his bridges with WWE and has wallowed in anonymity since. The championship bouts saw Eddie Guerrero retain the WWE Title against Kurt Angle, who was in need of another neck operation. The final contest of the night witnessed Chris Benoit achieve his dream by winning the World Heavyweight Title against Triple H and Shawn Michaels in a Triple Threat match, one of the greatest contests in *Mania* history. As the post-match confetti fell and fireworks exploded, two men who were told they'd be too small to ever make it embraced in the middle of a sold out Madison Square Garden as the two biggest stars in the number one wrestling company in the world.

Much like in 2003, post-*WrestleMania XX* left the overall talent roster with many gaping holes. Kurt Angle headed back to the injured list. Goldberg and Brock Lesnar departed for different ventures. The Rock began his latest movie role in *Be Cool*. Steve Austin's contract expired, and the two sides parted ways again after failing to agree on rights to the "Stone Cold" moniker for outside projects. Mick Foley stuck around for one more month before resuming his retirement. To shake things up, Vince McMahon announced a draft lottery to juggle the rosters. Rob Van Dam, The Dudley Boyz, and Booker T were among those moving to *Smackdown*, while Edge and Shelton Benjamin donned *Raw* colors. The interest in the lottery helped *Raw* draw a strong 4.5 rating, its highest in two years, but ultimately the talent shifts resulted in minimal impact on business.

The loss of Lesnar and Angle following *Mania* crippled *Smackdown*'s already thin roster and left Eddie Guerrero without a marketable heel opponent. The creative team looked in-house and chose an unlikely candidate. Bradshaw, the long, dark haired, barroom brawling Texan as one-half of the APA tagteam, transformed into John Bradshaw Layfield, a clean-cut business tycoon from New York City. Out of the blue, the "Million Dollar Man" takeoff became Guerrero's main foil, despite his having always been a mid-carder. Fans didn't buy JBL as a credible challenger, and *Smackdown*'s ratings suffered mightily. Despite the warning signs, JBL, even after causing an international incident by flashing Nazi gestures at a house show in Germany to attract heel heat, won the WWE Title from Guerrero at the June 27 *Great American Bash* pay-per-view in Norfolk, Virginia. The lack of interest in JBL led to a sad 238,000 pay-per-view buys. The era of JBL had begun, although no one seemed to want to take part in it.

Chris Benoit's summer run came to an end at the hands of Randy Orton, whose push heated up with a win over Mick Foley in a bloody street fight at *Backlash*. Benoit turned back all comers, including Triple H and Shawn Michaels in singles matches, before dropping the title to Orton at *SummerSlam '04* in Toronto. As a heel, fans began to cheer Orton's cocky and smug attitude. The decision was made to immediately turn Orton babyface via a group beatdown from his Evolution partners. The long-term plan called for Orton to main-event *WrestleMania 21* against Triple H. As part of the program, Orton quickly lost the title to Triple H at September's *Unforgiven*. The move resulted in a vacuum effect, as in all of Orton's babyface momentum got sucked away. Fans lost faith in Orton upon losing to Triple H, who deserved some blame in the decision-making. The crowd reactions left WWE reevaluating its *Mania* strategy.

MICK FOLEY: I think I was in New York City for one of my frequent literary journeys. A fan asked me if I heard what happened to Randy Orton. I knew he had just won the title the night before. So I asked what had happened, and the fan said that Evolution beat him up. I was baffled at why.

In some rare good news, fiscal 2004 numbers showed a healthy profit for the year, despite no upgrades in key business indicators. From $375 million in revenues, WWE posted a $48.2 million profit. The annual report underlined the difference between WWE and its defunct competition, WCW. Throughout the lean times, WWE effectively implemented cost-cutting measures across the board to maintain profitability. By contrast, WCW's mismanagement led to tens of millions in red ink despite respectable revenues. The profits notwithstanding, the WWE creative braintrust still needed to find the magic formula and fresh superstars to bring it back to the promise land.

> **RAVEN:** How are you going to write TV for fifteen-to-thirty-five-year-old males that either want to see what they're accomplishing or who want to see what they can never have if you're one of those people that's never had it or been there? If you've never been drunk, never been in a fight, never had sex, how can you write these things? The very first thing a writing class teaches you is write what you know. And all those writers, none of them have ever been laid, not to any extent, or none of them have been drunk on a regular basis. That's the single most important thing with any writing class is write what you know. And these guys are geeks.

To its credit, WWE adopted innovative ideas to stir interest. In October, the company presented *Taboo Tuesday*, the first interactive pay-per-view. Taking a page from the success of reality TV, WWE allowed fans to vote on the Internet for the opponents in the championship matches and stipulations for undercard bouts. Despite natural suspicions about stuffed ballot boxes, the results were completely legitimate, to the point that Intercontinental Champion Chris Jericho did not know his opponent or the finish of his match until the opening bell rang. Unfortunately, the idea bombed at the box office. The Tuesday aspect did not help, as only 3,500 fans paid for tickets at Milwaukee's Bradley Center and only 175,000 homes ordered the show for a 0.32 buyrate, the lowest for WWE in nineteen years on pay-per-view.

Another year without any long-term prospects would be an apropos classification for 2004. To avoid a similar twelve months in 2005, the company put its eggs in two baskets. On *Raw*, the haphazard booking of Randy Orton ruined his babyface push and cost him a *WrestleMania* main event. Instead, the other fresh face in Evolution, Batista, got the nod. To avoid the Orton pitfalls, creative slowly built up the Batista vs. Triple H storyline until the time was right. On *Smackdown*, the focus spotlighted John Cena, a superb talker with a chiseled body but below-par wrestling ability. His hip hop gimmick appealed to the young male audience, a demographic WWE had lost since the boom period ended and wrestling lost its "cool factor." Cena represented WWE's best chance to regain that departed audience.

> **JOHN CENA:** I love hip hop music. I like to freestyle. It's something I would do backstage at WWE shows, on the way to WWE events, and the creative team overheard me doing this and asked if you mind if we'd try it out TV. It started out pretty much as a joke. They didn't really give it much emphasis. But as soon as I got to do something on TV that was a little bit more comfortable and more my character, I tried to run with it. Now that I've run with it, the people have taken to it.
>
> WWE is really not savvy to the hip hop market, so they don't know how to tell me which direction to go in. It's cool. I really get to be myself. I think just giving me a chance, letting me do stuff like wear jerseys . . . very rarely do you see anything but boots and tights on WWE television. You don't usually see any logos or anything like that. They've really let me embrace hip hop style. If I want to go out wearing a steel chain, they let me do that. I'm wearing the pumps instead of boots. They let me be me and it's made a lot of noise.

To demonstrate WWE's faith in its new golden boys, Batista and Cena ended as the final two participants in the 2005 *Royal Rumble* on January 30 from Fresno, California. Batista won the event, earning him a World Title opportunity and setting the stage for his split from champion Triple H. Cena earned his title shot in a single elimination tournament on *Smackdown*. WWE Champion JBL awaited at the dance on April 1, 2005.

Vince McMahon led the troops into Hollywood for *Wrestle-Mania 21* at the Staples Center in Los Angeles. Following tradition, WWE brought back stars from the past to spice up the biggest show of the year. "Stone Cold" Steve Austin appeared on WWE television for the first time in more than a year as a guest on *Piper's Pit*, also marking Rowdy Roddy Piper's return to the big show. Hulk Hogan was summoned for induction into the WWE Hall of Fame, and an appearance in the red and yellow on the show. But the night would belong to Cena and Batista. The former pinned JBL to end his ten-month reign as WWE Champion and usher in the era of the "Doctor of Thugamonics." Batista also succeeded in his quest by exacting revenge on Triple H and dominating the contest to win the World Heavyweight Title.

> **JERRY LAWLER:** WWE has a philosophy that youth will not be denied. Sometimes I think just because of youthfulness and because some guys are young and WWE is so youth oriented, sometimes I think guys are put into a position that they're not necessarily ready for. I'm not knocking the guys in that sense. You won't find anybody any more charismatic than John Cena. He's got a great character. He's got a great look. It's his whole persona, it fits him to a "T." It's perfect, it's great. The only thing, and I think John would be the first to admit it, too, he's still not as polished a wrestler as he will be. Same for Batista. Neither one of these guys, and I guess that's probably something to look forward and good for WWE, are good as they are going to be.

The two new faces of World Wrestling Entertainment gave the company something to smile about when the pay-per-view's numbers arrived. The show shocked everyone with over one million buys.

As usual, the day after *WrestleMania* brought numerous changes to the company, but in a much different way. WWE announced plans to return *Raw* and its other cable television properties to the USA Network upon the expiration of its contract with Spike TV (the former TNN) in the fall. The deal also included the return of *Saturday Night's Main Event*, a 1980's staple, on NBC in the *Saturday Night Live* timeslot several times per year. The company took less money in the deal in exchange for the NBC specials and a potential ratings resurgence on the network where *Raw* had achieved its greatest success.

The success or failure of 2005 would rest on the wide shoulders of Batista and John Cena. Already in his late thirties, WWE hoped for a few big years out of Batista. But with a rap album release and a starring role in WWE-produced film, *The Marine*, the company believed in the 28-year-old Cena as a long-term star in the mold of Hulk Hogan and The Rock who would carry the company to its next great height.

PART IV

Kimberly Page and Fritz

One of the most unique individuals I have ever met in my life, in or out of wrestling, is Jim Mitchell.

The old adage in wrestling is that the best characters are those who are merely an extension of the real person. Well, that notion fits Jim perfectly. It's really not much of an stretch, because whether he's James Vandenburg or The Sinister Minister, whatever name you remember him by in wrestling, that was really Jim. Here is a guy who played an evil, demonic character, but was a true family man away from his profession. Still that didn't mean he was any different from his wrestling persona.

> **JIM MITCHELL:** I was tooling around town in my Lincoln one night, channel surfing on the radio, when I heard the melodious sounds of Brian Fritz, B. Randall, and Dickerman bitching at one another about some wrestling angle. At first, I figured it was a few garden variety douchebag local DJs discussing wrestling in between spinning records, with the usual lack of knowledge one expects out of garden variety douchebag local DJs. It became apparent that the guys weren't going to start spinning records, and the more I listened, the more impressed I became. The guys knew their stuff. It was only later that I found out that Fritz, Dickerman, and B. Randall really were garden variety douchebag local DJs during the day at the station. I told them to stick to wrestling, it was a far more dignified pursuit.

The one thing you always get after being around Jim is a great story. For me, it began the first time I visited his home. His office mirrored a scene out of a real life Odditorium at Ripley's.

The room was filled with various satanic memorabilia. Ceramic gargoyles and vultures littered the high corners. The walls were dressed with demonic posters that you would see at a carnival freak show, along with disturbing art featuring naked fat women. There were books on the subject of evil, and even a certificate framed on the wall from the Priesthood of the Church of Satan, signed by Anton LaVey, naming him an official member of the church.

Jim even had a pair of Chihuahuas, appropriately named Diablo and Vampiro. Those little hellions chased anyone and everyone throughout the house. In the backyard by his pool were two statues — one of the Virgin Mary, which belonged to his wife at the time, and the other of a devil, which, of course, belonged to Jim. Well, those dogs decided to besmirch the Blessed Virgin Mary by using it as a toilet while the devil remained in pristine, perfect display.

On top of all of this, there were always guns lying around in his office, which no one was allowed to enter without his permission. I think everyone else living there was too damn afraid to pass though the doorway for fear of having their souls overcome by demons. Jim loves his guns, and even showed me a huge safe he has to hold his enormous collection of firearms.

Mix in all of this with a wife and three kids, all of them girls just to torment Jim. By day, he was Mr. Mom, helping with homework and screaming about the laundry. By night, he was a satanic wrestling mastermind.

A classic Jim story happened back in 1999. I remember he was working on a new character for WCW so he could get back on television. The idea was for him to do a Jack Nicholson impersonation with plenty of clichés. Of course, he needed to film some promos to see if management liked what they saw. Well, Jim decided to call me over on Thanksgiving Day to be his camera guy.

He was decked out in his brand new, bright purple suit to emulate The Joker from Batman, spouting out the phrase, "You don't know Jack!" in his best impersonation. Between takes, he would throw back his favorite frosty beverage and, believe me, we did a lot of takes that afternoon. It got to the point where I knew the promo better than he did!

JIM MITCHELL: When Dallas Page was on the WCW booking committee, he came up with a really goofy idea for me to do a Jack Nicholson wannabe character. I thought it sucked, but I was in jeopardy of being canned as it was, and I needed the money. I was so embarrassed by the concept, that I had to enlist Fritz and Dickerman to help me film the vignette for Page, because they were the only guys in town I could trust to produce me and attempt to make a shit sandwich out of shit. The guys did their best to film and direct me through hours of drunken nonsense. I thought they were just being festive as they urged me to booze it up. In reality, they probably intentionally produced me to really suck so WCW would hate it, thus sparing fans from a Jack Nicholson clone managing The Maestro, and saving me from a lifetime of humiliation.

Dickerman and I first introduced Jim to Extreme Championship Wrestling. At the time, Jim lived out in Kissimmee, near Disney World in Central Florida. ECW ran shows down by the rodeo, which was only a few miles away from where he lived. He

Dickerman, Jim Mitchell and Fritz

had heard a lot about the promotion, and we convinced the evil genius to accompany us to the matches.

We headed over to his place early to hang out for a while before we had to leave. During that time, Jim showed Dickerman his gun collection. For some reason, he wanted to take one of his guns with him to the show. I guess he had heard about the crazy, violent nature that epitomized ECW and wanted to protect himself. Or maybe it was just second nature for him and he was used to packing. Well, we quickly informed him that the promotion searched everyone as they walked through the door, and would not even allow someone with a wallet chain, let alone a firearm, into the show. So, he put the gun away and we continued to hang out for another fifteen minutes before departing. I don't know what went though his head during that time, but when we decided to hit the road, there he was grabbing his gun again and tucking it away in his shirt.

"What the hell are you doing Jim?" I exclaimed. "You can't take a gun with you to ECW!" He finally got the message and decided to lock it up with the rest of his collection.

Later that night, the devil man looked a bit overwhelmed by what he'd seen at that show — the amount of violence and the high-risk moves. His eyes were bigger than a kid in a candy store. He immediately knew he would fit right in with that misfit crew. Several months later, The Sinister Minister was preaching his evil ways in ECW.

Jim has always been a great guy to have in the studio for the show, too. I remember one time Dickerman and I surprised him by having the lights down low with candles in the room, along with a skull and some porno magazines. The wicked genius was right at home. I think I even saw a tear roll down his cheek!

JIM MITCHELL: I had a blast in the studio on *Between the Ropes*. I used to love to the rib the guys. I'd saunter in, my tonsils awash in coffin varnish, with a sack or two of beer and drunkenly hold forth on various topics. The guys were always scared shitless that my blatant disregard for the station rules would get them in trouble. One evening I referred to Dickerman variously as Cockerman, Prickerman, Weinerman, Schmeckleman,

Shlongerman, etc. while watching B. Randall's hand nervously hovering over the dump button in case I went too far.

Jim is also one of the most articulate guys I have even known. He has an amazing mind for the wrestling business and is a walking clinic on how to deliver a promo. With the skills he has, he should be on the main stage as a manager for a young wrestler who needs a good mouthpiece by his side. At the very least, Jim should be training people in how to deliver a promo. Outside of wrestling, Jim is more than content working his karaoke gigs near his home. Plus, he is one hell of a singer. The guy is a dead ringer for David Lee Roth and can hit every note, on cue, of "Just A Gigolo." Now that's talent!

JIM MITCHELL: Fritz and Dickerman were often used as scapegoats while I was out philandering. Often times I'd wake up in the middle of night with a woman of questionable virtue and find that my soon-to-be ex-wife had been calling furiously, demanding to know where I was. One time I told her Fritz had been involved in a domestic dispute and I had to bail him out of jail. Another time I was involved in an automobile accident with Dickerman, but we couldn't call the cops because we were drunk, too drunk, so we slept it off in the woods. While my ex didn't trust me at all, as long as I had the *Between the Ropes* gang involved in my fictional misadventures, I could get away with murder: "Honey, I know it's 5:30 a.m., I smell like Chanel #5, and my Jockeys are smeared with lipstick, but me and Fritz were foiling a potential nuclear holocaust planned by Al Qaeda!"

"OK, as long as you were with Fritz, I know you're behaving yourself."

"Yeah, that Fritz is the best! He keeps me out of trouble."

* * *

One of the most down to earth, regular guys you will ever meet in wrestling is Steve Corino. He's just a normal guy who happens to be a wrestler. And he's as much a wrestling fan as anyone else. The guy loves the business. He must, considering all the scars he has to show for it. He has put his body through hell, but at the end of the day, he just laughs it off.

Steve is another guy I first met during his time with ECW. He was a guest on several occasions, and we always had a fun time with him. I kept running into him at various local shows he was doing, whether it was with ECW, NWA Florida, or the short-lived Major League Wrestling promotion. We always ended up sitting around at some restaurant late at night talking wrestling, usually about our personal favorite wrestlers and sharing our favorite moments from the past. Plus, we both have a passion for baseball. One thing for certain is that when the "King of Old School" travels, he will always have a Philadelphia Phillies' jersey with him.

Not only did Steve end up working on a somewhat regular basis down in Orlando, but the city is one of his favorite vacation spots. So he ends up coming in studio to be on the show whenever he's in town. It's gotten to the point that I don't have to even ask him if he plans to do the show. He just lets me know when he'll be in the area, and we plan for him to join us. In fact, we just refer to Steve as the "special cohost of *Between the Ropes*," since he has been in studio on so many occasions.

One thing you will always get with Steve, both on and off the air, are plenty of laughs. He has a tremendous sense of humor and does not mind throwing someone under the bus to get a laugh. Some of those jokes have come back to bite him in the rear end, too.

Near the end of ECW, Steve was a guest on the show and we talked about Missy Hyatt, who made an appearance on one of ECW's pay-per-views. Steve, like many other long-time fans, fantasized about Missy during her early years in wrestling, when she was one of the hottest women in the business. She was simply spectacular. However, age has caught up with her over the years, and she is no longer the smoking hottie she once was.

So, when we asked Steve about getting the chance to work with Missy, he said he was disappointed, and went into detail about why she fell way below his expectations. Well, Missy had a friend who lived in Central Florida who had tuned in to the show that week and decided to fill her in on what was said. And let's just say Missy was not happy. A few months later, Missy and Steve worked at the same independent show, and she gave him an earful about his comments. They've both worked it out since then, but it made for some good laughs on air.

I do know one thing, make that one person, who truly gets under Steve's skin — Keanu Reeves. Years ago, he got acquainted with the movie star while in Los Angeles, and happened to be at a restaurant with one of Keanu's ex-girlfriends. Well, Mr. Matrix did not like it, and decided to share his feelings with Steve right there and then. Things got a bit physical, and Keanu broke out his kung-fu skills and went medieval on Steve, punking him out in public! I don't think Steve has gotten over it to this day.

Actually, their encounter was much ado about nothing and the two never really came to blows. But the inside joke is busting Steve about how he got beat up by Keanu. He can't stand the guy, and refuses to watch any of his movies. That's holding a grudge!

There are plenty of other stories regarding Steve, some true and some not so true. Like the time Steve was driving through the mountains from Nashville to the Carolinas, and had not slept in a couple of days. To help the time pass and to stay awake, he decided to talk with another person in his car. The only problem was, he was alone! Yes, he had an entire conversation with an imaginary person — true story.

Another story involves the time that Steve, while he was the ECW World Heavyweight Champion, decided to show off his title belt at his local mall. As people would pass by, he would stop them, shake hands, and introduce himself — a true people's champion. Unfortunately, that story is not true, but I had heard rumors and asked him about it one time on the show. We still get a good chuckle out of that one, and I think Steve wishes it was true.

Steve has a true passion for the sport of professional wrestling and takes his work very seriously. He is a throwback, and I can only imagine how successful he could have been in the NWA during the mid-1980s. I just hope Steve's body can hold up considering all the punishment he has put himself through. He has worked so many stiff matches, from his time in ECW to various independent shows to his work in Japan. The guy has gotten the crap kicked out of himself around the globe! I just want to make sure Steve can enjoy a good life once he decides to hang up his wrestling boots.

STEVE CORINO: I have to first start off and say that Brian Fritz is a no-good liar! I never got punked out by that no-talent hack Keanu Reeves. Okay, maybe a little. But it is something he has brought up for five years now, and it never gets old.

I love coming on *Between the Ropes* and, if I lived in Orlando, I would probably beg Brian to let me be a part of it more. So I just kind of muscle my way on when I am in town.

When I met Brian in the ECW, he just had this laid-back coolness to him, and we hit it off right away. He is the type of guy that will do anything for you and I would do anything for him.

And of course, he still gets me in trouble every time I am on the show. Luckily for me, Missy Hyatt forgave me, but she still brings it up every once in a while!

Lastly, for the rumor about me wearing the ECW World Heavyweight title belt around the mall, that isn't true. But me and Brian are thinking about taking the AWA World Heavyweight Title and walking around Disney World with it!

* * *

Speaking of down-to-earth people, Pat "Simon Diamond" Kenney is another guy who comes to mind. He can talk anything from wrestling to sports to politics without skipping a beat, and is damn funny in the process. If that isn't enough, he's a huge Notre Dame fan. He lives, sleeps, breathes, and bleeds the Fighting Irish, which is fine by me. I'm a big Notre Dame fan as well, but I've got nothing on his passion for the school. Not only does he subscribe to the *Blue and Gold Newsletter*, which covers Notre Dame athletics, but he knows exactly when it will be coming in the mail each week, and will meet the mailman so he can break that bad boy open and read it from beginning to end.

Simon knows his Notre Dame sports, but he also loves all college football and the recruiting process of universities signing players from high school. He keeps up with all of it like an expert. In fact, when I hosted a high school football radio program on Saturday mornings, on several occasions I was joined by recruiting expert Pat Kenney of the *Blue Chip Illustrated*. Yes, Simon Diamond, incognito, from a fictitious publication.

For the past five years, Simon has appeared on *Between the Ropes* just before the college football season for an annual Notre Dame preview show. He runs down everything, including the roster, team schedule, and anything else that comes to mind. He also offers his prediction for the team's final record, which we always bust his balls about when he's dead wrong. Mind you, a lot of the show's regular listeners get really pissed off that we do this each year, screaming that they want us to just talk wrestling. But it's something fun we like to do to break up the monotony. The segment only lasts ten minutes, but that's enough to raise the ire of many listeners.

We also love to chat about baseball, whether it's Major League Baseball or the semi-pro team Simon plays for. Most people don't realize that Simon was almost a professional baseball player before going into wrestling.

To me, Simon is another underutilized talent when it comes to pro wrestling. He's a good-looking guy (not that I'm into dudes!) who can wrestle and talk. All he needs is an opportunity. At the

Fritz and Fighting Irish fanatic Simon Diamond

same time, Simon is not into politics, and does not want to go around tooting his own horn to earn a push. He enjoys wrestling and is good at what he does, but he doesn't need it. Simon lives a great life now, and simply wrestles as much or as little as he wants. And yes, I do call him Simon.

> **SIMON DIAMOND:** I met Fritz when I was in ECW. He was always a good guy and was able to speak sports, especially Notre Dame, which instantly "gets you over" in my book! He invited me on the show several times in ECW, then came up with a great concept. He had an idea several years ago where I would come on the show and talk about the upcoming Notre Dame football season. It went really well and I loved it. I would love to be a sports announcer, get paid for talking sports . . . are you kidding? I can't imagine the listeners of a wrestling radio show enjoying it too much, but I talk wrestling way too much anyway!
>
> Last year, Fritz joined myself and Jerry Lynn (one of my drinking team buddies) at TGI Fridays in Orlando for the Notre Dame vs. Tennessee game. Notre Dame upset the Vols and won 13-7 . . . at Tennessee! What made it even better was the fact my bosses, Jerry and Jeff Jarrett, are from Tennessee and big UT fans, and Red Stripe, my second favorite beer, was only $2 that day! Needless to say a Notre Dame upset combined with about twelve Red Stripe equals instant laughs. Fritz's poor friend Chris, who was a Notre Dame hater, had to bear the brunt of my jokes. Poor Fritz had to sit next to me and be my tackling dummy every time Notre Dame made a big play. It was all in good fun, and Fritz was a great sport about it.

* * *

One of our first listeners and earliest supporters within the wrestling industry was "The Voice of ECW," Joey Styles. In late 1998, Joey had heard about our show from the Internet and wanted to come on to promote the next ECW pay-per-view. I had to quickly let him down, since we already had a guest booked for the show. To say that set him back a little would be an understatement. I don't think Joey expected to hear me say we were too busy to have him on. But he took it in stride and came on a week later. In the end, he was a good sport and has always been a great guest on the show. In fact, Joey was one of our most-listened-to guests from our early shows, something I know he doesn't mind bragging about. Hey, I don't mind him bragging about it either.

> **JOEY STYLES:** Of the countless wrestling radio shows I had the pleasure of appearing on during my time with ECW, Brian Fritz's *Between the Ropes* was always my favorite. For whatever reason, I never felt like a guest, but rather like a cohost. With all the years I have known Fritz, you would think a guy living in Orlando for years would have made a few connections and helped me save a few bucks at those Disney theme parks. Now I know why that friggin' mouse is always smiling. I alone made that rodent rich! His suits are now nicer than mine!

TNA

TNA's Ultimate X

Chapter 31

The professional wrestling monopoly known as the World Wrestling Federation remained in full force as the calendar turned to 2002. Along with the ashes from the demise of WCW and ECW came dozens of displaced performers, most of whom had spent their entire adult lives in the wrestling industry. The WWF cherry-picked their share of free agent talent, leaving many more on the outside looking in. Fans were also out in the cold, as their viewing options were limited to one sports entertainment product.

Pro wrestling needed competition. Not just for wrestlers to be gainfully employed, not just for fans to enjoy an alternative product to watch, but for the health of the industry as a whole. Wrestling thrived under a no-holds-barred war as promotions attempted to outdo each other week after week for the fleeting attention of millions of fans. Without it, a malaise of staleness and monotony was a certainty.

While the rumor mill churned out ideas on which mogul would start the next great promotion to battle Vince McMahon and the WWF, the only real attempt came from an unlikely source — former WCW World Heavyweight Champion and WWF superstar Jeff Jarrett. A contractual dispute with the WWF before his jump to WCW in 1999 put Jarrett on the outs with McMahon. His future in the business became nonexistent as soon as McMahon completed his purchase of WCW in 2001. With nowhere to go, Jarrett devised a plan to launch his own professional wrestling organization.

Promoting wrestling was in the Jarrett bloodlines. His father, Jerry, operated successfully on a regional basis in and around

Tennessee for nearly three decades. Believing in the premise that the disenfranchised wrestling fan, who had grown tired of the WWF, wanted a new option, the younger Jarrett went to work.

The Jarrett product didn't aspire to threaten the WWF's empire. Jeff was wise enough to avoid a battle with a billion-dollar corporation he would no doubt quickly lose.

> **JEFF JARRETT:** It's a joke to even consider a bidding war with Vince McMahon. His stock speaks for itself. He's a publicly traded company. It is a true David vs. Goliath story.

Instead, Jarrett tackled a different opponent. He wanted to revolutionize the way wrestling was presented to the masses on television. As opposed to using a weekly television show to entice fans to buy tickets and order pay-per-view events, Jarrett chose to eschew the costly overhead associated with producing a national cable television series, and instead deliver his brand of controlled mayhem exclusively on pay-per-view.

> **JEFF JARRETT:** I basically thought to myself, "What is the next step? Where is the next evolution? Where is this business going?" Because over the years, I've seen it change drastically. In the '70s, it was a one-hour show on a local VHF station. And in the late '90s, two hours on prime time on the USA Network and two hours prime time on TNT. It's come so far over the years, and I was wondering is there another reincarnation, so to speak, of a national wrestling company, a traditional company? We explored those options and looked at it, and basically, it wasn't really feasible. It wasn't worth the gamble to do a traditional wrestling company. Nothing ever goes back. In sports, they're never going to take the three-point shot away in basketball. They're not going to revert back to how the game used to be played. Everything is evolution. Everything is going to change. I just saw this next step as an evolution in the business.
>
> Is it before its time? Who knows? I don't think so. And the reason I don't think so is that in the '70s in television, you had CBS, ABC, and NBC. And the next thing you know, you had a small UHF channel and then another one, and then FOX comes along. Everyone is saying there are too many TV

stations. It's never going to work. They can't survive. And the next thing you know there's cable television. And the people said that people will not pay to watch TV. Well, there's not a house in America now that doesn't have cable TV. Then the next thing, Ted Turner came along and said he's going to make an all-news channel. CNN rewrote the history books. And then you have MTV — music all day, ESPN — sports all day. And the list goes on and on. And then you have HBO. So on top of paying your basic cable, you're going to pay an extra charge to get HBO. And then you get another movie channel, and another, so you have three or four additional fees on your cable bill. Then you have a pay-per-view once a month. What we're doing is the next progression, as we see it, in the way viewing habits are. We're in a society that wants what they want, when they want, now, immediately, instant gratification. TNA is designed to do exactly that.

The Jarrett business model was unique to say the least. On paper, the concept seemed simple. For a nominal fee each week, fans would be treated to two hours of nonstop pro wrestling action free from commercials and the restraints of broadcast television. By utilizing established veteran wrestlers available on the open market, Jarrett had the hook to lure fans into sampling his weekly pay-per-view events. Once he captured the viewer's attention, the mix of well-known wrestlers with a new generation of fresh talent and well-written, compelling storylines would induce fans to tune in on pay-per-view every seven days.

MIKE TENAY: You can no longer go back to the 1960s, '70s, and '80s style of wrestling. The people have been educated to a different brand. I think the TNA promotion is going to provide the best of both worlds. We're going to respect that history, and at the same time we're going to have a real cutting-edge program with some very interesting storylines.

JEFF JARRETT: We want to make our Wednesday night TNA an exclusive show. We're not going to be oversaturated. We're going to be two hours on Wednesday nights of must-see TV, and give compelling storylines, drama, action, comedy, some brutality, a love story, certainly plenty of T&A. That's how we plan to capture them.

But the key was the hook. Under traditional wrestling business methods, the promoter relied on the free television program, no matter how big or small, to create feuds and matches to ultimately sell on pay-per-view. By forgoing the traditional television avenue, Jarrett faced the daunting task of convincing fans to plunk down cash every week for an unproven product.

> **JEFF JARRETT:** The business at its core is never going to change. In the seventies, how did you get people to come down to the matches on a weekly basis? There were twenty-two, twenty-three regional promotions, regional territories twenty or thirty years ago, and they had matches at the Tampa Armory every Friday night. They had matches at the Louisville Gardens every Tuesday night. They had matches at the Memphis Mid-South Coliseum every Monday night. It was a weekly event. Wrestling in the '80s became a weekly event on TBS. It was on cable, and people were paying for programming then. In the late '80s, you had one pay-per-view a year, and they went to two to four to five, and then you had one a month. In the late '90s, you had WCW doing twelve pay-per-views a year, WWF doing twelve pay-per-views a year, and ECW doing six to seven to eight pay-per-views a year. And they're all making money. Wrestling is that magical form of entertainment. It's not a maybe, it's a proven point. The wrestling fans are very loyal and very passionate, and they will pay for good programming.

Long before Jarrett could contemplate booking his first show, he faced the same roadblocks as all start-up companies, none bigger than money. After all, the WWF conducted close to half a billion dollars in business each year. WCW operated under the auspices of the AOL–Time Warner conglomerate. ECW, even with its limited resources and shoestring budget, had its share of corporate investors. Without the proper funding, Jarrett wouldn't last past week two. He needed help, and there was no better person to consult than his own flesh and blood.

Chapter 32

After thirty-eight years in the business as a wrestler and promoter, Jerry Jarrett had seen it all and done it all. In the days of regional wrestling, Jarrett made his name as a promoter by surviving for decades through cost cutting and conservative spending. His Tennessee office was one of the last to succumb to the national WWF and WCW powerhouses. Jarrett bounced around in his final years in the business. He had been handpicked by Vince McMahon to run the WWF had McMahon been incarcerated by the federal government for conspiracy charges related to steriod distribution in 1994. He also bid to purchase WCW in 2001, but pulled the offer after the Turner networks cancelled all wrestling programming. Jerry transitioned out of wrestling, using his business acumen to launch a profitable real estate development and construction company, Jarrett Construction, in his home state. But after a few conversations with his son, the wrestling bug returned.

JEFF JARRETT: I really think that's part of the good mix that I see. He [Jerry Jarrett] has wisdom and nothing replaces wisdom. He's been down the road. He's made his bumps, he's made his bruises, and he's survived them. More than anything, his wisdom has come into play. He was finished with the business. He had gone into other businesses — real estate development, commercial development, commercial construction. He had definitely segued into a different type of business. Once I started throwing the ideas out there, and me and him and others would discuss this plan from its very genesis, he had his doubts. But as one thing led to another and to another, he saw it coming together.

The Jarretts dubbed their pay-per-view-only product Total Nonstop Action, the initials a play on words suggesting the risqué areas of the female anatomy. The father-and-son tandem took to the task of acquiring sufficient funding for the TNA project. They both planned to invest portions of their personal fortunes, but it would take considerably more than that to absorb the early losses and stay in the game for the long haul. The Jarretts pitched their intriguing concept to investors, banks, country musicians, NASCAR drivers, and anyone else with deep pockets who would listen. Their first breakthrough came with a local Tennessee bank, thanks to a personal referral from their corporate lawyer. Luckily for the Jarretts, executives from SunTrust Bank were avid pro wrestling fans, and the bank was immediately receptive to backing the risky venture. They agreed to loan $1.1 million to J Sports & Entertainment, TNA's parent company, and furnish a $400,000 letter of credit to InDemand, the leading cable pay-per-view provider in the country and a crucial partner to the success of the weekly wrestling series. TNA seemed to be well on its way.

On the wrestling side, the Jarretts amassed a team to run its key activities, most of them ex-WCW employees. Bob Ryder handled talent relations and travel arrangements. Keith Mitchell was brought in to oversee television production. Former WCW color commentator Mike Tenay, Don West, a baseball-card shill on a shop-at-home television network, and former WWF and WCW creative writer Ed Ferrara were responsible for commentary, while Jeremy Borash conducted on-air interviews and did the ring announcing. Jay Hassman and Len Sabal were hired to negotiate pay-per-view agreements and spread the word about TNA to the cable and pay-per-view industry. When it came to creating story-lines and booking matches, Jeff and Jerry wrote the majority of the early shows, but also sought assistance from a controversial figure, Vince Russo. It was Russo who'd helped reinvigorate the WWF in the late '90s by ratcheting up the violence, swearing, and sexual content in his form of "crash TV." Yet, Russo's reputation took a massive nosedive after he jumped to WCW with Ferrara and became a significant factor in the company's ultimate downfall. Jeff went to bat to bring Russo aboard the TNA ship, but Jerry balked after seeing how Russo exposed himself as a fraud in WCW. Russo was eventually brought in and his distinctive style made an immediate impact.

> **JEFF JARRETT:** It's no secret that me and him go back many, many years. Vince has always been a very creative guy. He gets out of bounds a lot of times, but nobody can tell me that isn't what this product doesn't need. It's up to my father to keep him inbounds. There's probably a real good combination. Everybody knows his WCW track and his WWF track. He wrote television in the WWF heyday, and had segments over the 8.0's [Nielsen ratings], entire two-hour shows over the 7.0's twice, a multitude of 6.0's. I think there are a lot of things if you roll them up into a ball — the concept of a two-hour pay-per-view, the program can literally be total nonstop action. Russo will bring his element to the table of character development to the show. And the booking and structure of the show, that's what my dad made a living at for many years and that's his forte. That's how I think we can be more successful.

> **VINCE RUSSO:** Being a wrestling fan first and foremost, I would much rather watch a company that is going to try new things and try to revolutionize the business than a company that does the same old, same old. I'm not afraid to take chances. Yeah, some of them are going to work, and some of them aren't going to work. But the reality is the business needs to evolve in order to stay relevant. Right now, with Jeff and TNA, we're taking a lot of chances. I'd rather watch a product that is on the cutting edge and trying to shake things up and do new things and take a new approach than see the same things I've seen for thirty years.

While the creative issues involving Russo would be a problem for the Jarretts, they quickly encountered more pressing fires to extinguish. Less than six weeks after their first meeting, SunTrust Bank backed out of their investment deal. Citing Jerry's reluctance to personally sign for the cash flow loan, which may or may not have been the true factor, SunTrust opted to reverse its position on the loan request. The bombshell left the Jarretts and TNA in a precarious position, with their first event only two months away. Without the loan, there was a good chance that InDemand would cancel their fifty-two-week commitment and TNA would never see the light of day.

Two weeks of scrambling and hastily scheduled meetings finally resulted in positive vibes, following a conversation between Jeff and Richard Scrushy of HealthSouth, the national healthcare service provider based in Birmingham, Alabama. Scrushy, the CEO and founder, expressed an interest in becoming an equity partner in the TNA project. He followed up by securing the $400,000 letter of credit for InDemand, and funding the $1.1 million cash flow loan in exchange for a fifteen percent share of the company.

With the financial situation ironed out for the time being, the Jarretts geared up for their initial weekly pay-per-view telecast — Wednesday night, June 19, 2002, from Huntsville, Alabama. Although word had already leaked out among wrestling insiders, the company officially made the announcement in a May 10 press release. For $9.95, fans could enjoy two hours of the alternative TNA product every Wednesday night. TNA hyped the value of its eight hours of pay-per-view wrestling per month for under forty dollars compared to merely three hours of action for thirty-five dollars from the WWF, since renamed WWE. TNA also announced an affiliation with the National Wrestling Alliance to use the tradition of the NWA initials, and the NWA World Heavyweight and World Tag-Team Championships. The company also introduced a third title — the TNA X Division Championship — for more athletic, high-flying wrestlers.

> **AJ STYLES:** I think the X Division will be awesome, because the guys they are going to use throughout the tapings are the guys you're used to seeing on the independents, the good ones — Low Ki, Christopher Daniels, American Dragon. Those kinds of guys that you're going to see that have been all over the States and all over the world. These are the guys you're going to see throughout TNA. Total Nonstop Action, that's what they want. They're going to try to get the entertainment side of it, the Japanese side of it, and whatever other side there is in wrestling, they're going to try to hit.

The Phenomenal AJ Styles goes after Samoa Joe

You never get a second chance to make a first impression. The Jarretts had been around the block and knew the long-term success of TNA would hinge significantly on the inaugural event. A great show would bring viewers back. A bad show could drive them away for good, and drive the Jarretts to bankruptcy. It was imperative for TNA to make an impact, and they banked on stars from the past and undiscovered talent of the future to bring eyeballs to the television sets. The Jarretts contacted every major free agent of wrestling's past and present for the June 19 date. Some — like Sting, "Macho Man" Randy Savage, The Ultimate Warrior, and Scott Steiner — expressed interest, but played hardball in the end. Others — Ken Shamrock, Scott Hall, Buff Bagwell, and Rick Steiner — jumped at the chance for a payday and another chance at national stardom. New talent, including a high-flying Georgia wrestler named AJ Styles, and former NFL Super Bowl participant Monty Brown, added to the roster. And on top was the boss himself, Jeff Jarrett.

> **MIKE TENAY:** I think TNA is providing an alternate promotion to WWE at this point. And I think when you do that, you have to acquire the bigger name wrestlers that are available. The Scott Halls, the Rick Steiners, the Buff Bagwells, the Jeff Jarretts. So in doing so, maybe you attract that audience. Now when you have that audience, what you need to do is create new stars. I think that by having an AJ Styles, a Low Ki, bringing in Jerry Lynn — allowing them to run free in the cruiserweight division, along with some new heavyweights they have lined up, I think it gives them that opportunity to shine in front of a major league audience. But I think you need to have that big name talent out there.

To cut costs, the plan was to run two shows in one night, with the first one airing live and the second on tape the following Wednesday. Wrestlers were free to work elsewhere, except WWE, on the weekends for different independent groups to supplement their incomes.

> **ED FERRARA:** It's a beautiful schedule. It's a beautiful schedule for the boys, too. It's two tapings per month. It's every other week. It's Wednesday night. We'll be live, and then we're going to tape the next week's show after the live show. As far as the boys go, they can then go and work for anyone they want to. It's almost like the old territory thing. It allows the boys to get

the national exposure that they need and that they deserve, and then go off and work for whoever they want up until our next show, and then come back and work for us. If they don't want to work, they don't have to. And they don't have to be on the road 250 days out of the year, living out of a car and sleeping at Red Roof Inns.

Star wrestlers, such as Hall and Shamrock, earned upwards of $7,500 per show with TNA, while enhancement talent took home little more than three figures for the night's work. Between production, talent, and overhead costs, TNA budgeted 50,000 pay-per-view buys as the break-even point. Chances were good that the debut event would reach that mark, but it would take exceptional shows to maintain the momentum.

Chapter 33

The journey commenced on June 19 at the 7,000-seat Von Braun Civic Center in Huntsville. Ticket sales were downright poor as only 500 people spent money to attend in person. Since the company's main revenue stream was pay-per-view, ticket sales, or the lack thereof, were not a major problem. But being the maiden show to a virgin audience, TNA needed butts in the seats to create an exciting, live-event atmosphere for the audience at home. The company conducted considerable grassroots marketing the week of the show to paper the crowd with enough free tickets to present a respectable house. All told, 4,000 fans witnessed the dawn of a new era in wrestling and pay-per-view programming.

Perhaps an omen for the future, Total Nonstop Action's first extravaganza came to an abrupt stop minutes before the live broadcast started. The ring broke during a pre-show match, causing the crew to scramble to make repairs while the show was rewritten on the fly. A special legends ceremony away from the ring opened the show, giving the crew time to fix the malfunction. The opening match of the TNA era showcased the company's calling card — the X Division. In a six-man tag, Jimmy Yang, Sonny Siaki, and Jorge Estrada toppled Jerry Lynn, AJ Styles, and Low Ki in a fast-paced, high-flying six-and-a-half-minute contest. Midway through the show, fans were treated to a performance from country music star Toby Keith, and appearances by NASCAR drivers Sterling Marlin and Hermie Sadler.

ED FERRARA: It's a very calculated choice and I think it's a very smart choice. We're going for a cross-promotional type deal with NASCAR with

Sterling Marlin. There's a huge crossover audience between professional wrestling and NASCAR, which is like the biggest thing since sliced bread. Then you've got Toby Keith, who's a huge country star, and there you've got a big crossover audience. But I don't want people to think that this is going to be just a southern, country-western, race-car-driving promotion, because it's not. This is just for the first event. We're going to have other celebrities on future shows, and it's not going to be just country music. We're going to have some rock stars. We might have some rap stars. We're trying to appeal to the broadest fanbase possible, and for our premiere show, we're going for the gusto where we know there is a huge crossover audience.

The night climaxed with the Gauntlet for the Gold, a twenty-man battle royal style match to determine a new NWA World Heavyweight Champion. A blend of the aforementioned familiar names coupled with former WCW and WWE mid-card wrestlers, from Konnan and Lash LeRoux, to Brian Christopher and Ron "K-Krush" Killings, and newcomers Prince Justice, Del Rios, and Chris Harris came in and went out for over thirty minutes. In the end, former UFC and WWE superstar Ken Shamrock squared off with Malice, a near seven-footer with potential who had competed as The Wall in the dying days of WCW. Shamrock negotiated a belly-to-belly suplex on his much larger foe to earn the three count to capture the prestigious NWA World Title as part of Total Nonstop Action.

With the positives of the first night came several negatives, starting with The Johnsons, an independent tag-team from Florida dressed in flesh-colored bodysuits made to resemble penises. Then there were The Dupps, a backwoods, hillbilly family who enjoyed picking at various crevices of their bodies. Let's not forget The Rainbow Express, a homosexual tag team comprised of Lenny and Bruce who kissed each other on the lips as means of tagging into the ring.

TNA's debut garnered mostly positive reviews from the wrestling community, with the X Division dominating most of the critical acclaim. But did TNA do enough to convince fans to spend $9.95 the next week, and the week after, and the week after that? The pay-per-views numbers would answer that question, but it would take patience. A fundamental issue with the TNA business plan concerned the time it took for InDemand to calculate accurate buyrate information (usually several weeks) and pay programmers (usually several months). The company continued on with its weekly broadcasts while waiting to learn of the success of their venture.

TNA plugged along with its weekly pay-per-views, alternating between live and taped shows. Fan reaction continued to be mostly positive. AJ Styles became the first X Division Champion in the main event of the second show by beating Jerry Lynn, Low Ki, and Mexican star Psicosis in a four-way double-elimination match. For the July 3 show, TNA ran in Nashville, Tennessee, at the Municipal Auditorium. Live paid attendance was double that of Huntsville, with 2000 fans packing the smaller venue. Styles claimed his second championship by winning the NWA World Tag-Team Titles in a tournament with partner Jerry Lynn. Jeff Jarrett spent the majority of the first few shows working with Scott Hall, while several NASCAR personalities remained involved. But the X Division and the high quality matches it provided on a regular basis remained TNA's signature.

> **JERRY LYNN:** It's awesome, because there's so much tremendous talent out there on the indie scene, and they're trying to find out who the top workers are out there across the country and give them a chance to come and showcase their talents in the X Division. It's sort of like the X Games version of wrestling. We're going to try to use the X Division to show the extreme style of wrestling.

> **VINCE RUSSO:** One of the things that has definitely worked without question is the work ethic of these young guys, most notably the X Division. These guys, and probably the average age being about twenty-four years old, are reinventing the business on a daily basis. Right before my eyes, I'm seeing things that I haven't seen in thirty plus years as a wrestling fan. I respect these guys so much for this, because they're trying to put an effort into coming up with a style that nobody has ever seen before. I pat these guys on the back, and that's why I wouldn't trade in the world working for anybody else. These are the guys I want to be working with.

The country musicians and NASCAR drivers couldn't draw any mainstream press, but an impromptu angle on the July 10 event involving Jeff Jarrett and members of the NFL's Tennessee Titans got TNA some publicity on *ESPN SportsCenter* and in *USA Today*. The company needed to parlay that attention into pay-per-view buys. The figures for the early shows still remained a mystery, as conflicting reports flew back and forth. TNA soon got to the bottom of the situation and that's where they found their pay-per-view agents, Jay Hassman and Len Sabal. The Jarretts, Jerry especially, expressed great skepticism about Hassman's work, particularly after the first face-to-face meeting with InDemand. Their fears were confirmed in a conversation with Frank Romano of InDemand, who found that Hassman had been reporting fraudulent pay-per-view numbers to TNA. Hassman had sent bogus e-mails to the Jarretts claiming they were from InDemand. He also used the InDemand logo on forged flash reports with buyrate numbers significantly higher than legitimate projections.

Hassman informed the company that the first three events had drawn approximately 175,000 buys, and the Jarretts continued to budget accordingly. In actuality, the real number was close to 50,000 in aggregate, which put TNA deep in the hole after less than a month on the air. Hassman's deception continued with lies to InDemand about his relationship with TNA. A cursory investigation revealed that Hassman had maintained employment with Team Services, a marketing company that handled WWE's pay-per-view account. Hassman had told InDemand that he would give up the TNA account to Sabal to avoid a conflict of interest. Instead of informing TNA, he pretended to continue to act as their agent, cashing $10,000 monthly paychecks along the way.

JEFF JARRETT: We basically got the bomb dropped on us on July 10. We were definitely blindsided, but there were a couple of things leading up to the 10th that definitely made us question certain aspects of the marketing side of our product.

We're in 39 million homes, and that is InDemand and DirecTV. We were assured on numerous occasions that we would be in over 50 million homes. Of course, we weren't. We're lacking in distribution on one front. We did know and were assured that our marketing was going to be much broader based, and it wasn't.

Jay worked for us — solely for us, it was our understanding. We found out later he did not work solely for us, he worked for other companies and other agents of other companies. We're not real sure the amount of damage that has been done.

The depths and the steps that were taken that are without a doubt, very clear-cut and very concise, and very exact in some of the deliberate actions taken. It blows my mind.

TNA immediately set the wheels in motion for legal action against Hassman and Sabal, including contacting the U.S. Attorney's office while also exploring the possibility that there was covert sabotage by WWE considering Hassman's affiliation with Team Services. But Hassman's deception may have caused irreparable damages to the company. On top of the heavy losses through three shows, InDemand had done little to no advertising for TNA on its 1,900 cable systems, many of them unaware TNA even existed. Hassman also lied about negotiations with Cablevision systems in New York and the Dish Network satellite provider. Neither offered TNA pay-per-views because neither was ever contacted. With the future bleak, the Jarretts switched into desperation mode. To stop the bleeding, they drastically began to axe costs. Everyone from wrestlers and office workers to production and lighting companies took pay cuts or were let go. The company moved its live events into the smaller 1,500 seat Nashville Fairgrounds on a permanent basis to avoid touring expenses. The Jarretts slashed the budget to $75,000 per week with the hope of generating time to build the buyrates. Around the same time, the Jarretts internally began discussing a shift from their strictly pay-per-view strategy to finding a national television outlet to promote the Wednesday night shows.

Throughout the Hassman-Sabal scandal, TNA continuously updated HealthSouth on the status of their investment. The corporation stood behind the wrestling promotion for several weeks, then suddenly dropped another bombshell on the already wounded organization. In mid-August, HealthSouth decided to pull out of the project, effective immediately. The shocking news left the Jarretts stunned and reassessing their personal and professional financial futures. HealthSouth now claimed the project was too risky, and became agitated when word leaked out to the public about their relationship with TNA. The Jarretts surmised that CEO Richard Scrushy, who brokered the deal using company funds, had failed to obtain approval from the corporate board of directors and called for the pullout fearing potential reprisals. The Jarretts did their best to stall for time to find a replacement. They threatened to file for personal bankruptcy, which would have left HealthSouth holding the bag for the $1.1 million loan and the $400,000 letter of credit with InDemand. The threat worked and HealthSouth agreed to fund a final $150,000, inexplicably in exchange for another twenty-five percent stake in the company, to allow TNA time to locate new investors and keep the company afloat. The Jarretts planned to tape two shows on August 21, with the second to air on the 28th, a *Best of the X Division* special on September 4, and a week off on September 11 to remember the one-year anniversary of the national tragedy. This left them with one month to find enough money to carry on their dream.

Chapter 34

Meetings with banks, corporations, and personal investors proved fruitless, but a routine staff meeting with the company's publicist would potentially save the day. Jeff had hired Trifecta Entertainment, a Nashville public relations firm run by a young woman named Dixie Carter.

> **DIXIE CARTER:** I was asked to take a meeting with a group of people who were starting an upstart wrestling company. It had been presented to me by the president of Monterey Talent, which is a huge booking agency that does a lot of rock groups and country groups and things such as that. I took the meeting and heard a vision that I was very, very impressed with. I knew it had tremendous potential, and was hired on to handle the whole marketing, promotions, PR side of the company. I started with the company months before it started, about five or six months before we launched our first show in Huntsville, and slowly became more and more involved.

After updating her on the company's status, Jeff asked Dixie to contact him if she knew of any possible investors. Within days, Dixie surprised Jeff with encouraging news. Dixie's father, unbeknownst to anyone in TNA, owned Panda Energy International, a Dallas, Texas–based energy company specializing in the electric power industry. Bob Carter, Dixie's father, acted as CEO and Chairman of the Board, while her siblings held top management positions. Dixie revealed that her father followed the TNA pay-per-views and felt the Jarretts presented a solid product. She arranged for a meeting in Dallas to discuss Panda Energy buying into TNA.

DIXIE CARTER: Jeff had come to me and said, "This is the situation, but we're going to be looking for additional investors. I feel confident we're going to find something." I believed in the product enough to take it to somebody who I knew is an outside-the-box thinking person. I knew the industry only had one competitor in it who had a 100 million dollar plus market cap, but a few short years ago there were two competitors in the business and it was thriving. I really believed that there was something there. I took it to them and it's been really good, a good investment.

In early September, the Jarretts flew to Dallas to meet with the Carters and Panda's key officers at company headquarters. The day-long discussions went so well that Panda flew the TNA contingent home on the private corporate jet. Following several days of follow-up conversations and due diligence, Panda sent their offer sheet. In exchange for fifty-one percent of TNA and extricating HealthSouth from the picture, the Carters agreed to fund the letter of credit to InDemand, repay the final $150,000 loan from HealthSouth, and loan money for each new show thereafter. But they also felt HealthSouth should assume responsibility for the original $1.1 million loan. Panda would control the board of directors for TNA and create a dual presidency with a Panda choice and a Jarrett choice. The Jarretts were anxious to accept, but approval from HealthSouth, in the midst of a company downturn following the indictment of Richard Scrushy in a $2.7 billion conspiracy and fraud scheme, would be a stumbling block.

HealthSouth demanded control of Jeff and Jerry's remaining stock in TNA in exchange for assuming the $1.1 million loan. Panda refused a partnership with HealthSouth. They advised the Jarretts to inform HealthSouth that they had pulled out of the deal, in an attempt to call HealthSouth's bluff. With Panda out and the Jarretts filing for bankruptcy, HealthSouth would be on the hook for $1.65 million and potential lawsuits for $1.3 million in unpaid contracts. Realizing the potential consequences, HealthSouth blinked. They asked for only a portion of stock to try to recoup their $1.1 million. Panda agreed to offer five percent of the company, but now would not reimburse the $150,000 loan. HealthSouth's stock would also be capped at $1.25 million (the total of the original investment) with no voting rights and a provision that they could never sell their shares. After vicious rounds of negotiations, HealthSouth and Panda approved the terms on September 6. Panda now controlled TNA, and the Jarretts were absolved of personal financial liability. When the deal closed and stock transfers were completed, Panda controlled fifty-six percent of the TNA, the Jarretts owned thirty-nine percent, and HealthSouth held five percent.

With the future bright and its financial woes behind them, TNA relaunched, so to speak, on September 18. Dixie Carter and Chris Sobol from Panda stuck around as liaisons to help with the business end and file reports back to Dallas. Panda upped the budget to $90,000 per show, mainly to upgrade production and recruit more name talent. The idea of taped shows every other week was abandoned. Prior to the September 11 hiatus, Ron "The Truth" Killings won the NWA World Title from Ken Shamrock. Killings, who had worked in WWE as K-Kwik under a rapper's gimmick and K-Krush in TNA's early days, stamped his place in history as the first African-American NWA World Champion.

> **RON KILLINGS:** It's an unexplainable feeling. The best way I can tell you is it's a remarkable feeling. It was a surprise to me. But I think I deserved it. I think I paid a lot of dues in this sport. If it came, I think I was man enough to step up to the plate and handle it. I'm grateful to the NWA and I'm grateful to the fans who see me as Ron "The Truth" Killings, the NWA champ. I'm happy to be the champ.

> **KEN SHAMROCK:** I was treated real well by Mr. Jarrett. He pulled me aside and explained to me what they needed to do, because their program was having some problems. They got kind of backstabbed with some pay-per-view with how many buyrates they were getting. I'm not quite sure what the problem was. He sat down and told me they needed to shake things up a little bit and wanted to switch the title. As far I knew, they wanted to hang with me with the title until after the UFC, and then after that we'd go in a different direction. But they had to shake things up a little bit and I was really happy they pulled me aside and talked about it, and I had no problem switching it.

To add some additional star power, Scott Hall and Buff Bagwell were re-signed at lower per-show salaries. Sean Waltman, better known as X-Pac in WWE and Syxx in WCW, made his long-awaited debut as Syxx-Pac, as did Brian James, a.k.a. Road Dogg from WWE, as BG James. TNA made another attempt at celebrity involvement with Dustin Diamond. Yes, the same Dustin Diamond who portrayed Screech in the teen sitcom *Saved by the Bell.* Diamond knocked out a midget timekeeper in a forgettable boxing contest. Forgettable would also be the word to describe the story-line of Bruce, an effeminate character claiming to be Miss TNA Champion. Jerry Jarrett continued to handle the majority of the storyline writing following a falling-out with Vince Russo. Ed Ferrara quit the company over money. The X Division remained the company's bread and butter, with good-to-great matches every week. The X Division Title bounced around from AJ Styles to Low Ki to Jerry Lynn to Syxx-Pac. Chris Harris and James Storm brought stability to the NWA Tag-Team Titles, after winning the vacant straps on the September 18 show.

Behind the scenes, a storm was brewing over creative control of the company. Unbeknownst to Jerry Jarrett, Vince Russo attempted a power play to seize control of storyline booking from Jarrett by privately speaking with Dixie Carter behind the scenes. Russo had tried to sell her on his vision of wrestling and his previous accomplishments with WWE. The tension came to a head at a late October meeting where for several hours Dixie and Russo criticized the company's product under Jerry's watch. Incensed, Jerry walked out and threatened to walk away from the entire project. Had he done so, much of the talent, including Hall, Waltman, Curt Hennig, and Mike Tenay, would have followed, essentially crippling TNA.

SEAN WALTMAN: I missed a shot after I dislocated my hip right at the time the whole power struggle thing with Vince Russo and all that crap was going on. I was in Jerry Jarrett's corner. I have a lot of faith in Jerry as a producer in wrestling. I like him because of his traditional values and his open-mindedness when it comes to knowing that he's a sixty-year-old man, and he's not on the cutting edge of knowing what people like that are eighteen to thirty-five. He'll take people like myself or other people that do know, he'll take our word for things when it comes to that. What Russo stands for is opposite of what I stand for. I think he has spit in the face of everybody that goes out there in the ring and busts their ass.

Jerry later sent a detailed letter to Chris Sobol outlining his vision of wrestling and the weaknesses of others involved in the company, namely Russo. He made it unequivocally clear that he had no intention of working with Russo as a writer. Within a week, Panda made the decision to stick with the Jarretts and follow their vision forward. But the entire incident soured Jerry on Panda's understanding of wrestling and its ability to manage a wrestling company.

Ironically, Russo's attempt to depose Jerry Jarrett's old school concepts of pro wrestling in favor of his "crash TV" style of sports entertainment would become the central TNA storyline by year's end. The angle kicked off with Russo's debut as an on-air talent on the November 26 event. Under a mask, Russo ran out to help Jeff Jarrett capture the NWA World Title from Ron Killings. Battle lines formed among wrestlers supporting Russo's shock-and-awe version of sports entertainment and those believing in the tradition of the National Wrestling Alliance. Russo dubbed his heel group, Sports Entertainment Xtreme, or SEX for short, to challenge the babyface NWA.

CHRISTOPHER DANIELS: I think the thing that people need to understand now is that Vince is playing the character on the television show. It's not like he's behind the scenes making these things happen. I think TNA has taken the advantage. We've played a lot to the hardcore fans and hardcore fans, know what Vince Russo's history is. I think TNA is trying to take advantage of that, and take advantage of the fact that the hardcore fans don't like Vince Russo, and they put him in the position where they made him the leader of the heel group.

Despite overtures and unwanted help from SEX, World Champion Jeff Jarrett remained loyal to the Alliance. Russo built his

The Fallen Angel, Christopher Daniels

troupe with antiestablishment talent, led by Christopher Daniels, Elix Skipper, and Low Ki, collectively known as Triple X. Russo enlisted AJ Styles, BG James, The Harris Brothers, David Flair, Mike Sanders, and X Division Champion Sonny Siaki as well. SEX's crusade against the NWA led to battles with traditionalists Curt Hennig, Jerry Lynn, Ron Killings, Chris Harris, and James Storm, and the NWA World Champion. As Russo and SEX continued to spit in the face of the NWA, legends Rowdy Roddy Piper, "The American Dream" Dusty Rhodes, "The Living Legend" Larry Zbyszko, and The Road Warriors joined the war. "Bullet" Bob Armstrong and J.J. Dillon assumed leadership roles against SEX, while Mike Tenay remained the voice of the NWA on commentary. Russo recruited his own old-school talent in "The Russian Nightmare" Nikita Koloff, and The Rock & Roll Express. By the start of 2003, SEX vs. the NWA had reached fever pitch.

The first major confrontation came on the January 15 event, where Russo laced up the boots in teaming with Triple X to defeat Rhodes, Jarrett, and The Road Warriors when Koloff interfered on behalf of SEX. The following week, Triple X won the NWA World Tag-Team Titles from Harris and Storm, but despite stacked odds, SEX could not dethrone Jarrett, who survived a bloody four-man battle royal against BG James, Don Harris, and Christopher Daniels. The big story came post-match, when Raven, after quitting WWE and walking away from guaranteed money to join TNA, attacked Jarrett. The World Title picture soon revolved around Jarrett and SEX representatives Raven and AJ Styles, who had taken out Larry Zbyszko the previous week.

> **LARRY ZBYSZKO:** It was fun working with the younger guys because they've got the moves. A kid like AJ, and some others, they can fly around with the best of them. But that lost art of psychology and how to make the people go nuts, which means how to motivate them to buy tickets, and also means how to get yourself imbedded as a character. Do they love you or do they hate you? If they love you or hate you, you'll make money. If they don't care, get the hook. I love to do it with them, because I like to take what they don't know and give it to them so they can combine it with what they can do.

On the February 19 pay-per-view, Jarrett successfully defended his belt against Styles. One month later, Raven and Styles did battle in a Ladder Match to determine the number one contender for

Jarrett. With help from fellow SEX member Glen Gilberti, Raven grabbed the contract. Dissention crept into the SEX camp, with Styles pondering his future.

As business heated up in the ring, business behind the scenes remained stable. Attendance was decent, with close to capacity crowds at most shows, although free tickets outnumbered paid tickets by a three-to-one margin. The company had already begun looking into television deals. They hired the former President of the TNN cable network, Brian Hughes, to help open doors in the television industry. The company briefly spoke with officials at WGN, a Chicago-based superstation with national penetration on satellite and some cable systems, but discussions halted at the network's $65,000-per-hour price request. TNA did follow through on producing a weekly syndicated show, TNA *Xplosion*, featuring recaps of the previous week's pay-per-view and first-run matches. *Xplosion* started on tiny local stations in small markets throughout the country, but soon added affiliates in larger markets such as Nashville, Atlanta, Memphis, Pittsburgh, and New York City. Internationally, the company found some additional revenue by selling their shows to television networks in Australia, Asia, and parts of the Middle East. The weekly budget held firm at around $90,000 per week, even with the influx of expensive veteran talent. Politically, Vince Russo's push for creative control escalated by slowly convincing Panda, specifically Dixie Carter, that his vision was superior to that of Jerry Jarrett. Dixie had become the sole liaison for TNA when Panda fired Chris Sobol in March.

As the warm weather of spring and summer arrived, several news faces hit the TNA scene. Former WCW World Champion and WWE superstar Vader, as well as former WWE star D'Lo Brown, came in as major babyfaces for the NWA. AJ Styles had had enough with SEX and turned babyface to feud with his former mates. Several new factions sprouted up throughout the promotion. David Flair broke away from SEX to pair up with Erik Watts and Brian Lawler as a team of second-generation wrestlers called NWA Next Generation. A group of ex-ECW competitors, including The Sandman, New Jack, Perry Saturn, and Justin Credible, worked together. Jim Mitchell's faction of evil, The New Church, stayed prevalent, with Slash and Brian Lee heavily involved in the tag-team picture and Mike Awesome working as a single. The paramount theme continued to be Russo's quest to squash tradition and snatch the title from Jarrett's clutches.

The most highly anticipated match in TNA's brief history took place on April 30, as Raven challenged for the NWA World Title. The largest crowd in company history for the Nashville Fairgrounds (a.k.a. the TNA Asylum) — approximately 1500 fans, with over 1000 more turned away — saw Jarrett retain the gold in a match filled with outside interference. The success of the show from a business standpoint led to a new company mindset of building up major matches over several weeks before delivering. Although not at break-even level yet, pay-per-view buys had climbed over recent months, from the 8,000 to 10,000 range at the end of 2002 to a consistent 10,000 to 12,000 per week. The April 30 event with the well-hyped title match broke all TNA pay-per-view records to that point. The company planned to focus on June 18, TNA's one-year anniversary show, as the next blockbuster event and an opportunity to top the Raven vs. Jarrett numbers.

> **RAVEN:** I think the buildup has been tremendous. A bunch of my buddies were like, "When's this match? What's next?" I was like, "Don't be in a hurry. We're going to tell a story. When we get there, it's going to be much more gratifying if you wait for the story to begin." Let's face it, after three months, now the story begins. I don't think we've done anything to cheat the people. I don't think the people can say you screwed us by not having the match. When I won the title shot, I said, "I'm waiting thirty days. I've got plenty of time. I don't have to do it now. I want to get my forces together." And now, here comes the first match after four months. Now me and Jeff can go another three months easy. You have to know how to top yourself and be creative to do it and have enough psychology that you can keep the people where you want it.

Heading into the anniversary event, the World Title picture involved Jarrett, Raven, Glen Gilberti, AJ Styles, and D'Lo Brown.

On June 4, Jarrett defeated Gilberti in a title match when, of all people, Vince Russo helped the champion retain. The following week, Russo revealed his true colors by smashing Jarrett with a guitar to help AJ Styles win the NWA World Title in a three-way match also involving Raven.

> **AJ STYLES:** It's unbelievable. It's different when you're NWA champ, because it's the oldest. When it comes to history, it's the oldest and it's the best. It's unbelievable. It was a great match. It really was. It came off with a little different ending than most people were expecting, but it doesn't matter. I still have the heavyweight title. A lot of people talk about a rub, and I definitely got a rub tonight. They rubbed the heavyweight title right on me. I'm so stoked about being the NWA World Champion. They're passing me the belt and for them to do that, they're saying that AJ Styles is going to put butts in the seats being the heavyweight champion. To me, that blows my mind.

Perhaps even bigger than the title change and Russo-Styles reconciliation was the announcement of Sting joining TNA. The franchise babyface throughout WCW's entire existence had been on the sidelines since the sale of the company and had agreed to participate in the anniversary event out of respect for Jerry Jarrett, the man who gave Sting his first break in the business.

> **STING:** I have a soft spot in my heart for those guys because Jerry [Jarrett] hired me originally and after he found out how bad we were, Hellwig [a.k.a. The Ultimate Warrior] and me, they finished us up. I remember we were in the Memphis Coliseum in the dressing room. I had separated my shoulder really bad. Hellwig was in the ring, and Jerry Jarrett was in there with me, and he's got his clipboard and he says, "Sting, we have to finish you up." I said, "Finish me up. What does that mean?" He said, "I got to let you go." But he didn't just let us go, he gave us a job. He called Bill Watts and got us booked again. I just felt obligated to him and have a soft spot in my heart with him.

Chapter 35

Few in wrestling felt TNA could survive its first few weeks under the weekly pay-per-view format, let alone a full year. Yet, through perseverance, hard work, and a whole lot of luck, TNA embarked on year two. Despite losing several million in the first twelve months, the company felt optimistic with the backing of Panda Energy.

JEFF JARRETT: We can be real happy and glad of our one-year anniversary, but the fact of the matter is, we're going to be here next Wednesday night starting off year two. That's really what excites me.

We definitely had some unbelievable moments that seemed like the darkest of darkest days. It was almost like a wrestling match. The good guy had those insurmountable odds, but at the end of the day he started that slow build back. That's where we're at. We took some bumps and bruises. We were blindsided and everybody speculated why, why, why? We never sat around and felt sorry for ourselves. We pulled our bootstraps up and came back and tried to kick ass the best we could. Those were some dark days, six or seven months ago, but they are behind us, and we've got great partners and everybody is invested, not just monetarily, but really the effort and the heart and the game plan and the business plan.

The June 18 anniversary event was a good start to year two. Over 1000 fans bought tickets to the show, the largest paid crowd in company history. TNA debuted a new set to sweeten the look of the Asylum. In the main event, Sting, the biggest wrestling star to work for TNA, and Jeff Jarrett pinned NWA World Champion AJ Styles and the returning Syxx-Pac.

JEFF JARRETT: Stinger made his return. Tremendous ovation. Sting is a legend in this business, maybe a new legend, so to speak. He worked on top for years and years and years in WCW. He was the one guy who stayed through it all, never wavered. He's got a heart of gold and we were tickled to death to have him part of our show tonight. He was elated to be here and he could feel the energy just within our dressing room, just within our company, and through our crowd. He told me after the match, "You know Jeff, there's something real special about this." And I couldn't agree with him more.

The show also featured two strong title matches, as Chris Sabin retained the X Division Title against Paul London, while Triple X retained the NWA World Tag-Team Titles against Harris and Storm, now using the moniker America's Most Wanted. The two teams followed with a classic steel-cage rematch the following week, with new champions crowned. Elsewhere, "The Franchise" Shane Douglas, a former ECW World Champion, debuted to work a program with babyface Raven.

SHANE DOUGLAS: I'm on record as being very critical of Ric Flair's career after forty. I would be hypocritical to say it's okay for Shane Douglas at forty-five and still be wrestling in the ring. I do believe that I can still offer a ton of advice and do the things that weren't done for my generation. I don't want to sound like I'm on a soapbox or crying or whining. But we missed out. By we, I mean our generation. We carved out of the business our own place. Steve Austin carved his way. Brian Pillman, God rest his soul, carved his way. Shane Douglas carved his way. It was not handed to us. But along the way, we learned a lot of stuff, and it really made us better prepared to lead dressing rooms. There's a reason Steve Austin is seen as a leader in WWE and his character is so darn compelling. The same things hold true for a company like TNA that has some young, raw, fire and pissing and guts wrestling talent that just needs to be pointed in the right direction. They don't need to sit there and emulate Shane Douglas, because they can do moves that I could never dream of doing. The thing is, will they do it facing the camera the proper way? Will they do it selling it the right way to the crowd? When they do a promo, can they incite a fan to love them or hate them? Those are the things we can still teach them.

The overriding storyline switched directions in the summer with dueling directors of authority — Don Callis, previously known as Cyrus in ECW, as the heel, and Erik Watts as the babyface.

DON CALLIS: They had liked what I'd done in ECW, and wanted to have me come in. I just completed my MBA degree, and they found that kind of intriguing as a gimmick. Because now in corporate America, the people that come in as the corporate heat-seekers are the management consultants that tell you what's wrong with your company. So I thought that was kind of a neat tie-in. The angle started with the hardcore thing, but it's really more about the character trying to do things to make changes to gain him power. I don't think it's simply an anti-hardcore gimmick. I think it's real easy to come in right off the hop and say this guy is the commissioner or president or whatever, and he's got the power. There's nothing kind of devious or brilliant in a heel sense about that. If you can come in, and the character makes people believe they have power by the way they act, then I think that's the tricky bit about it.

AJ Styles fought off the title challenges of D'Lo Brown, including a two-out-of-three falls match, with the third fall being a Ladder Match that ended in a draw, as well as a steel cage showdown won by Styles.

D'LO BROWN: We went out there and really busted our asses to put on the best form of entertainment we could. I think everyone was pleased with it. Nothing but positive feedback from everyone you talk to. I'm doing things now that I wasn't allowed to do for a long time in another company, WWE, and basically I've been given the freedom to go out there and do what I deem is necessary to provide good entertainment in the match. These things, they're crazy, but they're not that crazy. If I can get the crowd to chant, or wonder what AJ and I are going to do next, that's what I want to do. If they're just sitting in anticipation wondering what we're going to do next, we've done our job, and we're both very happy with that.

To no one's surprise, the X Division, even minus Styles' participation, remained the lifeblood of TNA. Taking things up a further notch, the company introduced the Ultimate X match, where two cables were crisscrossed above the ring in the shape of the letter "X." The participants would climb the ropes, leap to grip the cables, and work their way to the middle of the "X" while hanging in the air to grab the championship belt. The first match of its kind on the August 20 pay-per-view was met with great praise, as Michael Shane won the title against Chris Sabin and Frankie Kazarian. Earlier in the night, the first Super X Cup, an eight-man tournament featuring X Division–style wrestlers from around the world, kicked off. With the Nashville Fairgrounds already booked for the annual state fair, the Super X Cup would air in its entirety as a taped show on September 3 after being filmed before the August 20 and 27 live events. This tournament concept evolved from the legendary Super J Cup international junior heavyweight tournaments in Japan throughout the 1990s. TNA's version featured X Division mainstays Michael Shane, Frankie Kazarian, Chris Sabin, and Jerry Lynn; Canada's Terry Hart; Juventud Guerrera from Mexico; Jonny Storm from the United Kingdom; and Japan's Nosawa. The semifinals saw Guerrera pin Hart, and Sabin pin Kazarian, with Sabin winning the trophy in the finals. The entire tournament on pay-per-view came off as the best show in TNA's fifteen-month existence.

The high quality of the recent pay-per-views, coupled with better attendance and an apparent upswing in pay-per-view numbers, instilled confidence among management. As a result, TNA decided to offer contracts to all of their regular performers. Previously, only key talent, including AJ Styles, Raven, and Jerry Lynn, were signed. With TNA gaining momentum and WWE taking notice, as evidenced by their signing of X Division star Paul London, female wrestler Alexis Laree, and one-legged wrestler Zach Gowan (who'd had his first TV appearance with TNA), management offered everyone exclusive wrestling contracts. The agreements spanned one year, with TNA holding an option for year two. It included a set salary per TNA appearance, but no guarantee on the number of dates. Obviously, contracted talent was prohibited from signing with WWE for the duration of the deal. Wrestlers could work weekend independent shows, but only with office approval. Talent choosing not to sign would forfeit their opportunity for national exposure with TNA. All key talent except Elix Skipper, who would later sign, and Low Ki, who chose Japan as his first priority but still appeared sparingly, inked their names on the dotted line.

The creative situation took another turn as Dutch Mantel, who'd made his name revitalizing promotions in Puerto Rico as booker, joined TNA. Vince Russo's power had steadily decreased, while Jerry Jarrett's concentration turned to other areas. Jerry had his eye on a talent acquisition that would provide TNA immediate credibility with the television industry and put the promotion on the map with fans. This man had ignited WWE's popularity surge in the mid-1980s and keyed the turnaround of WCW in the mid-1990s. The Jarretts believed he could do the same for TNA. This man was none other than Hulk Hogan.

The Jarretts flew to Tampa on September 12 for a meeting at the Hogan estate. They laid out a long-term plan building to the company's first three-hour, Sunday night pay-per-view on November 30 called *Bound For Glory*. Hogan seemed receptive to the idea. Before the paperwork was signed, TNA and Hogan shot a major angle in Japan to set up his arrival in TNA. Following Hogan's victory over Masahiro Chono at New Japan Pro Wrestling's October 13 Tokyo Dome event, Jeff Jarrett stormed into the victor's press conference and smashed him with a guitar. Jarrett continued to hammer away on the bloody Hogan until Chono stopped the attack. Footage of the beatdown in Japan aired on TNA's October 15 pay-per-view.

However, six days later, Hogan called an audible. He contacted TNA on October 21 and asked to postpone his match until February due to a knee injury for which he'd scheduled surgery ten days later. On the pay-per-view, TNA made the questionable move of having Jimmy Hart, Hogan's wrestling manager and best friend, announce that Hogan had signed a contract with TNA, which was untrue. The promotion followed through with plans of having Jeff Jarrett officially turn heel and defeat AJ Styles to win the NWA World Title for a second time, originally hoping to headline with

Hogan vs. Jarrett for the title on November 30. But with Hogan out of the picture, at least temporarily, TNA canceled *Bound For Glory*, hurting their reputation with pay-per-view and cable operators in the process.

With the major plans for Hogan shelved until February, the company shifted gears. The latest direction included the return of Sting, who didn't come alone. Sting convinced TNA management to bring in Lex Luger, whose personal life had been in a shambles following the controversial drug overdose death of his girlfriend, the former Miss Elizabeth, in his home, and Luger's subsequent arrest for steroid possession. On the November 5 event, Sting defeated Jarrett via disqualification, leading to a tag match the next week pitting Sting and AJ Styles against Jarrett and Luger. The finish saw Styles pin Luger, with the storyline being that Styles had proved he was on the level of major stars like Sting and Luger. The pinfall set Styles up for a December 3 title rematch with the champion, but interference by Kid Kash helped Jarrett retain.

As 2003 drew to a close, TNA received some bad, although not unexpected, news. Hulk Hogan again pulled out of his TNA pay-per-view match during a meeting with Jerry Jarrett in Tampa. Hogan claimed his knee was not responding well after surgery, and he would be physically unable to wrestle in February. Jarrett and most others in TNA were skeptical of Hogan's intentions from the start, and the company had prepared for life without him despite looking into a Sunday, February 29, 2004, date at a military base in Fort Campbell, Kentucky. While Hogan told Jarrett he still wanted to wrestle for TNA in May or June, most believed Hogan would never step in a TNA ring and had other interests — either a return to WWE, or helping kick-start his teenage daughter's music career.

The effects of not being able to use Hogan to headline a three-hour Sunday night pay-per-view were lessened by an internal decision to pursue a major television deal. TNA's syndicated show, *Xplosion*, had recently been picked up on the Empire Sports Network in Buffalo, and soon also started on the Sunshine Network in Florida, both regional sports stations with limited national availability on satellite services. However, TNA sought a larger network to promote their Wednesday pay-per-views. Finding little interest in a wrestling show among most significant networks, TNA rekindled discussions with SuperStation WGN out of Chicago. The inherent problem was the fact that WGN was far from a national network, available outside of the Chicago metropolitan area only on certain digital cable and satellite systems. But TNA desperately needed to advertise their pay-per-views to a television audience. WGN's 60 million potential viewers fit the bill. The time would not come cheap, though. WGN wanted approximately $50,000 per week to air TNA in a 10am eastern Saturday morning timeslot. The promotion had turned down the exorbitant fee earlier in the year, but now changed its tune with the hope of increasing pay-per-view numbers and at the same time, delivering strong enough ratings to improve their standing in the larger television community. As negotiations moved along, TNA promoted a forthcoming major announcement on its shows, expected to be the WGN deal to start in January 2004.

Before any official announcement, the year ended in the ring with a bang. Ron Killings and BG James, two-thirds of the 3 Live Kru trio with Konnan, defeated America's Most Wanted to win the NWA World Tag-Team Titles. On the final live show of the calendar year, Sting returned to defeat Jeff Jarrett in a nontitle match.

Chapter 36

The initial TNA 2004 pay-per-view saw the return of Ultimate X, with Chris Sabin winning the X Division Title over Michael Shane, Christopher Daniels, and Low Ki in another awesome bout. But the major TNA news came outside the ring. The company made an announcement on the January 14 show, but it had nothing to do with WGN. TNA announced the signing of Jonny Fairplay, the star villain on the CBS *Survivor: Pearl Islands* reality show in 2003. Fairplay, a lifelong wrestling fan who would recite wrestling catch-phrases weekly on *Survivor* while antagonizing his fellow contestants, inked a $100,000 one-year deal. TNA hoped to piggyback on Fairplay's celebrity status, albeit transitory, to bring exposure to TNA. As for WGN, TNA ultimately got cold feet on spending over two and a half million dollars annually for a non-national television program in a weak morning timeslot. The company did, however, explore a three-hour Sunday night pay-per-view again with an April date in Fort Campbell, Kentucky. To replace Hogan as the top drawing card for the megashow, the company initiated talks with Kevin Nash and Scott Hall to come in as a tandem. Nash and Hall's jump from WWE to WCW in 1996 had helped set WCW's business on fire for several years. Eight years later, TNA hoped the magical aura would still exist. They also considered bringing in legend "Macho Man" Randy Savage to participate as well. Ironically, while negotiating for these major names at major price tags, the company slashed costs again by deciding to air one taped weekly pay-per-view each month. They planned to tape additional matches and segments over the previous three weeks' live events, to air on the taped show the fourth week. The savings of close to $100,000 would help TNA get closer to the previously unattainable break-even point.

Around the same time TNA signed Fairplay (and received little mainstream buzz for their investment), the company backed into its biggest media exposure ever. On the January 28 event, star NFL linebacker Brian Urlacher of the Chicago Bears made an appearance to second Erik Watts for a match with Don Callis that would determine who would be the sole TNA director of authority. Before the match, Callis called Urlacher to the ring and tried to eject him from the building. Callis' security guards, Kevin Northcutt and Legend, jumped Urlacher, who fought back and double clotheslined both men out of the ring. Urlacher then press-slammed Jonny Fairplay over the top rope to the floor in a scene that aired all over the country on ESPN, CNN, FOX Sports, NBC, and many local television and newspaper outlets. TNA was thrilled with the free publicity, but the Chicago Bears viewed it much differently. Upset with Urlacher risking injury while under a long-term, $56 million contract, the Bears publicly chastised Urlacher's decision making and prohibited him from physical involvement in any future wrestling angles.

The first of the monthly taped pay-per-views aired on February 11, built around the America's Cup, a one-night X Division competition pitting stars from the AAA promotion in Mexico against TNA stars in a series of four singles bouts, two tag-team matches, and an eight-man elimination final. Taped over the previous two weeks, the show was another critically acclaimed success. Team AAA won the Cup by a score of 13-9 after Juventud Guerrera pinned Jerry Lynn to win an elimination match that included Mr. Aguila, Hector Garza, Abismo Negro, Chris Sabin, Elix Skipper, and Sonjay Dutt. TNA followed up with a second America's Cup for the taped March event. This event pitted Mexico against Canada, with the Mexican squad retaining their trophy over Teddy Hart, Petey Williams, Johnny Devine, and Jack Evans from north of the border.

TNA underwent another company overhaul in early March with a decision to move to a cleaner, family-friendly product focusing on the athleticism of their performers. They marketed

TNA as "Wrestling Reinvented" with the hope of securing a television deal, specifically with Fox Sports Net.

> **MIKE TENAY:** I've been pretty outspoken, even when our product was quite a bit edgier. . . . To get to the most people and expose the masses to our product, let's face it, that's the bottom line. I've really been encouraged by the direction of the company in the last few months, especially as it pertains to language and actions of the wrestlers in the ring. I've seen it all. I started watching wrestling in 1962, and I've pretty much watched wrestling every week for over forty years. I can tell you that while there was that year or two-year run where that edgier product was really bringing the numbers, and I have to admit it definitely worked, when it was new, when the WWF at the time kind of went with an edgier product and WCW countered with a similarly edgier product, the numbers were certainly there. But I think the people have seen that. I think that's been done. I think what we need to rely on is the most basic aspects of the business — creating good feuds, getting wrestlers and characters over, and having people appreciate what they bring to the table. I think that's when you'll see we have the chance for the most success. There's really not an upside to going so edgy with your product that you turn off families. Why would you even consider doing that? If people want to see adult type aspects of professional wrestling, they can go watch adult films or something that really can probably satisfy them much more than we can by teasing it. I think we need to be much more family friendly and more family oriented.

In the ring, NWA World Champion Jeff Jarrett faced the challenge of AMW's Chris Harris, who split from tag-team competition for a chance at singles stardom. Harris came up short, after Jarrett used the guitar in another very good match on the March 17 event. To clarify the World Title picture, a four-way match took place on the March 31 show, with Raven going over AJ Styles, Ron Killings, and Abyss to set up a match with Harris to determine the number one contender. On the same night, Frankie Kazarian pinned Amazing Red to win the X Division Title vacated by Chris Sabin due to a knee injury. The following week, in a taped show, Kid Kash and Dallas defeated Low Ki and Christopher Daniels in the finals of a tournament for the NWA World Tag-Team Titles. The show also featured the third America's Cup, with Mexico squaring off with the United Kingdom. Heavy Metal replaced Juventud Guerrera on Team Mexico, while Robbie Dynamite, Frankie Sloan, James Mason, and Dean Allmark comprised Team U.K. under the guidance of David Taylor. This installment was not as well received as the previous two, but Team Mexico defended their crown with a comfortable win in the elimination match to seal the victory.

The April 14 event centered on the highly anticipated Harris vs. Raven match, with Harris winning a wild brawl to earn another shot at Jarrett's NWA World Title. The contest was slated for April 21 inside a steel cage, but Raven attacked Harris early in the show, injuring the challenger's shoulder and preventing him from competing. AJ Styles was put in the spot by new babyface director of authority Vince Russo, and won the title in the cage to the delight of the Asylum faithful.

While fans rejoiced over Styles' title victory, TNA celebrated its first national television timeslot. Weeks and weeks of negotiations with FOX Sports Net culminated in a 3pm Friday afternoon timeslot on all FSN affiliates beginning June 4. TNA would be paying for the timeslot, approximately $30,000 per week, but hoped to quickly impress the network with its ratings and earn an upgrade to a precious prime time slot. As part of the new era, the company chose to downplay the NWA portion of its name, while keeping the championship lineage, and market itself as TNA Wrestling. The television series would be TNA *Impact*. To enhance the look of the product for the network, TNA struck a deal, with the aid of Jimmy Hart, with Universal Studios in Orlando, Florida, to tape the weekly show at Soundstage 21.

JEFF JARRETT: Over the last three or four years, wrestling has had a black eye in the public, so to speak. It has been looked at from a different light for several reasons. When we started TNA, we were a weekly pay-per-view series and we still are today. Our product, our brand of wrestling, our style of wrestling, our style of presenting sports entertainment/professional wrestling is something that the public has definitely grabbed a hold to, and

I think this is the continuation of our success. I think from top to bottom, everyone here is excited. When the idea was first presented to Universal Studios, and they researched it and really dug deep into what our product is all about, they couldn't be happier. The same goes with Fox Sports Net. Once you research what we're about, know what we're about, I think both brand names have really looked long and hard at it and welcome us with open arms. It's been over three years since anyone has been on a national television outlet since the demise of WCW. We couldn't be more excited about the future.

JIMMY HART: Universal has always loved wrestling. Back in WCW, we were there for a couple of years. When they left, Universal was very disappointed. Then we had a small stint there with the XWF, and the people just opened their arms to that. When the powers that be in Total Nonstop Action Wrestling went to Universal, it was just a no-brainer. Pam Warren up there, who is the lady that has always been in charge of everything that we've done with wrestling back with the WCW days, she knows what kind of clientele it brings in there. It's just awesome. They've really welcomed this with open arms.

TNA intended to maintain its Wednesday night pay-per-views in Nashville, then fly the crew to Orlando to tape *Impact* on Thursday nights for a Friday afternoon airing. Fans would be admitted to the tapings for free, with the intention of drawing locals and tourists to fill the 800-seat studio. Wrestlers grew excited at the prospect of two paydays per week and national exposure on free television for the first time. In another attempt to differentiate itself with the public, TNA planned to utilize a six-sided wrestling ring, made popular in Mexico, for all of its matches. The company wanted to do as much as possible to showcase its unique brand of wrestling to the new Fox Sports Net audience.

JEFF JARRETT: From the beginning, all we've tried to do is create an alternative wrestling product. We tried to be successful, and I think it's, more or less, a congratulations, a trophy or a trademark we can hang on our mantle. Over the last two years, from the top to bottom, everyone in Total

Nonstop Action has definitely put out the effort. I think Fox has noticed, I think Universal Studios has noticed, I think the wrestling fan has noticed. I can't wait to make another impact with the Fox Sports Net show starting up in June.

The announcement of the television deal came on the May 12 pay-per-view. One week later, the NWA World Title changed hands, as Ron Killings captured the gold for a second time in a four-way match over champion AJ Styles, Raven, and Chris Harris. But the excitement was tempered by pre-show events, as an ambulance rushed Jerry Jarrett to the hospital after he complained of chest pains. He subsequently underwent quadruple-bypass surgery. While Jerry's role had decreased significantly from the early days, the stress of recent business dealings caught up with him. With Jerry on the mend, the final taped event aired on May 26 as the World X Cup, with teams from Japan, Canada, Mexico, and TNA competing in an array of mostly gimmick matches. Team Japan was eliminated first, leaving Chris Sabin from TNA, Petey Williams from Canada, and Hector Garza from Mexico to determine the winner in an Ultimate X match. Sabin won the crazy match to bring home the World X Cup for himself, Jerry Lynn, Christopher Daniels, and Elix Skipper. Of course, the show received rave reviews across the board. TNA hoped to carry over the energy to its first television taping.

Before the inaugural tapings in Orlando, there was the June 2 pay-per-view in Nashville. For the third time in six weeks, the NWA World Title belt relocated, this time back to the waist of Jeff Jarrett, who was victorious in the first ever King of the Mountain match against Killings, Styles, Harris, and Raven. The confusing objective was to score a pinfall and then climb a ladder to hang the belt above the ring. Jarrett's victory made him the standard-bearer heading into the *Impact* era.

Chapter 37

The June 4 debut of TNA *Impact* on Fox Sports Net got the promotion off on the right foot. Fans packed Soundstage 21 for the historic show, and witnessed a solid collection of matches in the new six-sided ring. For the television program, matches were given a ten-minute time limit, with title matches under a half-hour restriction. If a match went the distance, a wrestling judge in attendance, usually a legend from the past, would render a decision. On television, the participants' names were listed on the top of the screen with a running clock in the "Fox Box" to offer a sporting event feel. On the bottom, results of the Wednesday night pay-per-views and other TNA news scrolled occasionally to update new viewers. As expected, the X Division became the focal point. The opening match saw Hector Garza, Sonjay Dutt, and Amazing Red take out Petey Williams, Bobby Roode, and Eric Young of Team Canada in a fast-paced six-man tag. The main event also featured X Division stars, with AJ Styles winning a four-way match over Michael Shane, Elix Skipper, and Chris Sabin to earn an X Division Title shot. The debut show also included a title change, as the reunited America's Most Wanted captured the tag-team belts from Kid Kash and Dallas. New NWA World Champion Jeff Jarrett also made an appearance in an angle with Ron Killings.

> **RON KILLINGS:** The reaction was overwhelming and the energy is, like, totally the highest it can get. Everybody is really excited and pumped, and ready to go ahead and prove themselves and make this thing happen.
>
> Orlando, Florida, gave us a nice welcome. The crowd was just outstanding, and ready for a change, and ready for some new *Impact* wrestling.

With everyone getting accustomed to the new schedule, the company geared up for its second anniversary event on June 23. A capacity crowd (with about half paid) witnessed the TNA debut of former WWE superstar Jeff Hardy, who fought AJ Styles to a no-contest in an X Division Title match after interference by an injured Kid Kash.

> **JEFF HARDY:** The most important thing for me is I'm starting to find it fun again. I'm enjoying it, and that's something I lost, and got totally burned out on, and I didn't even want to wrestle anymore with WWE. I'm starting to have fun again, and that was the main thing as far as I was concerned in coming back.
>
> The year that I wasn't wrestling, there wasn't a week that went by that my brother didn't stop by my house and say, "Hey man, you thought about going up there to TNA? They really want to get you up there and I think it would be a good thing." Week after week he would tell me that, and I thought about it every week. But then I was doing the motocross thing too, and I kind of fell out with that, not altogether, but I just took a break from it. I wanted to do it again. I've always been told I had a God-given talent to do this, and I think I better use it while I can.

Also on the card, Jeff Jarrett regained the NWA World Title over Killings, with another controversial finish after an illegal guitar shot. AMW regained their titles over the Japanese team of Nosawa and Miyamoto. The anniversary show received mixed reviews, but the product seemed to be experiencing an upward surge thanks to *Impact*.

> **MIKE TENAY:** I think TNA has really made some incredible strides in two years, especially as it pertains to the young talent that we've exposed to the general public. I think we really have so many huge things in our future that I think the balance of 2004 is going to be an incredibly positive year for everyone associated with TNA, and we certainly have to expose a lot more of the wrestling fans all over the world to the TNA product.

The early ratings for *Impact* led to a celebration at TNA headquarters. With no network promotion, and airing in poor timeslot, the June 4 show drew a 0.22 rating, translating to about 151,000 homes. The TNA ratings nearly tripled those of one of FSN's marquee programs, *I, Max*, on weekday evenings. The numbers rose for the second week to a 0.32 rating and 220,000 homes, before falling to a 0.20 and 0.15 for the June 18 and 25 shows, respectively. The July 2 *Impact* bounced back to a new high of 0.33 off an appearance by Dennis Rodman, who sat ringside for the six-man-tag main event between 3 Live Kru and Team Canada. The company hoped for an Urlacher-type media buzz, but Rodman refused to physically involve himself in any angle. Instead, he walked to the ring with 3LK and sat idly by.

Both TNA and Fox Sports expressed enthusiasm over the ratings and content of *Impact*. However, the additional exposure had not seemed to help the Wednesday pay-per-view numbers. The buys had dropped to an abysmal 7,000 per week. Even worse, a contractual impasse prompted DirecTV to discontinue offering TNA events starting with the July 7 show. While the company finally closed a carriage deal with the Dish Network, the loss of the larger DirecTV distribution shut out 12 million potential homes. With pay-per-view dwindling to disastrous levels, TNA made the call to cease the weekly experiments in favor of traditional, three-hour Sunday night pay-per-views. The decision put the final nail in the coffin of TNA's initial business approach — weekly pay-per-views at an affordable price without expensive television costs — which had turned out to be a failure on almost every level. The move to weekly television and monthly pay-per-views, a necessity for company survival, underlined the fact that word-of-mouth and the Internet alone could not carry a wrestling promotion in new the millennium. National television was a priority, and to TNA's credit, the shift was made before it became too late.

The final Wednesday night pay-per-view was scheduled for September 8 at the TNA Asylum. The company planned to air taped shows in the normal timeslots for the rest of the month. The first three-hour pay-per-view, TNA *Victory Road*, was announced for Sunday, November 7. In the meantime, TNA moved the weekly *Impact* tapings to Tuesday nights to allow additional post-production time. In the ring, throughout July and August, the company pushed Jeff Hardy as the next contender for Jarrett's NWA World Title. The Naturals, Chase Stevens and Andy Douglas, won the tag-team belts from America's Most Wanted in an upset on July 7. This set up the first six-sided steel cage match on the July 2 show, won by Stevens and Douglas. The X Division Title had co-holders after a disputed finish in a July 28 Ultimate X match. Michael Shane and Kazarian both laid claim to the gold. A twenty-man gauntlet match on August 11 cleared up the confusion, with Petey Williams winning his first TNA title. Vince Russo and Dusty Rhodes feuded over storyline control of the company, while Terry Funk, Harley Race, and Larry Zbyszko formed a championship committee to determine title bouts.

Jeff Hardy challenging Jeff Jarrett for the NWA World Title headlined the final Wednesday pay-per-view from the TNA Asylum in Nashville. Fans filled the building to watch Jarrett again successfully defend his title with aid of a guitar.

TNA settled on the Impact Zone at Universal Studios in Orlando as the site for *Victory Road*. The company could guarantee a full house and a rabid crowd in Orlando, a necessity for its first effort on a Sunday night. To lure new fans on pay-per-view at a full $29.95 price tag, TNA bit the bullet and shelled out big money for some major names. Kevin Nash and Scott Hall agreed to deals at $5,000 each per appearance. The duo would make an appearance at *Victory Road*, and eventually wrestle on future pay-per-views. The main event for the show was locked in as a Jarrett vs. Hardy title rematch (a Ladder Match with Hall in Jarrett's corner and Nash backing Hardy). AJ Styles vs. Petey Williams for the X Division Title, Team Canada vs. 3 Live Kru for the NWA World Tag-Team Titles, a Last Man Standing match between AMW and Triple X, a twenty-man X Division gauntlet match, and a Raven vs. Abyss vs. Monty Brown three-way comprised the remaining top matches on the show.

JEFF JARRETT: The pressure is on. On one hand, I'm very optimistic. It's been a long two and a half years at times, I feel. At other times, it's flown by. A lot of hard work has gone into the *Victory Road* pay-per-view. Our expectations are no different than our big Wednesday night events. This is our first Sunday event. As far as the in-ring, everybody better pull out all the stops and go for it, and I fully expect they will.

I think the cable and satellite industry, in some sense, has a feeling of this being a relaunch. We've gone with TNA like any startup business. We crawled before we walked, and we tried to walk before we run. I feel like *Victory Road* is our first step that we're running. We evolved into this. We went from the Wednesday night events, and then we added Fox Sports Net, and next week we have two prime-time specials. I think it's the evolution of the company that we can continue to grow at a time that sometimes is not fast enough, and other times it feels like it's just a very, very slow growth process. But any business is that way. Especially with the climate of the wrestling business as a whole, it's been a tough, hard process. As far as a relaunch or rebirth, I think this is just the next step for us, because December 5th we're coming right back with our second three-hour event, called *Turning Point*.

Chapter 38

To celebrate the *Victory Road* weekend, TNA staged a fan convention the afternoon before the show at the nearby Doubletree Hotel in Orlando. Nearly 500 fans came out at $49 per person, which included guaranteed admission to the pay-per-view and an opportunity to meet the wrestlers, take pictures, obtain autographs, and participate in Q&A's with the talent. TNA management expressed a new sense of confidence after the success of the Fan InterAction event. *Victory Road* further fueled the optimism, with a solid show featuring strong matches up and down the card. Hector Garza won the opening X Division gauntlet match in an attempt to create a popular Hispanic babyface character. An eight-man tag saw Ron Killings, Erik Watts, "The Empire Saint" Pat Kenney, and Johnny B. Badd defeat The Naturals, Kid Kash, and Dallas. The minis from Mexico battled in a comedy match. Konnan and BG James of 3 Live Kru won the NWA World Tag-Team Titles from Eric Young and Bobby Roode of Team Canada. Rowdy Roddy Piper held a *Piper's Pit* segment with surprise guest "Superfly" Jimmy Snuka, ending with Kid Kash taunting Snuka and then knocking out Sonjay Dutt with a coconut. Trinity beat the debuting Jacqueline in a women's match. Monty Brown won a three-way hardcore match over Abyss and Raven. Petey Williams retained the X Division Title over AJ Styles in the match of the night. Dusty Rhodes was named new director of authority over Vince Russo, based on fan balloting from the TNA website. Christopher Daniels and Elix Skipper of Triple X defeated America's Most Wanted in a poor Last Man Standing match, after Skipper suffered a concussion early on. In the main event, Jeff Jarrett grabbed the NWA World Title in a Ladder Match against Jeff Hardy, when Kevin Nash turned on Hardy to join Hall and Jarrett. To even the sides, "Macho Man" Randy Savage made a surprise appearance at the end of the night to run off the heels.

Perhaps more important than the success or failure of *Victory Road* was the success of a two-night TNA special on Fox Sports Net as part of wrestling week on *The Best Damn Sports Show Period*. Two ninety-minute specials would air in prime time in place of *Best Damn* on November 10 and 11. If the specials did well in the ratings, FSN would consider a timeslot upgrade that TNA had been pushing for. The specials were taped in Orlando prior to *Victory Road*, with the *Best Damn* cast, including Tom Arnold and Leeann Tweeden, in attendance. The company aimed to demonstrate the amazing athleticism and wrestling ability of its talent roster to new viewers. On the first show, they did just that with the free television debut of Ultimate X, with Chris Sabin beating Elix Skipper and Sonjay Dutt. AJ Styles pinned Alex Shelley, and Christopher Daniels defeated Kazarian in singles bouts. The second show featured Styles going over Abyss in a tables match. A five-way X Division match saw Petey Williams survive over Shark Boy, Michael Shane, Jerrelle Clark, and Sonjay Dutt. The main event for the second night saw Jeff Jarrett beat Jeff Hardy on the third consecutive occasion, this time inside a steel cage.

For all of the good, the *Best Damn Wrestling Event Period* had its share of low points. The interaction by the *Best Damn* hosts, originally there to provide legitimacy to the product, turned out to be a negative. Tom Arnold's commentary, particularly during Ultimate X, came off as indifferent to the action and disrespectful to the wrestlers. His match with Puppet the hardcore midget was a disaster. Chris Rose sporting a "Wrestling Is Fake" T-shirt made the product look foolish and incensed Rowdy Roddy Piper, who legitimately sprayed him in the face with a fire extinguisher, instead of the stomach as mutually agreed upon, as retaliation during a *Piper's Pit* segment. Only former NFL linebacker Bryan Cox, a big wrestling fan to begin with, made a positive contribution. He teamed with Monty Brown to defeat The Naturals in a tag-team match, and looked surprisingly good in the ring.

With the *Best Damn* tie-in and prime-time slots, TNA hoped to draw ratings in the 0.50 to 0.60 range. FSN promised a weekly Monday night timeslot in association with *Best Damn* if the two specials averaged a 0.35 rating. Unfortunately for TNA, the ratings fell well short of these marks. The first night drew a 0.26 rating, while the second night garnered a 0.18. The ratings beat *Best Damn's* averages for those nights, but were still labeled a disappointment. FSN shelved talks for a Monday night wrestling timeslot.

For the December 5 *Turning Point* pay-per-view, again in Orlando, TNA planned a six-man tag main event with Jarrett, Hall, and Nash facing Hardy, Styles, and Randy Savage. However, "Macho Man" changed his tune on joining TNA. Upset by the innocuous presence of Hulk Hogan, who he personally despised, backstage at *Victory Road*, Savage refused to return to TNA, despite a $25,000 payday offered for the November 7 appearance. He also no-showed the November 9 *Impact* tapings. Savage had not signed a contract, so the blame lied with TNA for even using him. The two sides negotiated thereafter, with Savage demanding his own personal security guards, limo service to the shows, and a private locker room on top of his gaudy appearance fee. Desperate to follow through with the *Turning Point* main event, TNA acquiesced.

Before *Turning Point* arrived, the company underwent another creative upheaval. Vince Russo quit to enter seminary school (seriously) with his last date being *Victory Road*. Jeff Jarrett and Dutch Mantel had been writing most of the creative direction. In mid-November, Dixie Carter, with nudging from Jerry Jarrett, named Dusty Rhodes the sole storyline booker. Rhodes had an ultrasuccessful run as matchmaker for the national Jim Crockett Promotions in the mid-80s, but his repetitive ideas and inability to develop new talent had killed the promotion and forced a sale to Ted Turner in late 1988. Dusty's first order of business was to move the *Impact* tapings to a bi-weekly format, taping two shows in one night to save money, and doing away with the *Xplosion* tapings.

With business sliding somewhat and ratings down for *Impact*, TNA needed a home run with the *Turning Point* pay-per-view. They hit a grand slam, with the strongest pay-per-view from any company in recent memory and arguably the greatest steel cage match in wrestling history. Despite not being promoted as the main event, the Six Sides of Steel pitting America's Most Wanted against Triple X (with the losing team forced to permanently divorce) ended the show and delivered a classic.

> **ELIX SKIPPER:** It was a great feeling and honor that they trusted us enough to carry us at the end. We've done it before. We're just doing it again. It's really no big deal. Everybody kept saying, "Are you guys going to try to top the first cage match?" And that wasn't our intention. Our intentions were just to have a really solid match, and in doing so we ended up topping the first cage match we did.

The high point of the match featured Elix Skipper walking across the top of the cage, à la a high wire artist, and hitting a huracanrana on Chris Harris from the top to the ring, more than ten feet below. Several other memorable, high-risk spots followed, with AMW going over in the end.

> **ELIX SKIPPER:** My biggest deal was first I did a powerbomb from the top of the cage, and I had blood all over me and blood all over my shoe. I was like, "I could do it. I could do it. It's no big deal." I didn't want to know how high the cage was, because I knew it was really high. I didn't want to know none of those details. All I wanted to know was how I was going to get up in the corner and how I was going to walk across. I never even figured out, once I did the huracanrana, how I was going to land. Landing was the last thing I was worried about. All of those details came after I actually did the move. As I'm coming down, I was like, "I got to spin really quick." And as I'm spinning I hit my head on the cage and then I hit the floor. I'm doing a body check, and my fingers are still moving and my feet are still moving. I was like, "All right, I'm alive. I'm okay." It was so many things. I got really upset, because when I first went to stand up on the cage, I slipped off. To me, it felt like forever, because I'm sitting there thinking, "I can't believe it. I'm not going to be able to do it." Then all of sudden, you see me pop straight up and take off because I got really hot, and next thing you know I end up doing it out of nowhere. That's one of

those moves that once you do it, people are going to remember it forever, and you don't have to do it again.

The actual main event saw Randy Savage appear in the ring for only a minute, but pin Jeff Jarrett to give his team the win and theoretically set up a title match at the next show. But history repeated itself two nights later at the *Impact* tapings. Again, with no contracts signed, Savage would not agree to lose to Jarrett at the *Final Resolution* pay-per-view, and walked out. This time, TNA did not chase him down, and business moved forward without him.

Chapter 39

2005 opened with some hope for TNA's future. The pay-per-view numbers for *Victory Road* were strong, with 35,000 buys tallied, by far the highest number in company history. *Turning Point* did slightly lower numbers at first, but ended up surpassing the *Victory Road* figures off replay telecasts, thanks to the awesome cage match. Fox Sports Net also agreed to a timeslot upgrade, although one not as significant as TNA hoped. *Impact* moved to Friday afternoons at 4pm. More importantly, FSN added two replay broadcasts — Friday night at 2am and Saturday night at midnight. The company also finalized T-shirt and action-figure deals to generate additional revenue. Things were looking up heading into the January 16 *Final Resolution* pay-per-view.

For the third straight month, the Impact Zone in Orlando hosted a great pay-per-view. Ultimate X played a major role, as AJ Styles' victory over Chris Sabin and Petey Williams for the X Division Title became an instant classic. The match preceding Ultimate X also turned out to be a masterpiece, with AMW winning the NWA World Tag-Team Titles from Team Canada's Eric Young and Bobby Roode. The main event saw Monty Brown challenge Jeff Jarrett for the NWA World Title after winning a three-way match against Diamond Dallas Page and Kevin Nash earlier in the night to earn the shot. Jarrett, however, used his entire bag of tricks to thwart Brown's challenge and retain the gold.

The new timeslots for *Impact* promised to double the TNA television audience. The 4pm Friday slot held steady with the January 7 show drawing a 0.19 and the January 14 show reaching a 0.27. Few viewers, if any, caught the 2am Friday night airing, but Saturday night at midnight quickly became the highest-rated show. The January 8 show pulled a 0.20, with the next week up to a 0.33. The shows following *Final Resolution* did near-record numbers, with a 0.32 and 0.33 on Friday and Saturday, respectively. With mostly new viewers sampling the product on Saturday night, *Impact*'s overall viewership increased close to 100 percent. FSN took notice and offered a two-hour prime time special for April with another *Best Damn Sports Show Period* tie-in.

Against All Odds, on February 13 from Orlando, marked the fourth TNA Sunday pay-per-view and the fourth strong outing. Once again, the X Division stole the show as AJ Styles retained the gold over Christopher Daniels in an outstanding thirty-minute Iron Man match by a 2-1 score after sudden death overtime. The match ranked as high as any bout in TNA history. Jeff Jarrett successfully defended his championship again, this time against former ally Kevin Nash. The match included run ins by a returning Sean Waltman and a debuting Billy Gunn, of WWE fame, under the name The Outlaw. TNA also made another stab at celebrity involvement by putting Jeff Hammond, host of NASCAR events on FOX and a TNA correspondent, in the ring. Hoping to gain some exposure in the auto-racing community, Hammond and BG James defeated Michael Shane and Kazarian after Hammond pinned Kazarian, who promptly quit the company in disgust.

Diamond Dallas Page assumed the role as the next challenger for Jeff Jarrett at Destination X on March 13, and became Jarrett's latest victim. The show ended the streak of strong pay-per-views, with only Christopher Daniels' X Division Title victory over AJ Styles, Elix Skipper, and Ron Killings living up to expectations in a series of three matches.

> **DUSTY RHODES:** Christopher Daniels, to me, is a modern day Rick Rude. He's a throwback to the old heel and the way a heel should be.

The heat came down on Dusty Rhodes as the company's momentum took a tumble off the poor March event. To cut costs, the company filmed three weeks of television instead of two at the *Impact* tapings, leading to burned-out crowds by the third set of matches. To spice up business, management went in a unique direction for the *Lockdown* pay-per-view in April. Rhodes initially booked two steel cage matches at the top of the card, but the TNA head honchos pushed for an entire night of steel cage contests, a pro wrestling first.

TNA *Lockdown*, on April 24 from Universal Studios, presented eight bouts, all inside the Six Sides of Steel, for a surprisingly good show. AJ Styles and Abyss highlighted the night with a wild bout both inside and outside the cage, won by AJ to earn to a shot at the NWA World Title. A six-man contest featured Diamond Dallas Page, Sean Waltman, and BG James defeating Jeff Jarrett, Monty Brown, and The Outlaw. James replaced Kevin Nash, who missed the show with a staph infection in his lower leg. America's Most Wanted and Christopher Daniels retained their respective championships as well.

Perhaps the biggest story of the night came out several days later. In the opener on pay-per-view, Chris Candido suffered a broken leg after landing awkwardly on Sonny Siaki. He underwent successful surgery the next day, and even worked the *Impact* tapings on Tuesday, helping The Naturals win the NWA Tag-Team Titles. Two nights later, Candido suddenly passed away from a blood clot that originated in his surgically repaired ankle and traveled to his heart. The tragedy shocked TNA and the entire wrestling community, many who noted the sad irony that the tragedy had come after Candido had beaten his drug-addiction demons and cleaned up his life. With dozens of his wrestling brethren in attendance, one of the NWA Tag-Team Title belts was laid upon the casket at the funeral as a touching gesture from Candido's final employer.

Business moved forward with significant changes behind the scenes. Long-time Panda executive Frank Dickerson was shifted to the wrestling division to act as Chief Executive Officer and Chief Financial Officer. Dickerson and Dixie Carter took greater control of the decision-making. Their first order of business was to remove Dusty Rhodes as the sole creative booker of storylines. Rhodes ultimately resigned on May 10, and in his place went a committee of Scott D'Amore, Mike Tenay, Dutch Mantel, Jeremy Borash, and Bill Banks. This group would devise the plans for the May pay-per-view.

> **SCOTT D'AMORE:** There are a couple of different approaches to how you handle the booking and writing of wrestling. We are people that think it's important to have things make sense, and have things go from episode to episode with a logical progression. We like to think that we can add a little bit of excitement and a little bit of, "Oh shoot, what's happening happen next?" kind of feel. Basically, I think it's a little bit of old school wrestling, with just a splash of shock value. We're not shocking them with violence or with sexual overtones or anything. The shock TV idea was that everything goes against the grain. I always use the example that when I took ninth-grade wood shop, I learned that if you sand against the grain, eventually you have a crappy piece of wood. In wrestling booking, if you go with the grain and with the grain, and then at the right time you go against the grain, you've got a little bit of shock value and something that might stir a little interest and doesn't ruin the overall direction.

TNA traveled the celebrity route again for Hard Justice on May 15. Former Ultimate Fighting Championship Light Heavyweight Champion Tito Ortiz, a pro wrestling fan, was summoned to referee the Jeff Jarrett vs. AJ Styles NWA World Heavyweight Title match. Ortiz maintained law and order, and counted Jarrett's shoulders to the mat to end his eleven-month reign.

> **AJ STYLES:** It was a big thing. This wasn't something they threw together. They made a big deal about this. That really pumps you up. Going for the World Title, this is a prestigious belt, almost everybody on the planet that enjoys wrestling knows the NWA World Title and the prestige that it has. It's the only belt that's actually gets defended all over the world. It's quite awesome to have that belt now and beat Jeff Jarrett.

Styles, the new NWA Champion, signed a three-year contract extension before the show, keeping him locked into TNA through 2008. Christopher Daniels, who retained the X Division Title against Mexican sensation Shocker, signed a similar long-term deal as the company attempted to secure its future.

However, TNA's immediate prospects, particularly on television, were nebulous, with the one-year contract on Fox Sports Net expiring at the end of May. The company spent $30,000 per week for the Friday afternoon slot, recouping only $10,000 in advertising revenue based on a 0.22 average rating for the year. The company no longer wanted to pay for time and sought alternatives. With WWE programming leaving Spike TV in the fall, TNA opened negotiations to keep wrestling on the network. They also revisited discussions with WGN, this time for a coveted two-hour Monday night timeslot to theoretically ignite a second Monday-night wrestling war.

> **DIXIE CARTER:** Fox Sports Net was a great opportunity for our company, the first time we were given a national platform. We succeeded and exceeded all of their expectations. We were their highest-rated show, including their national prime-time programming. We knew we had something really special. It wasn't just a dream to us anymore that we could do this on television. We knew that we had great pay-per-views, but we really felt like we really needed to reach the masses to expose our brand to a greater number of people. We really felt like Fox Sports Net had its limitations, in the size and the way the network is set up. We started talking to a few other people, and based on what we had done there [on FSN], everybody showed interest. We were very, very lucky.

While WGN offered a precious timeslot, the network had several drawbacks. WGN aired in approximately 60 million homes, two-thirds of Spike TV's penetration, and without affiliates in New York City and Los Angeles. The company came within centimeters of signing a deal, but talks broke down at the eleventh hour over monetary issues. While Fox Sports Net was still an option, the network was demanding a six-month commitment at the same weekly price. The focus shifted to Spike TV, which took a liking to the TNA product and picked up *Impact* for an 11pm Saturday night timeslot to replace WWE *Velocity*. Wrestling would be paired with the

The monster Abyss splashes Lance Hoyt

Ultimate Fighting Championship for a Saturday night combat block of programming.

DIXIE CARTER: I think they [Spike] were getting out of the wrestling business. Once you've had what you perceive is the top of the game, you think,

"I don't think we're going to go there from a programming standpoint." But they were interested enough to take the meeting with us. I think from the very, very first meeting, they were intrigued by the uniqueness of our product, how innovative it was, how different it was from what they currently had on their air. They felt like, "We could stay in this business and grow a brand together with a company who wants to work hand in hand with us." Man, what could happen if two partners work together. They've been believers from the beginning. They're as excited about us being on Spike as we are.

Despite the absence of a television outlet, TNA presented *Slammiversary*, a pay-per-view extravaganza for its third anniversary on June 23. The night culminated with a new NWA Champion, as Raven won the second King of the Mountain match over AJ Styles, Monty Brown, Abyss, and Sean Waltman. Earlier in the night, Christopher Daniels and The Naturals retained the X Division and NWA Tag-Team Titles, respectively.

With its third anniversary in the rearview mirror, and optimism for year four, TNA has continued to survive. The infrastructure appears to be in place for a successful future, but the company faces the same roadblocks as all businesses — time and money. Estimates place TNA more than $20 million in the red over the three years since its inception, with losses mounting weekly. TNA, however, has survived disasters already and, perhaps with a little magic and lady luck on its side, can soon turn the corner into a profitable secondary wrestling promotion. For the sake of the industry as a whole, one can only hope.

PART V

Fritz and Debra

The law of averages dictates that if you've spoken with more than 200 wrestling personalities, there is bound to be at least one poor interview in the mix. Over the years, we've had our share of strange interviews, and perhaps none more memorable than an October 1999 chat with George "The Animal" Steele.

Even people who are not wrestling fans have heard of "The Animal." With his trademark green tongue and grunting interview style, Steele is best remembered as a wild-but-lovable babyface in the mid-1980s WWF, who often snacked on a ring turnbuckle before vanquishing an opponent. His career pinnacle came in 1986–87 as a foil for WWF Intercontinental Champion Randy "Macho Man" Savage. The Animal became smitten with Savage's beautiful manager, Miss Elizabeth. Even though Savage portrayed the villain, his lovely, innocent valet was a popular character with the fans. Steele and Elizabeth were wrestling's equivalent to King Kong and Jessica Lange. While he never won the girl, Steele did help Ricky "The Dragon" Steamboat wrest the title from Savage in a classic bout at *WrestleMania III*. "The Animal" retired from active competition two years later, but still did some matches here and there on the independent scene.

One such match was slated for October 10, 1999, for a pay-per-view venture called *Heroes of Wrestling*. Pro wrestling was white hot at the time, and having seen the revenues earned by the WWF and WCW, Fosstone Promotions jumped into the already-saturated wrestling pay-per-view market with a nostalgia show featuring past-their-prime stars from the glory period of the 1980s. To help

Fritz and classic Randy Savage foe Ricky "The Dragon" Steamboat

promote the event, the company asked us to have Steele on our radio show.

We had a few worries, since we had never heard Steele do a media interview anywhere. One of our biggest fears when doing an interview is speaking with someone who responds with curt answers and offers little detail. But Steele was a well-educated man, a Michigan high school teacher in his other life, so we didn't expect any problems when it came to conversation.

At the time that we spoke with George "The Animal" Steele, the show still had its original cast — myself, Dickerman, and B. Randall. The three of us came into the studio a few days before the show to tape this interview with the hairy veteran. Not one of us had ever heard Steele speak out of character. We all wondered what we would get out of him. At worst, we thought we could conduct a ten to fifteen minute conversation with him.

Truth be told, I've never been a big fan of George Steele. I thought most of what he did in wrestling was ridiculous. But at the same time, I realized that there was a role for him, and he was popular with most fans. Just not me.

Still, I thought he would be a good interview considering how long he had been in wrestling. I believe the wheel was invented around the time he broke into the business, so he had to have at least some entertaining road stories.

We were all intrigued to find out what he had to say about a variety of things. We could talk with him about how he'd devised his weird persona, the green tongue, how he was a fat guy who more or less chased guys around the ring but never lost any weight ... deep, thought-provoking questions. And I know Dickerman was dying to get some intimate details on the beautiful Miss Elizabeth.

It all sounded fine on paper, but the final product was anything but. This interview sucked. Big time.

We got an early hint of where things were headed when "The Animal" didn't call in on time. If only we hadn't had the patience to wait him out. Twenty minutes passed before he finally called in. We spoke with him for a brief moment, hit record on the tape, and started the interview.

We hoped for a talk with a colorful figure from wrestling's 1980s heyday. Instead, we got a bitter old man who seemed more interested in catching a midday nap than speaking with us.

The conversation started out poorly, as we asked about the *Heroes of Wrestling* pay-per-view and his role on it. He answered in his old, gruff voice about getting back into the ring. Mind you, he was way past his prime at this point in his life. Unfortunately, this was the high point of the interview.

As we continued, we asked George about his career in wrestling, and when it came to his time with the World Wrestling Federation, things quickly went south. He decided to keep things short. I mean *really* short, like three-to-four-word answers. He wouldn't go in depth about anything. The three of us just looked at one another in amazement.

As if things couldn't get worse, the phone line began cutting in and out. There was nothing we could do about it. Steele noticed, and started barking about it. Now he starts talking! Why couldn't he have done that after we asked him a question? We knew the problem was on his end, with what was probably an archaic phone that he'd refused to replace. We tried to move ahead but the connection became worse. George grew more irritated, then the line went totally dead.

You would think that in a situation like this, the person who made the call would immediately call back. Not George. We waited for about ten minutes and decided that was enough. If only we were so lucky, because, of course, the phone started to ring just as we were walking out the door.

I don't think any of us really wanted to answer that phone, but I did, and we continued. To say it was awful would be like saying George "The Animal" Steele was a well-groomed man. He gave us almost nothing. I think the man was living his gimmick. That's how little he was sharing with us.

After what seemed to be an eternity, the interview concluded. Now, George might have been having a bad day. Heck, he might have been missing a big game of bingo down at the local VFW hall to do this interview. Who knows? All we'd wanted was a good conversation with someone who was supposed to be one of the legends of wrestling. Instead, we got an angry old man who seemed turned off by the surrounding world.

All of us knew this interview could never see the light of day. There was absolutely no way we could put this on the radio. Just to make sure I wouldn't have a lapse in judgment, I immediately erased the interview from the tape. Too bad I can't erase the memory.

DICKERMAN: As a kid, I was a big fan of "The Animal." He had that green tongue and was always acting crazy eating the turnbuckles. I'd even say for a while he was my favorite wrestler. I was pretty damn excited to talk to George. There was so much I wanted to ask him, whether it was about his old stuffed friend, "Mine," or his constant lust for Miss Elizabeth. How did he get that green tongue anyway? When it came time for the interview, instead of getting the wild and unpredictable Animal, we got a grumpy old man who'd apparently forgot his Geritol for the day. We wanted to have a lighthearted interview, but George would have none of it. When he wasn't giving snide two-word answers to our questions, his century-old rotary phone kept cutting off. He would come back every time the phone cut out grumpier than the last time. I don't know if he ran out of prunes and had to make an extra trip to the store on his Rascal that day, but George was in no mood to be interviewed.

Believe it or not, there was something worse than our George Steele interview — the actual *Heroes of Wrestling* pay-per-view. If you never saw the show, consider yourself lucky. It has been universally panned as the worst wrestling event of all time, which covers a LOT of ground. Nearly every bout on the card, including the sixty-two-year-old Steele's showdown with fifty-one-year-old Greg "The Hammer" Valentine, was a Worst Match of the Year candidate in 1999. Not only were the matches a problem, but actions like Jake Roberts provocatively playing with his pet snake — between his legs — made the entire night a disaster.

Years later, we each look back on that experience and share a good laugh about it. George Steele remains our poorest interview to this day. No one has eclipsed it yet, and I don't see how it could be surpassed. We still reference it from time to time on the show as a mythical tale from ancient history. Any time we talk about a bad interview, we still say, "Well, at least was he no George Steele!"

* * *

Any time you're on the air, there are bound to be some awkward moments. Lord knows we have had more than our share in our seven years doing the show. Honestly, all you can do is try to be as prepared as possible, because you never know what is going to come your way.

Back in January 2001, I was given a contact number for the Honky Tonk Man, and thought he would be an interesting guest. After all, he is the self-proclaimed greatest Intercontinental Champion of all time! Well, I think there is a good reason why he is probably the only person toting that line.

I got in touch with good old Honky on the phone and he agreed to join us on the show. All he asked was that I send him an e-mail with the exact day and time he would be coming on so he would not forget. Easy enough, right? Well, somehow my math was off by an hour when I was figuring the time for his part of the country. He had been waiting by the phone all night when we finally did get in touch with him on the night of the show.

After cutting a blistering diatribe on the producer over the snafu, I decided to speak with him off the air to help cool down the situation.

"Can't you even get the time right?" he yelled at me. "Thank God you don't work for the airlines, or else you'd screw up hundreds of lives at one time! I was going to give you an hour of my time. Now you'll be lucky enough to get fifteen minutes with the Honky Tonk Man!"

He sure was a pompous jackass, and quickly moved down the ladder on my list of greatest Intercontinental Champions. Dickerman wasn't exactly thrilled with his attitude. In fact, he was ready to just hang up. But I'd gone to the trouble of lining up the interview, so I figured we should at least try to speak with him. But he was on a short leash. The slightest thing and we were going to discard him like yesterday's newspaper.

Once he was on, everything went fine, and Honky decided to keep his attitude in check. But the guy does think the world of himself and has very little for everyone else. Let's just say that we quickly crossed him off the list of future guests.

> **DICKERMAN:** This interview took place before Honky was all over the Internet trying to "shoot" on anyone and everyone. We weren't expecting him to be so confrontational, but knowing Honky as we do now, it was to be expected. At the time, I was pretty upset about his attitude, but with time, my opinion has softened. He did end up being a good interview, and we did screw up the time. He didn't need to get so pissy, but hell, at least he showed up for the interview, which is more than I can say for others.

Former WWF and WCW star Tom Zenk was another interesting character. In fact, the Z-Man made it onto the program twice in 2000. He had just opened his Website, and was more than willing to share his poignant and sometimes outrageous opinions on his career and the wrestling business as a whole.

The first time he joined the show, in July of that year, things went great. He came off fairly intelligent and possessed a good sense of humor. He was a fun guy to speak with, even if is his point of view on some things seemed to come out of left field. But we liked him, as did a lot of the listeners, and decided to have him on again in December.

Tom was more than happy to come back on the show, too. But things got interesting the night of the broadcast. When I called him up, his mother, of all people, answered the phone. That sure seemed a bit strange, considering this is a guy in his forties possibly living at home. More importantly, it didn't exactly sit well with us that he was sleeping.

I told his mother about the situation and she promised to have him call the show once he woke up. That was all I could ask for at the time. About twenty minutes later, the station hotline rang with Tom on the other end. But once we got him on the air, we truly found out why he'd been sleeping . . . he was drunk!

Tom was a bit sloppy as he fumbled to put his words together in a coherent manner. The guy was three sheets to the wind, but we were strangely amused and kept him on the air. He was really going wild with some crazy opinions, and veering off on tangents left and right. Thank goodness he never got out of control with his language, but I would put good money down that he never remembered a word he said that night. Once it was over, we decided it would not be in our best interest to have the Z-Man on again. In short, that is how Tom Zenk came to be known as "Tom Drink" on *Between the Ropes.*

DICKERMAN: The Tom Drink interview was a classic. I don't know if he was looking for some liquid courage for all his Dusty Rhodes bashing or what, but for some reason, he decided to tip back a few before appearing on our show. Fritz always looks back at that interview with disdain, but the listeners and myself seem to love it. If I could convince Fritz to have Tom on again, I'd be all for it. Too bad nobody can find him.

Those weren't the only instances where we've been caught off guard. One time, we had the chance to speak with the legendary Jake "The Snake" Roberts. Since we were taping the interview, we could afford to take our chances with him. You never know what state of life Jake is going to be in. Sometimes, he is the most brilliant wrestling mind you can ever speak with. Other times, his mind is caught in a thick fog.

The conversation with Jake seemed to get off to a good start as we chatted about his career. But several minutes later, Jake decided to nonchalantly drop a bombshell on us when, out of nowhere, he stated that as a child he'd been raped by his father. How do you follow up on that?

Dickerman and I both had blank looks on our faces as we wondered what we should say next. Jake continued to ramble on about something before we shook off his shocking comment. It was the most unsettling moment I have ever had when interviewing someone and I was relieved when the interview came to an end.

> **DICKERMAN:** How the hell do you go from talking about André the Giant being afraid of snakes, to being raped by your father? Jake was a hell of a wrestler, and has a great mind for the sport, but he is one messed-up dude.

Of course, I've been guilty of asking people some questions that haven't made them feel very comfortable. Case in point happened in an interview I did with Kane. It was right before the 2002 WWF *Survivor Series*, and the Big Red Machine was making the rounds to promote the pay-per-view. It was also at a time where he was involved in a controversial storyline in which he'd supposedly killed his former girlfriend, Katie Vick, and Triple H was insinuating that Kane had sex with the dead body.

Naturally, I wanted to get Kane's feelings about all of this, and the first question I blurted out was about him being part of a necrophilia storyline. I guess it was the first time he had been asked the question that morning, and was not at all at ease with having to discuss the topic.

There was a long pause before he tried to deflect the question as best he could. I knew at that moment that I shouldn't have been so direct, or should at least have gotten the conversation rolling before asking a hard-hitting question like that. Kane responded that he was only part of an angle, and it was up to the company to determine what storylines air on television. He was so flustered that he ended up rambling on and on. After that, we continued on to some other subjects, and he was professional about everything, but I knew he was more than happy when our time ran out.

* * *

It is absolutely amazing to me that *Between the Ropes* has lasted as long as it has. If anyone had told me when we began that the show would still be on after seven years, I would have thought they had been kicked in the head one too many times. But here it is, and still going strong. To be honest, there are times when I wanted to stop doing the show, because I was somewhat disinterested in wrestling or had become too preoccupied to put forth a good effort every week. But every time that I allowed those thoughts to creep into my head, I took a step back for a moment and knew that I wanted to continue to be on the air. The bottom line is that I enjoy the two hours I spend each week on the air talking pro wrestling. Plus, I've had the opportunity to work with some great people along the way.

Dickerman is, without a doubt, the funniest person I have ever met in my life. The man is pure comedic gold. Sometimes, he is a bit over the top. Well, actually, most of the time he says something that makes you cringe after you burst out laughing. I'm still waiting for the day when someone comes after the guy for something he has said. But in the end, it's never anything mean-spirited. It's just his brilliant, yet sometimes warped, sense of humor. He makes the show so easy to do, and is a huge reason why it has continued on for so long. Without him on the show, it would most likely be over, because it could never be the same. He livens it up so much with not only his humor, but his keen knowledge and pointed comments. He's also never one to shy away from an opinion and will simply blurt it out rather than just skirt an issue. Above all else, Dickerman is as good a friend as you could ever

Dickerman, Fritz, Tully Blanchard and Vito DeNucci

have. In fact, he is like a brother to me, and to have him be a part of my life means the world.

Then there is the big man of the show, Larry "Vito DeNucci" Brannon. In case you didn't know, Larry is a former three-time NWA World Tag-Team Champion. If you didn't, he'll let you know!

All kidding aside, Larry has been a great addition to the show over the last couple of years. We've had our ups and downs during that time as well, and have been known to have some pretty good disagreements with one another. I think most of that is the two of us just truly getting to know one another, and understanding where the other person is coming from. In the end, we've both learned from each another and are better for it. That is not to say that he doesn't mind getting in my face from time to time while sharing a difference of opinion. But that is how he is wired, and I wouldn't change a thing.

I think the true tower of power behind the show is Chris Murray. He has been a part of it since day one, and was the first

Chris Murray and Vito DeNucci

believer in what we were doing. Chris has worked countless hours helping out with the show, from helping book guests, to promotion, to advertising, to anything else that needed a helping hand. Chris has always been there, and I cannot thank him enough. He's a good friend and another major part of the success of the show. On top of all that, Chris is a freaking genius and it's always good to have someone like that in your corner at all times.

Over the years, I would like to believe that the show has gained a good level of respect, from not only listeners, but from wrestlers themselves. We always respect the guests, and value the time they are sharing with us. There is a way to talk about controversial subjects and elicit true opinions without badgering or sideswiping someone on live radio. If you treat someone well, show the person respect and make that person feel comfortable, you can delve into the more interesting topics and draw more detailed answers.

Of course, we joke around a lot on the show, and we can push the limits from time to time. But in the end, we know what we are talking about — or at least I hope we do! There are times to joke around and there are times to be serious, and I think we offer a nice balance.

After seven years, I know that *Between the Ropes* has a solid reputation, which makes me realize all the hard work has been worth it. It is truly a great feeling when I first speak with someone in the wrestling business, and they have heard of either myself or the show. Or the proud feeling when I am at a live event and a fan comes up to me and says he enjoys the show. It doesn't get any better than someone appreciating your work and supporting what you do.

Sometimes, I wonder how much longer the show will go on. The wrestling business has its up and downs, but ultimately, it's not going anywhere anytime soon. Until I get that itch to try something different, I plan on being there to talk about the latest in wrestling. And I hope you'll be there to join us week after week.

The Future

Fritz and Traci Brooks

Midway into the first decade of the 2000s, sports entertainment faces a fascinating outlook. The onus for the foreseeable future lies on the broad shoulders of Vince McMahon. Entering his sixties, and showing no signs of stepping down, the Chairman of the Board will charter World Wrestling Entertainment's course. Where will that journey lead? The fans, ultimately, will make that decision.

While business has bounced back slightly from the depths of 2002 and 2003, significant work remains to return the sport to its late-1990s glory days. That responsibility lies not just with the creative staff, which must step up its ability to produce quality storylines under the guidance of Stephanie McMahon, but with the wrestlers' ability to connect with the audience. Stone Cold and The Rock in the '90s, preceded by Hulk Hogan and Ric Flair in the '80s, broke out of the pack to achieve sports entertainment immortality. Wrestlers must develop their own mannerisms and their own styles to truly become the person behind the character. Only then can the fans truly connect with a wrestler, whether he's a heel or as a babyface, and create that elusive emotional bond. Who will be next? In WWE, John Cena and Randy Orton possess many of the tools necessary to reach that stratosphere. But until the next breakout star emerges, the days of sold out house shows and record television ratings will seem a distant memory.

While youth will be the primary building blocks of WWE's future business, nostalgia will also play a big role in the company's next great venture. WWE 24/7, the McMahons' foray into an all-wrestling cable network, will showcase the company's vast video library from its own wrestling programming and that of WCW, ECW, the AWA, and smaller territories from the past. Down the road, the success of WWE 24/7 could dictate the home of *Raw* and *Smackdown* on television.

Yet wrestling's greatest popularity came as a result of one factor — competition. For now, the best opportunity for fans to relive the excitement of 1998 will be determined by the accomplishments of Total Nonstop Action Wrestling. With deep corporate pockets, years of experience, and a plethora of awesome in-ring performers — all indispensable ingredients — along with a national television home on Spike TV, the potential exists for the new promotion to crack WWE's stranglehold.

Brian "Spanky" Kendrick and Fritz

Will someone else step up to the plate? Will another multimillionaire mogul or corporation fund a rival startup to WWE, or even TNA? Perhaps the dreams of wrestling fans seeking a new version of the "Monday Night War" will be answered by a Ted Turner or a Mark Cuban, or a television network looking to jump onto the next pro-wrestling cycle.

"Cycle" is perhaps the most apropos word to use when discussing the future of sports entertainment. Since the invention of television, for which wrestling programming was an early staple, the ebb and flow of the business has followed a cyclical path. For every peak, as in the late '90s, there was a valley resembling the postmillennium period. Each time, the sport returned to even greater popularity. If history serves as any guide, the next great wave, likely bigger than the last, could be just around the corner.

Between the Ropes AUDIO INDEX

The comments and quotations throughout the book have been excerpted from the *Between the Ropes* radio program from the following broadcasts:

CHAPTER 2 Sting — September 22, 2004

CHAPTER 3 Randy Savage — December 12, 2001
Eric Bischoff — February 12, 2004
Randy Savage — December 12, 2001

CHAPTER 4 Sting — September 22, 2004
Mike Tenay — May 5, 2004
Bret Hart — July 27, 2005

CHAPTER 5 Ric Flair — July 7, 2004
Terry Taylor — September 15, 2004
Chris Jericho — July 20, 1999
Terry Taylor — May 17, 2001

CHAPTER 6 Bobby Heenan — September 4, 2002
Eric Bischoff — February 12, 2004
Chris Jericho — July 20, 1999
Diamond Dallas Page — November 9, 2000
J.J. Dillon — December 3, 2003
Ed Ferrara — January 9, 2002

CHAPTER 7   Bret Hart — March 22, 2000
Ed Ferrara — January 9, 2002
Shane Douglas — April 17, 2002
Eddie Guerrero — June 29, 2000
Shane Douglas — April 17, 2002
Billy Kidman — May 4, 2000
Booker T — June 22, 2000

CHAPTER 8   Hulk Hogan — March 22, 2000
Jeff Jarrett — May 15, 2002

CHAPTER 9   Mike Sanders — January 11, 2001
Stacy Keibler — July 2, 2003
Larry Zbyszko — April 28, 2004
Scott Hudson — July 26, 2001
Ric Flair — November 21, 2003

CHAPTER 10   Shane Douglas — January 12, 2005
Shane Douglas — May 25, 1999

CHAPTER 11   Eddie Guerrero — June 29, 2000
Steve Austin — November 12, 2003
Mikey Whipwreck — July 27, 2000
Chris Jericho — January 12, 2005

CHAPTER 12   Buh Buh Ray Dudley — January 5, 2005
Paul Heyman — December 15, 2004

CHAPTER 13   The Sandman — July 19, 2001

CHAPTER 14   Shane Douglas — May 25, 1999
Rob Van Dam — July 20, 1999
Shane Douglas — May 25, 1999
Rob Van Dam — July 20, 1999
Joey Styles — May 30, 1998

Kevin Kelly — September 8, 1998
Mick Foley — February 10, 2000
Mick Foley — June 29, 2000

CHAPTER 24   Vince McMahon — February 10, 2000
Vince McMahon — February 10, 2000

CHAPTER 25   Jim Ross — February 7, 2001

CHAPTER 26   Jeff Hardy — April 9, 2003

CHAPTER 27   Buff Bagwell — June 12, 2002
Jim Ross — June 11, 2003
Jim Ross — June 4, 2003

CHAPTER 28   Steve Austin — November 12, 2003
Eric Bischoff — February 12, 2004
Paul Heyman — December 15, 2004
Shawn Michaels — January 22, 2004
Jim Ross — June 4, 2003
Chris Jericho — September 18, 2002
Billy Gunn — May 18, 2005

CHAPTER 29   Steve Austin — November 12, 2003
Billy Gunn — May 18, 2005

CHAPTER 30   Jerry Lawler — August 20, 2003
Jim Ross — March 11, 2004
Mick Foley — January 19, 2005
Raven — April 23, 2003
John Cena — July 30, 2003 and April 14, 2004
Jerry Lawler — April 6, 2005

CHAPTER 31   Jeff Jarrett — May 15, 2002
Jeff Jarrett — May 15, 2002
Mike Tenay — June 5, 2002

Jeff Jarrett — May 15, 2002
Jeff Jarrett — May 15, 2002

Chapter 32   Jeff Jarrett — May 15, 2002
Jeff Jarrett — July 31, 2002
Vince Russo — August 28, 2002
AJ Styles — May 22, 2002
Mike Tenay — June 5, 2002
Ed Ferrara — July 31, 2002

Chapter 33   Ed Ferrara — July 31, 2002
Jerry Lynn — July 3, 2002
Vince Russo — August 28, 2002
Jeff Jarrett — July 31, 2002

Chapter 34   Ron Killings — August 14, 2002
Ken Shamrock — April 2, 2003
Sean Waltman — November 27, 2002
Chris Daniels — January 22, 2003
Larry Zbyszko — April 28, 2004
Raven — April 23, 2003
AJ Styles — June 11, 2003
Sting — September 22, 2004

Chapter 35   Jeff Jarrett — June 18, 2003
Jeff Jarrett — June 18, 2003
Shane Douglas — July 2, 2003
Don Callis — August 13, 2002
D'Lo Brown — July 30, 2003

Chapter 36   Mike Tenay — May 5, 2004
Jeff Jarrett — May 12, 2004
Jimmy Hart — May 12, 2004
Jeff Jarrett — May 12, 2004

Chapter 37   Ron Killings — June 9, 2004